In gratitude to all who are on the path to wholeness and who are remembering the truth of who they are

A Lionhearted Bear Publication

A CIP catalogue reference for this book is available from the British Library.

ISBN: 978-0-9571642-6-0

First published in 2018 by R.A. Moseley.

This paperback edition is printed and distributed by Create Space.

HAMARTIA *

By R.A. Moseley

* Please note that this book contains strong language that is only suited to an adult audience.

# CONTENTS

## *A JOURNEY OF INITIATION*

# THE INHERITANCE

# Chapter I

*Friday, 14th May 2010*

C ome on. Big boys don't cry,' remarked Joe with a gentle, but dismissive, pat on John's arm.

Though light hearted in tone; these words were loaded with shame. They pressed John to fight back the tears; although he was unable to stop his bottom lip from quivering. It was the second time this week that his mother hadn't been there to meet him at the school gate and naturally he felt upset because of her absence.

Instead Joe was waiting for him; the father of his friend Benny. Even though they lived on the opposite side of town; Joe had kindly offered again to drop John off on his way home. But John did not feel any of this kindness as he climbed in alone into the back of the car.

As they drove away, John's mind stirred rapidly into a fitful state of worry. Compounding matters; Benny and his father paid him no attention as they chatted happily amongst themselves. John turned his head sideways and stared blankly out the window. The depressing thought came that only a few minutes ago he had felt the same happiness having come to the end of another week of school. But now his mood had turned to the deepest black.

Joe pulled to a stop outside John's home. Moodily, and with only a muttered word of thanks, John climbed out from the car; dragging his schoolbag behind him off the seat. Then they were gone and he was left alone with a feeling of apprehension because he anticipated what was now about to happen. He opened the front door cautiously, found the downstairs rooms empty, and then proceeded upstairs to his parents' closed bedroom door. Heat built up inside as a feeling of distress came upon him like a rolling wave. For John had stood here only a couple of days before, and had banged and shouted at the locked door to no avail. On that day his mother did not appear until well after teatime with only a meek apology and an implausible excuse that she must have fallen deeply asleep. His mother's words would never be questioned by John; but nevertheless he could not help but think that he must have done something wrong to upset her. Now he was back standing here and finding that the door was locked again. John did not bang and shout this time. Instead he went silently to his room, curled up into his bed, and started to sob.

Back on the other side of the locked door, Anna, his mother, was not sleeping even though she tried to pretend that she was. She had heard John arrive, had watched the door handle turn, and had felt the silent distress of her seven-year old son on the other side. It hurt that he did not fight today for her love and merely turned away in resignation. Surely nothing pains a woman more than to hear her child suffering; but yet she felt paralysed and powerless to act. Such was the weight of depression on her shoulders; it had immobilised her completely.

So Anna lay there and prayed that her son would find a way to soothe himself until she could muster the strength to raise herself from under the dark cloud that had smothered her. She knew that Warren, her partner, would not be home for hours; and she had long lost her trust in him to reveal her fragile state and to ask for his support. His business had taken over his life to the point that they rarely talked beyond scratching the surface. They were passing strangers; bound only by their parentage to John. Warren provided the financial support and Anna covered the rest. She hated this arrangement that they had fallen into over the years. But it seemed to her as if this relationship dynamic had formed its own groove and could not change course. Any anger she once felt had long petered out.

Anna had been hiding these feelings of depression for a few years; but now it was gnawing away more insistently at her soul. With John at school, most days were spent alone at home with only housework and Warren's paperwork to occupy her mind and give her purpose. But these days she could hardly rouse herself even for that. Anna had been a proud maternal woman and had played well the role of the strong dependable mother when she devoted herself fully to John in the early years. But inside she had been incubating a wound of loneliness; there was an empty hole at the core of her being that she had been masking for years.

She sensed what had triggered the grief and sadness that now weighed her down; even though she could find no remedy to ease it. It was a mother's burden of guilt and shame for having brought a child into this world with a partner who she had soon realised was not a man who was ever going to be fit for the purpose of parenting. She hated herself for even thinking this; but regardless John was always there as a constant reminder of it. She had played the proud and committed mother; but she knew instinctively that no matter how hard she tried that she could not play the role of both parents in her son's life. Looking at Warren now she could only see what her son would be thirty or forty years down the road; and she was too ashamed to admit that the image haunted and embarrassed her in equal measure.

Anna knew that she was hardly alone in raising a child with a partner who was largely absent from the home. These days a father need be nothing more than a single sperm from a frozen container. But she felt alone in her worry for John and his development; something that had long been her sole concern in life. There were simply no other male role models around for her to call on right now.

These worries brought back memories for Anna of going along to mother's circles whilst John was still small. She found that these were places where women came to get sympathetic approval for playing the role of the multitasking 'supermom'. Anna found that there was a competitive undercurrent amongst the group as if they were proud of how many balls they were trying to juggle at the same time and proud of how insanely busy their lives were. And all the while they bagged their male partners who seemed to them to be lagging shamefully behind; lost in their work and struggling with various addictions and afflictions. These groups served these women by making them think that because this was common that it was healthy. In these circles this imbalanced dynamic of relationship had become normalised. These groups also became a place for further rigorous male-bashing where women entrenched the insidious belief that a man in the home can be replaced with three things; a dildo for her, a fat cheque for the bank, and a large cuddly toy for the child to throw around in order to satiate their 'father hunger'. It appeared as if this was where the era of feminine empowerment had reached and Anna was instinctively repulsed by it. She had not stayed a part of these groups for long.

In looking back further, Anna punished herself for her naivety in thinking that having a child with Warren would somehow give her partner the push into a stronger masculinity. She had desperately wanted equality; a man who would stand toe-to-toe with her through the ups and downs...and not an adolescent she would have to mother too. It was risky and deluded because Warren simply didn't have the tools or the will to cross that bridge. Sadly, Anna only came to realise this when John began to grow inside of her; with the conception taking place only a few months after her and Warren had started dating. As a fierce romantic she had seen only the potential of their new life together and had fallen hopelessly in love with the perfect idea of who Warren could become. She believed that the price of that romanticism was now John's to bear. Anna was a woman with many regrets.

At the time they had met, Warren had been a travelling salesman drifting aimlessly from town to town and struggling to make his way. But he had captivated her with his strong ideals and his passionate dreams for the future. And whilst he put these into motion as he settled down to establish his business during the pregnancy; as the years passed he had simply failed to mature from these roots he had placed into the earth. Even though he had gamely struggled on, the one place that both Anna and John needed him to be was the one place that always eluded him; that place being here in the present.

As she lay immobilised on her bed with these depressing thoughts of the past haunting her mind; Anna reached for and began to grasp once more at the one desperate idea that had made itself available to drag her out of this trough she had fallen into. It seemed to her a mad illogical thought that had begun to form and take shape in recent days because it appeared risky and counterintuitive. If she'd of asked the opinion of one-hundred people then one -hundred people would surely have come back and told her that it was selfish and wrong; that it would only make matters worse for John not better.

But nonetheless it was an idea that more and more felt right to her. This is because if she couldn't change Warren into becoming a better parent then she had to change herself. And to change herself she needed to leave the home. Not only that, she needed to leave *on her own* without John. Her health and wellbeing was clamouring to be put top of the list. Anna had to find a way to fill this empty hole that had formed deep within her soul and to find the person who had once lived there. And she knew that she couldn't do that with John by her side. Although her son may hate her for it, she could only hope that he would one day come to understand what had driven her to this point. She did not know how long it would take and when she would return. She did not know if Warren would even allow it. But certainly things could not continue as they were; and this was true for all of them.

However, a fresh wave of guilt soon dragged her back under the covers as she grappled with the implications of this weighty decision. Down there, Anna tried to soothe herself with hopeful thoughts that maybe Warren would step into the breach and that it would indeed be good for all of them. She knew that she was not blameless in this toxic triangular relationship that had formed and that she had surely contributed to. After a couple of miserable attempts at fathering in those first few months of John's life; she knew she had judged Warren as incapable and had never truly given him a chance again. She offered no encouragement for him to step in as she had condemned him silently as weak and incompetent. She had stubbornly refused to leave John alone with him for any length of time; to the point where Warren had distanced himself and disappeared into his work.

And so Anna soothed herself in thinking that leaving the home would, perversely, help restore her faith in Warren by handing him the reigns. The guilt that had stirred began to ease. Tentatively she began to form plans for a fresh new start.

# Chapter II

*Friday, 1st April 2016*

Warren was at his desk and was submerged under a fresh wave of stress and concern. In his left hand he held a children's plastic block of cheese, which he had bought for himself and his office after a conversation with his son a couple of years earlier. It was a reminder to him of everything that he was trying to create and protect. Most importantly of all it helped focus and motivate him in the work he did for he was a man concerned for the future and for the world his son John would have to grow up and live within. Warren wanted to protect his only child by leaving the greatest possible legacy. He was driven in this ambition because he had never reconciled in himself the decision to bring a child into a world that at best he considered unfriendly and at worst hostile.

Before Anna and John came into his life, Warren had been a charming dreamer; but he dreamed out of a deep rut of depression that ran through the core of his being. No seed that he had tossed into the wind had landed and bore fruit; his life had long been a magnet for failure and disappointment. Sometimes he merely lamented his fate and bleated in frustration as to the point of his existence. At other times paranoia seeped in as dark thoughts consumed his mind that the world was conspiring against him to make his life a living nightmare. These were the thoughts that motivated him with a stubborn resolve and a desire for revenge.

But then Anna had magically appeared and Warren had been

literally consumed and swept away by her breezy romanticism. She had seen beyond his gloomy mindset and had glimpsed the powerful man that was waiting there. Her faith and belief in what she saw gave Warren a conviction and zest for existence that he had not tasted since he was a young child. Out of that giddy optimism John was conceived; and swiftly afterwards Warren also conceived his first real business venture. After years of aimless wandering it appeared as if life was pushing him to finally settle into this world and to put roots down into the earth.

However, the bright honeymoon period couldn't be sustained. As soon as John was born, Anna's energy and focus naturally shifted away from Warren and towards their son. He soon felt like an incompetent makeweight in his own home as the two of them shared a love and bond that often excluded him. John had not responded well to his own tentative and unconfident touch and care and Warren felt ashamed because he sensed that he was seen at best with indifference and at worse as a threatening stranger to his son. It only took a couple of occasions where Anna had pushed him aside in order to soothe their son for Warren to meekly retreat back into a world of work where he felt far more useful.

But in that arena too, all his conviction and zest soon disappeared for he did not know how to give himself the gift of loving encouragement that Anna had once brought into his world. He was just not mature enough to rise up to the changes that had taken place in his life. It is at this point in the script that Warren would normally run and move on to the next dream and the next failure. But John's addition had changed the equation and so for the first time in his life Warren felt committed to stay and to stick it out.

That commitment came with a heavy price. Warren remained at war in himself as he wilfully fought to make his business a success when his thoughts and beliefs remained entrenched in its failure. And as he paddled furiously upstream; all the while he carried an unspoken burden that his life had become a bitter disappointment to Anna because he could never live up to the expectations she once held for him. He had seen it in her eyes and the pitiful way she looked at him once the romantic hue had been rubbed off the lens. He felt her shame of him as a man, as a lover and as a father. Over the years that followed Warren gradually distanced himself more and more and avoided any efforts to salvage their broken relationship. It was simply too challenging and uncomfortable for Warren to change his ways or be reminded of his failings. John was the only thing that bound them all together and Warren's single unwavering commitment was to perform his duties and to take financial care of his son.

For years Warren had half expected to come home and to find Anna and John gone. There was a part of him that was waiting for her to relieve him of duties that he would never have the courage to walk away from himself. He had deliberately left the door open; but for a long time she remained steadfast in keeping up the pretence of their perfect family life. And then when the time came that she finally did walk through that open door, soon after John had turned seven, what surprised and upset him greatly was that she didn't take their son with her. Warren had not been relieved of his duties and given his ticket of leave as he had hoped; instead he had been placed as John's primary caregiver. When the realisation of this finally sunk in; Warren was left feeling that Anna had placed him in one big set up.

More than five years had now passed since that day and Anna had not shown herself once in that time. The bitterness and fury had not eased at all for Warren as he was convinced that her leaving had only stacked the odds higher against John and his journey into adulthood. Her leaving note spoke only of her self absorption; words that surprised Warren as Anna had always portrayed the image of a strong and independent woman who always put others first in life. He could see that something must have snapped inside; but Warren was not willing to look and consider the part he had played in her unravelling.

However, Anna's departure didn't help develop the bond between father and son as she had so wished for. Within a day of her leaving, Warren had arranged for a nanny to come into the home as a replacement; whilst he continued to bury himself into his business. It seemed as if this addictive pursuit was the only outlet for Warren to cope with Anna's shame around his practical inability to relate and care for their son.

Even though he'd had some commercial success in the very beginning; the tide had soon started to turn against him. It seemed to Warren that every effort he made to preserve and enhance that block of cheese only served to provoke a furious reaction from the economic systems that bound him. Every time he went to stand tall it felt to him as if it came along and cut him down to his knees. Regulations, legislations, taxes; these all stood as centurions barring the path to his success. He had quickly realised that red tape only serves to strangle the underdog in the commercial world and he was now struggling for air and turning blue. His block of cheese had so many holes nibbled into it that it was already shifting past the brink of collapse.

In his right hand he held the block of wood upon which his name and title was carved so lavishly. '*Warren Waideman; Chief Executive*,' it read in gold lettering. It had once given him great pride to touch it. Today, in a flash of sudden rage, he turned around and threw the object at the pane of glass of his closed office door; shattering it in the process.

Downstairs, on the open warehouse floor of the watch factory that the office overlooked, many faces turned in unison at the sound from above. But those faces swiftly turned back to their work as if nothing out of the ordinary had happened. Warren's employees were well used by now to his fits of rage if ever the rug started to get pulled away from under his feet; as it so frequently did. Only the elderly foreman, who had known Warren for many years and had no fear of his mood swings, took action by grabbing a dustpan and brush and walked up the steps to the office door.

'Is there a problem sir?' he asked sagely.

'The bank is going to let me hang when I show them these latest figures. I'm sorry Jim but I simply can't see a way for us to keep this going any longer. We're truly fucked now.'

12

'I see,' Jim answered without any sign of emotion from this proclamation. 'Well sometimes you just have to let the axe fall and move on to something new. There must be something better for us all out there if that is the way the dice falls.' Jim had always been an optimist who had an unwavering faith and who had often played the role of counsellor to his boss; often, it has to be said, to no avail. There perspectives on life were simply too far apart with nothing to bridge them, and so at moments like this Jim could not help but wonder why he had worked so long for a man who held such a paranoid and pessimistic worldview. He was truly the chalk to this man's block of cheese.

'Stop being so damn cheerful Jim! Don't you get how fucked the situation is right now for you as well as for me. By the end of the week we are all going to be out of work and no-one is going to come along and rescue us from this pit we are in. Let me tell you that you're not going to find it easy out there to pick up something else no matter what you may dream. Right now there are thousands of kids scrapping for a handful of jobs and all with degrees to their name. At your age, where do you think you are going to go?'

Jim gave a weary sigh and had no desire to defend his credentials or his prospects right now. He found it frustrating because beneath Warren's fearful gloom he knew that this was a man with a big heart and who had started this business with noble intentions. In truth he had joined up because Warren's ideas at the time were so new and fresh from any other business venture in town.

For Warren had been repulsed by the import of low quality, poorly manufactured, goods from the developing country of Aidni to the east. In fact his business idea came to him after purchasing a cheap imported watch from a large department store that within a few hours only worked intermittently. Warren had taken it back to the store thinking that he must have bought a dud. But the manager simply shrugged his shoulders and told him: '*You get what you pay for. What did you really expect from a cheap imported watch like that?*' It was a dismissive question that cut through into Warren's soul. As a business minded man, it was simply unfathomable to him that such an object could have its place in a wealthy modern world. He had marched out of that store in a fury.

It was an incident that pushed Warren into action; aided with Anna's boisterous support. He decided that day to set up his own watch making business with the intent of producing reasonably priced watches that could at least be relied upon to tell the time. His honourable vow was that he would never ever sell a watch that he was not prepared to guarantee was going to work for at least ten years.

That passion had been infectious in the beginning as good people like Jim were magnetised towards it. There were many regulative hurdles that had to be overcome to get the business going but Warren threw himself against all of them with a lot of savings and an enthusiastic workforce behind him. There was a golden period in those first couple of years; but fighting against an economic system involved a long war rather than a single battle and inevitably it took its toll. Having come to know the man over many years, Jim always saw Warren as a figure of loyalty; loyal to his ideals and loyal to anyone who helped support him. But he also knew that Warren's drive for success also contained a dark shadow of paranoia and pessimism that had sadly sabotaged his ambitions.

Jim was aware too that none of the ten remaining employees downstairs enjoyed working for the company anymore and they were all tired of Warren's constant griping at the way the world was nibbling at his cheese. This was something he uttered regularly at weekly staff meetings, which often descended into a diatribe. Warren had tried to create a siege mentality of us against them; and yet his staff no longer had interest in the fight and just wanted their pay cheque at the end of the week. This cooling of enthusiasm only encouraged Warren to turn on his employees and put them in the 'them' camp at times. He would ruthlessly dock staff wages if business was slow and he'd had a bad week in order to ram home the message to get on his side or get out. Over the years necessary cutbacks had seen his workforce diminish by half.

Because of a sluggish job market; many of his remaining staff had been working here since the early years. But there was an atmosphere of fear and trepidation that was now toxic around the place. Jim had become the glue who kept the focus on the dream they had all come together to create. And in staying on all these years he was perhaps guilty of being a hopeless romantic in thinking that he could be the one to soften Warren's tyranny and to deflate his tempestuousness. But although he had perhaps failed in this regard; he was not a man to dwell on the past or worry about what was to come. Right now, Jim was concerned more for Warren's future than his own.

## Chapter III

*Thursday, 4th December 2031*

John was stood at the kitchen sink and was busy scrubbing the dishes. However, it was not only the hot water on his hands that was causing his temperature to rise as once again his guest had disappeared to his bedroom after dinner and had left him to clear up after them both. He complained angrily to himself:

*'Damn him that lazy bastard! Does he not know how selfish he is; leaving me here to do all this dirty work after him? I've sure had a harder day of work than he and damn it I'd love to put my feet up too. Tell me who was it who got up first to light the fire so we could both have a hot shower this morning? And who fucking did this and who fucking did that the rest of the day? Well that will be me of course! And now add this chore to the long list! So no I can't go take a well earned rest can I because if I don't bloody well clean up then I'll be damned if anyone else will!'*

After slamming another pot down onto the draining rack he stopped for a brief moment and glanced outside of the window. It was pitch black and had been so for a good few hours. December was already here and in another couple of weeks it would be the time of the longest night. The skies were clear on this still moonless evening and the stars were shining bright. Out here on Diarra, a remote island in the far north, there was no light pollution and so he was one of only a few souls left in Arasmas, one of four countries on the planet, who could easily cast their gaze upon those most distant galaxies in the cosmos. But alas, the vastness of the view did distant galaxies in the cosmos. But alas, the vastness of the view did little to shift his perspective as the hot inner fire continued to blind his sight. John swiftly turned his head back to the last unwashed pot and yanked it down hard into the soapy water; causing a splash. At that moment a noise to the side caused him to stop and lift his head. It was then he noticed that Myrkais, his guest, had suddenly reappeared and was standing at the kitchen door. His presence startled John out of his own mumblings.

'Can I give you a hand by drying the dishes?' Myrkais asked with noticeable trepidation in his voice as John's cold and steely eyes turned to meet with his.

John almost scowled aloud. But he checked himself and then responded almost cheerfully.

'Don't worry about it Myrkais. You go and put your feet up!'

John immediately turned his attention back to the pot in the sink as if drawing a line under the conversation. In observing this Myrkais raised his eyebrows awkwardly in response. Only someone very insensitively out of tune would have failed to spot the inconsistency between the words expressed and the energy of the person expressing them. It was so blatantly inauthentic that all Myrkais heard was the grating sound of sarcastic menace that ran beneath these kind and dutiful words of generous service from his host. Myrkais was tempted to probe further into this evident discord and to try and clear the tension that was left hanging in the air; but he soon thought better of it and so quietly vanished without a further word. After he had gone John slammed the pot onto the draining board, grabbed hold of the tea towel, and began mumbling to himself again:

*'Can I give you a hand? Can you believe the cheek of such a question? He sat there eating his dinner and didn't have the sense to just get on with cleaning up afterwards. Can he not put two and two together? If I cook dinner for us both then surely it is not too much to expect for him to clear the table without having to come in at the last minute like that and asking such a pathetic question? And anyway he came too late didn't he. I don't mind him washing the*

*dishes but I really can't stand him drying them. He never knows how to put things away just as I like them to be put away and so it really isn't worth him coming in here now to help when I will only have to come back and tidy up after him later. It really is like looking after a child sometimes.'*

Once the kitchen had been tidied to his exacting standards; John gave a weary sigh before turning off the light. He expected that the rhythm of household chores would all begin again with him tomorrow and at this moment that thought simply drained him even more. But whilst the hot fire of anger may have been raging inside of him; outwardly, John was too submissive to speak with his guest and to shake him from his evident laziness himself. He excused his submissiveness by projecting the thought that this was not his problem and that he had made it perfectly clear in the beginning with Myrkais how things should be done around here in sharing the workload. John simply could not accept or take responsibility for any part he was playing in this difficult relationship dynamic that had been building between the two of them these past few weeks. And judging by this latest conflict; the situation seemed to have reached a critical impasse of dissonance. In truth, the only positive action John could take was to cross his fingers in the hope that one day soon Myrkais would get the message and start toeing the line by pulling his finger out and behaving exactly how John was expecting him to behave. But for now, with no other outlet for the fire to go, that inner complaining voice simply continued unabated.

*'I mean how many times have I told him how I want things to be done around this place? Six months he's fucking been here now and yet he still seems to expect me to nag him like I am his own mother. How hard can it be to pull your own weight?'*

John went on grumbling into the lounge and turned on the radio before taking a seat by the fire. It needed stoking but he decided to save his supplies of wood for another day and instead pulled a woollen blanket over his knees and onto his lap. Myrkais had again vanished upstairs to his room. John mused that he was

18

probably avoiding any possible reaction to his shocking laziness. As he settled down for the evening he was only half listening to the debate that was unfolding about some politician who'd been caught whilst involved (predictably he thought briefly and cynically) in some corruption scandal. Softly soothed by the glow from the last embers of the fire, his temperature slowly began to cool even whilst the debate became more heated.

In this quieter space John's now more relaxed mind wandered freely and he started to reminisce of his own first difficult winter here on this inhospitable island when it had been hard to pull himself out of a childish survival mentality of 'me, me, me'. Feelings of sympathy towards Myrkais then gently arose with them. But it didn't take long for these warm feelings to be shoved back down with righteous indignation.

*'It's crazy to think how pathetic I must have been out here back in the beginning whingeing about the fucking cold and the fucking wind. It's all the way the modern world has been designed with its creature comforts and life of ease! Get too fucking cold nowadays and all you have to do is press a fucking button to deal with it. Or else put on your latest snazzy thermo insulated piece of clothing designed by some clever dick who has fucking nothing better to do than create something that leaves you barely a smidgen warmer than the brand new fancy piece of clothing he fucking created last year. And he fucking thinks that this smidgen of difference is a worthwhile way to spend all his fucking time…and we all stupidly think that's a valuable way to spend our fucking money as we dump last year's now outdated model in the fucking trash.*

*'It seems so fucking long ago now that I was one of those fucking suits in the city running around on the hamster wheel. Not that I was ever enslaved by the necktie and duped into thinking that I was living the suburban fucking dream. In times like this it makes me sick to have him here reminding me of the living dead I once had to deal with. He looks so fucking clean; almost like he has never lifted a fucking finger in his whole life. Take one look at him? Was I really like that when I first came here? Of course I know as*

well as anyone that there's no sweat and toil in moving a few numbers around a computer screen…and yet you can easily make yourself a cool million if you do it right. Call that fucking progress? Well I don't. Oh I know I played the game too; but that was the quickest and easiest way to get rich and get the fuck out. Apart from going out there and robbing people of course. I can't tell the difference between the two but people call one thing illegal whilst calling the other perfectly civilised and normal. Doesn't anyone see it is the same fucking thing just wrapped up in a different package? Well at least I knew it was all bollocks whilst I played it and didn't have my pants up my arse thinking I was doing a respectable fucking job. And at least I didn't think that I was on the evolutionary fast track like the rest of my fucked up colleagues. Oh how fucking smug they looked sitting in their fancy cars…but tell me where were they going? On the road to fucking nowhere; that's where. They will surely go all the way to retirement before they realise it's all been one big fucking con and all they are left with is an empty house that they have finally paid off but no longer care for because the kids they never saw have already flown the nest. And their wife has also probably long given up waiting for their man to show up and has divorced them too. Then they will sit alone in their five-bed fucking manor house and suddenly ask themselves; what the fuck were the last forty years about? Not so smug then are they when they discover that even though they've finally got their balls back from the bank; they are shrivelled up and gone rotten because their best years are long gone behind them. Well that life was never going to be for me! And now out here I have to get on and do some real fucking work to make my way. This is where real progress happens. Man's work is what it is. And that little fucker needs to learn what this is all about much like I had to learn what it was all about.

'Oh yes it was easy of course in the summer months for him to come here and live the fucking dream with long summer days helping warm his back and helping him to forget the whole fucking rat race that surely once spun his yarn. But I wonder if it has fully sunk in yet that the winter here is bloody beastly…because I for one saw *those rose-tinted specs of his shatter once that first storm rolled in off the ocean and battered this land. Where was the joy of island living then! You need fucking backbone to make it out here; that's what it is. Well really it is the fucking darkness that gets to you as much as the wind, the rain, and the fucking never ending chill. But you soon toughen up to it. You fucking have to if you want to make it out here because Mother Nature shows no tolerance for the fucking depressed. I just fucking wish he would get over it and get on with it because I simply don't need to put up with all this pathetic weak-minded shit around asking me whether I want a fucking hand drying the fucking dishes. Fuck that.'*

So sat by himself on this darkest of nights; John was starting to indulge in his first real doubts about the experiment that he began six months ago when he'd first invited Myrkais to join him here on Diarra on a work exchange agreement.

As John readily conceded; in the beginning the experiment had worked well, surprisingly well even. For, as intended, the extra pair of hands had enabled John to harvest a generous surplus of food from his increasing allotment. In fact a perfect blend of rain and sunshine, coupled with warmer conditions than normal, had ensured that it had gone way beyond his expectations. And all this had been achieved even with Myrkais missing most of the growing season; having only arrived in early June.

This success meant that in the autumn months he was able to take this surplus and trade it with others who were part of a newly formed exchange network he'd been persuaded to join early in the year. Surprisingly, it was in this remote far north-western corner of the country that this network was developing fast. The area seemed to be an attractive hotbed for those seeking respite from the trappings of the modern world and the financial systems that governed it. In the first year this localised network had already grown a hundred-strong and provided a whole host of services ranging from food, fuel, building materials, labour, and many others. Most on the list were hobbyists who quietly did a bit extra on the side of their regular day job. Or else they were retired enthusiasts who were struggling to get by on their meagre pensions. In truth there were very, very few in the whole of Arasmas who could take the bold step that John had taken in cutting ties so thoroughly from the trappings of the modern world; or very few that at least had the money behind them to give it a real shot.

For John, Diarra had always seemed the perfect place to come and tap in to that independent spirit that typically comes down the generations of island dwellers who always had that natural separation from the mainstream herd of society. On paper it was indeed the perfect place to carve the self sufficient life he wanted to create for himself.

Being a part of this exchange network was like making a return to an antiquated bartering system that had existed before the money system had taken over. It was the brainchild of a small group of dedicated individuals who had realised that it made good old fashioned economic sense for them to specialise in something they were passionate about and to trade the surplus; rather than trying to spread their spare time thinly by doing a multitude of small things in order to get a little bit closer towards a simple self sufficient lifestyle. This network was undoubtedly ruffling a few feathers in the government tax office; but for now there was apparently nothing they could do to get their own grubby hands involved in this scheme and to stop this group from slipping through their well crafted net. But John suspected cynically that if too many people started joining him by quitting their jobs and escaping the system full-time, that new legislation was sure to be passed to kybosh the scheme in order to get all these people back onto the hamster wheel and back earning and spending money.

The other beauty of this exchange network was that John did not have to organise the exchange of his surplus food in return for something he wanted. Instead his bounty went into a communal pot which John received credits for when they were sold on; and these credits enabled him to 'purchase' anything he liked out of the pot. The only bone of contention was how much items were to be valued at; but generally the credit figure mirrored what the item could fetch on the open market. It ran on a first come first served basis and he found that it didn't take long to shift his vegetable boxes once they were ready to go. Of course, if John wanted something specific from the pot then he also had the option of contacting the seller directly to see whether they could organise a trade between themselves. It was a very efficient and flexible scheme that was becoming more popular by the week; aided by the fact that those who had set it up had no desire or need to make any profit from their involvement and only charged a small administration fee.

As intended, in return for his surplus of food, John had been given the promise of timber supplies from a nearby woodsman; supplies which he hoped were drying out nicely in the woodsman's shed. With this hardwood he had plans to improve the cottage over the next year to better his living conditions here. There was a lot of work to be done though to bring these ideas to fruition as John had made plans to put in place new window frames throughout the old cottage to help keep out the draft; plans to build a shed to store his firewood so as to keep it dry; and plans to rebuild the rickety old compost loo out the back. This not only leaked when it rained; it had also been so badly designed that it was really nothing more than an unhygienic open cesspit.

However, despite these ambitious plans, the jury was still out as to whether John could pull it all off by the end of next summer. Right now it seemed to him as if it hinged on Myrkais and whether he could renew his level of enthusiasm for what was being created out here. The mood had swung very quickly for it had only been a month or so ago that John had been filled with optimism from those days spent loading his small motor boat full of their bounty and sending it off in a delivery truck from the mainland. However this golden moment in time was already starting to slip from a mind that was becoming blacker by the day. John had already calculated that Myrkais was now no longer contributing positively to the running of the house and was only eating into his precious winter food store. Even though there were still many jobs to be done around the place; as the days had grown shorter he had also watched Myrkais' initiative and work ethic diminish. For John; even though winter had yet to fully arrive, springtime could not come around soon enough.

## Chapter IV

*Tuesday, 3rd February 2032*

Winter still held the island in its vice like grip and for John it had proved a trying couple of months as he continued to struggle with the challenges of sharing his home. Myrkais seemed to him to be completely oblivious to what impact he was having as, to John, he appeared utterly absorbed inside his own little dream world. To John he now seemed to float and wander around the island like a depressed ghost. Everything he did around the house and garden got under John's skin; or more to the point everything he now didn't do. In Myrkais' evasive presence, John was left feeling like a prized idiot who had been dumped upon with the worst employee in the land. The whole negative experience was a distraction that took away his energy and motivation for the tasks at hand, and he could only watch in a daze whilst his guest wisped around doing, in John's opinion, whatever the fuck he pleased.

Today though things had quite possibly reached their nadir and John felt as if he had been placed firmly in the eye of the storm. It was late and he was lying in bed; but the prospect of sleep seemed a distant one with his mind running wildly around in circles. He had no clue how to tame this beast and to bring it rest and so it went forth unleashed and without restraint. All John could do was lie there and hope that it would eventually run itself down into exhaustion. But his wishful thinking wasn't to be fulfilled on this night.

*'I can't fucking believe the way he stoked up the fire this evening. It was fucking roaring like mad when I came out from clearing the table. And he takes one look at me and then fucking scurries away to his room like a naughty child. It's the middle of the night and it is still fucking burning now. I am sure of it. And for whose benefit is it? Does he not know how short of fucking firewood we are and that if we are not careful I will have to fucking go out and buy another fucking load. That will be more fucking money to pay out. He is becoming a fucking liability. Does he not know that you don't drag in and put big fucking logs on the fire like that! And all because he can't be arsed to fucking chop them. And then not just one but two of the fuckers in one go! It fucking drives me mad how fucking selfish he is. This shitty city boy doesn't have a clue. He needs to fucking leave. Why does he not find somewhere else to go; find someone who is happy to put up with his endless bullshit? For what fucking point is there in me ramming home again the importance of economy in how we do things around here. He doesn't fucking listen. It isn't even fucking cold this evening and he has gone and turned the lounge into a stifling fucking sauna. Prick. He has absolutely no respect for me or the fact that this is my fucking home.'*

And so this sorry tale went around his head again, and again, and again. In fact it went on for hours that night as these thoughts fed into others as he chewed over and over again all the ways he had been wronged by this guest in his home these past few months. It was a long list of complaints that he carried and would not let go of easily. And so his mood grew as black as the night.

In the morning John raised himself from the bed bleary eyed and he remained weighed down by a heavy burden. He walked down the stairs with a steely resolve to finally hold Myrkais' feet to the coals and claim back some control of his affairs. John had reached the point where he could no longer go on feeding the beast that was his mind and he was ready for some peace and solitude from its incessant negative ramblings. The only option he had at hand was to finally serve Myrkais his eviction notice and send him packing. John, being at the end of his tether, hadn't thought any further ahead though and that all of his bold plans for the year were about to be engulfed by his black fiery mood. Indeed, at this rate, they would simply be burnt to ash and added to the pile that was left behind in the fireplace from last night's extravaganza.

But despite this steely resolve, no eviction notice was forthcoming that morning or any time soon after that. For the moment Myrkais came into his field of vision; John's resolve immediately crumbled and his notoriously soft underbelly wobbled. It was as if a huge bucket of water had come and doused his flaming tongue into silence.

For John hated conflict and he, typically, had always been unable to dialogue and to speak of difficulties in his relationships. John had learnt a long time ago that a quiet stoicism was the only safe way to navigate across the human terrain. And if it wasn't possible for him to just get his head down and plough on then he would rather walk away and put the difficulty out of sight. However, escaping wasn't going to be an option for him today on an island that he owned. There is only so far he can go to get away on a bit of dirt that spans little more than a mile across and a mile wide.

John had learnt early in life that revealing his heart's truth only left him exposed and vulnerable; opening the door for pain to enter. His desire for safety outweighed his desire for connection and so he had never learnt how to communicate what he held true inside. In many ways he hadn't grown up from that three-year old boy who pushes and shoves at those around him and throws a tantrum if he doesn't get his way. The only change is that John, as the adult, has learnt to control his behaviour and now only throws a tantrum in his own head. In appearance it seemed a positive step of improving maturity to bury his feelings and to be the person who smiles and nods at the appropriate moments.

But despite John's efforts to maintain that image of quiet stoicism; Myrkais could intuitively sense the negative vibes that were literally poring out of John's skin like liquefied lead. And so this morning, like many times before, Myrkais took one step into view in the kitchen and quickly ducked out of sight before a word between them could be spoken. He too was acting instinctively by prioritising his desire for safety over his desire for connection. John observed all this and sat down righteously at the table with his morning cuppa.

*'Ah did you see the way he fucking ran off like that. Yes he knows who is in charge here and he surely understands he is on borrowed time if he does anything wrong by me again. And he probably hasn't got anywhere else to go the sad fucker. No wonder his missus told him to leave if that is what he is like to live with. He reminds me of all those sad sacks I used to work for in the city. They were bastards to deal with but at least they were useful in helping me to fulfil my plan by making the million out of them that I needed to buy this place. Fucking stupid idiots who didn't have a clue about how the finance game really ticks. Like him last night; they were the ones who foolishly threw down a couple of huge logs on my fire thinking it was a grand investment. But at least then I was the one who told those gullible fuckers to do it… because I was the one who cunningly pocketed the heat out of that fire whilst they were simply warmed by the bright orange glow it radiated for a while. And there was nothing they could do when the glow faded and they realised they had been duped and left in the fucking cold. So really I'd be stupid to chuck him out now when spring is around the corner. Surely he will perk up by then. Yes I think I will be able to make the most of this for now and maybe by the end of autumn I will tell him to leave. I know I'm not so far off getting this place to where I need to get it too and then I can finally give him and the world the finger without worrying about the consequences. I just need to focus on that goal and make sure I get him lined up and in place to move me towards that end. It will be worth putting up with all this shit in the meantime, surely, like it was worth putting up with all the shit in the city to get me to this place. It will all work out okay. Yes I think so. Anyway it's time to get on and stop wallowing in all this self pity crap. I need to remember that he's the sad pathetic fucker in all of this; not me.'*

# Chapter V

Tuesday, 13th April 2032

J ohn was breathing heavily and sweating profusely as he lugged piles of wood down to his boat from where they had been dropped on the mainland. As arranged, the supplies of timber he had been promised last year had arrived the previous evening; and he was up and ready at first light to gather them. However, any feelings of excitement that John may have felt from finally receiving this gift did not last beyond the crossing and his first glimpse of this treasure. For in looking at the stack it soon dawned on John that he was going to have to develop some new carpentry skills over the coming months to bend these solid pieces of timber into shape. The reality of the task seemed daunting and it was not a prospect that gave him an injection of enthusiasm or joy.

'*It's going to take me at least another ten trips to get all this shit across,*' he grumbled to himself as he calculated how much was left to do after stacking up the first boat load. '*I'm knackered already and yet I've got to get it all done today because, knowing my luck, if I leave it out here another night it's bound to get nicked. Where's my fucking helping hand when I need him?*'

The unspoken answer was that his helping hand was no longer around for Myrkais had made his exit the previous week and had left John and Diarra behind him. In the end it was Myrkais' decision, not John's, as a surprising turn of events had shown to Myrkais that he had other options available and that he did not have to stay hiding on this remote bolthole as he had been. For John, hearing the news inevitably stirred up mixed feelings. On the surface there was this initial strong feeling of relief that the decision had been taken out of his hands and that he would have the island back to himself again after all these months of having his personal boundaries trampled on. For this reason he had let Myrkais depart meekly and with goodwill.

But beneath that wave of relief, John was seething with anger because to him the timing of Myrkais' departure was truly awful. After his guest had gone he no longer tried to shield a deep and dark black mood that had been hanging without respite ever since. It didn't take a lot for John to be triggered back unconsciously into his mind's repetitive loop of complaint; and this burdensome task was just another excuse to press the blame button again and dredge up the contents of this recurring story for the umpteenth time this week.

*'I should have given him the fucking boot earlier. What a weak bastard I am. For six months he has been here giving fucking nothing to the place and draining my resources dry. Now spring is fucking here, this wood is fucking here, and he is nowhere to be found. Where's his fucking consideration after all I did for him in inviting him here and looking after him? All I have to show for it is a bare cupboard and some fucking timber. Timber that I should have just paid out for last year rather than messing around with this stupid fucking plan of mine. I've also gone and expanded my fucking allotment and planted seeds thinking he will be around and so what am I to do with just my two hands and this impossible amount of work? Don't even think of re-advertising for extra help you weak bastard! The whole idea was a fucking stupid mistake and don't you dare let me fall into that same hole twice. Fuck that and fuck this stupid exchange network.'*

John climbed in the boat and sat anxiously as the motor strained under the extra weight it had to bear. He began to have doubts as to whether it was such a good idea to try and transport it across using his small motorboat. Cautiously he decided to half the load for the next trip even though he knew it would double the time. At this rate it was going to be a long day's work and he had grave concerns having heard that a storm was forecast later that afternoon. With haste he continued on as best he could.

If anyone had happened to pass by in that moment, a first glance would easily give the impression that John was far out of his depth to be doing the work of sustaining a life out there on the island of Diarra. His appearance didn't really fit the stereotype of other hardened dwellers in the area. John had not long passed his 29th birthday; and with smooth chubby cheeks and thick-rimmed glasses he retained a boyish look more suited to the city than a hard solitary life on the land. John lacked the weather-beaten complexion from the harsh climate of this north-western coast that helped the locals blend in around here. Even after three years he stood out noticeably as an outsider. Also, in weighing in at more than one-hundred kilograms, John was heavily overweight for someone whose frame doesn't quite extend to the six feet mark. Weight had been a problem for him since his early childhood. And even though he was living an active lifestyle on Diarra with a healthy diet; the excess had stubbornly remained around his waistline.

Exacerbating matters, John often had severe difficulties with his breathing. At best his breathing was short and shallow and he only had to walk a few yards before he was puffing heavily. Today those difficulties were accentuated with the amount of workload he was pushing himself to take on. As an exuberant child John had suffered incidences of hyperventilation; and so these frightening episodes typically caused him to be extremely cautious about over exerting himself. He was more confident with his cardiovascular movements in the city; but on Diarra it was a completely different matter. For this reason alone he had not dared to venture across the full length and breadth of his kingdom; even though it was only four miles to circumnavigate. Rarely did he go far at all from his home on the eastern shore.

However, these first glances of boyish fragility would easily mislead for beneath his delicate constitution; John's inner character was filled with solid and impenetrable steel. This hard inner core had not been formed by chance but as a protective layer out of harsh circumstances he had endured as a child. John's father died when John entered his teenage years, and his mother had left them both some years before that. As his grandparents had also passed away early in his life; his only remaining family was an uncle, his father's brother, who had taken him in and then quickly dispatched him to a boarding school.

Because of these circumstances John had developed the independence to take care of himself early in life and that was as necessary then as it is now in forging a sustainable life for himself in this bleakest of places. So even though his cardiovascular movements were extremely limited on the island; his arms were still strong and powerful to do the heavy manual work that his life out here involved. And he was a willing worker because as far as John was concerned; order was vital and that meant everything had to be maintained in its rightful place by the force of his will.

As with his environment; John was also utterly meticulous in how he presented himself each day. He had an inbuilt disdain for the feral mannerisms that could have so naturally befitted a lone island dweller who had come because of a lack of interest in the sterile routines of the civilised world. John had no desire to 'let himself go wild' for it may risk unlocking the deep feelings he had long caged inside of him. He was a tireless fusspot who demanded that everything was positioned in what he believed was its rightful place. Life was tightly controlled and yet that perfection was proving exhausting to maintain on this exposed slab of black rock with its harsh and changeable climate.

But it didn't stop John from trying and his first symbolic act of the day was to remake his bed before leaving the bedroom. He also shaved every single morning and typically slicked back his long black hair with a comb to reveal a high forehead and ghostly pallor. These were small matters but they helped stop John from letting down his guard and teetering over the abyss into melancholy and depression. However, the daily struggle to keep the wheels of life turning did little to lift his spirits. John rarely smiled or showed any outer sign of emotion and his lips barely twitched when he spoke. In the background he consistently emanated an unpleasant negative vibe that would simply be called joyless. Feeling grateful for the small precious gift of being alive was something that had rarely touched him.

What drove this will was a desire to prove the strength of his manhood and to emulate a father who had allowed this world to get the better of him and had committed suicide. A litany of betrayals from a disappearing partner, merciless competitors, his employees, the banks, and the governing authorities, had all piled up and pressured him into this abdication. A bankruptcy notice had proven to be the final straw. John was utterly determined to avoid going down the same path and the shame of failure that lingered in the shadows there. His one ultimate aim was to reach a place of *absolute* self sufficiency out there on Diarra; as hard as that may be to achieve without real sacrifices needing to be made. And though that may sound a noble goal to aim for in life; in truth John only wished to conquer this place so that he could finally keep his middle finger permanently raised against the world and to say confidently to anyone who dared to send even a welcoming hand across the water: '*I don't need anything from you so just fuck off.*'

Although it was hostile; this driving motivation had already reaped many rewards and John was righteously proud of all that he had achieved in his short time on the island. He had arrived here with no horticultural knowledge or hands on experience and so he learnt all he knew from reading books. After much experimentation in that first year; he eventually turned to old-fashioned subjects like organic horticulture, permaculture, and biodynamics in order to establish a thriving allotment for himself. As much as he could be belligerent and rigid in trying to control his world; John was also an eager and curious student who was willing to experiment and find the best way to coax as much as he could from his land. And he was willing to try any method that would help him achieve his goal.

Four solar panels on the south facing roof of the cottage, and a small wind turbine at the back, had been installed by a previous owner to generate just enough electricity for the home; although he had learnt from experience that he needed to use it sparingly in winter. Frustratingly, the wind was often too strong here to put the turbine to use during these months; and daylight hours were short. John hadn't though got around yet to redirecting any excess to his stove top and he still relied on gas bottles from the mainland for cooking. He also had ideas of installing a solar hot water and heating system as at present hot water was only available from pipes heated by the wood stove; which had proved an inefficient and cumbersome system. In the summer months John generally took cold showers right through to reduce the amount of wood he required; but eventually he wanted to reduce his need for wood to whatever he could forage on the island. Even though many of these improvements would be quick and simple projects for a contractor; John was keen to learn and to do the bulk of it himself. Because of this, these were things that had been postponed onto his task list for the next year.

And though John had grown used to a diet driven by seasonal produce from his allotment; he continued to spend a significant amount of his dwindling supply of savings to buy groceries from the mainland. Meat was one thing he was struggling to cut out from his diet; although he remained confident that when the time came that he would be able to adapt to live purely off a vegetarian diet. John hadn't the heart to start rearing and killing animals on his land and would choose to eat a plate of veggies if it came to it. He also had in his mind ideas of planting a small plot of cereals and grains to enhance his diet; but this remained way down on the long-term project list.

For now, with Myrkais no longer on the island to support him, many of these ideas and plans had once again been shifted onto the back burner. The focus for John was on getting this wood onto the island and under cover before the storm arrived. After ten hours of solid physical effort he did achieve his task for the day; before swiftly collapsing at home in exhaustion.

# Chapter VI

## Wednesday, 21st July 2032

*S*hit. Get in you fucking bastard. I don't have time to deal
*with you being a pain in the arse. I've get seven more of*
*you fuckers to get done and Mother Nature ain't going to*
*be kind and hold back winter so that I can fiddle around*
with squeezing you into this fucking misshapen hole.'

A further three months had passed by since taking his delivery
of wood and John had only just prepared, and was fitting, his first
window frame. It had taken him more than a week to get to this
point and he knew that he had already passed the peak of summer
and that time was moving against him. Being inexperienced, John
had begun, pragmatically, with the simpler tasks of building his
wood shed and completing a new compost toilet. But both of these
projects had still taken the best part of two months to complete.
Now he was on to this final project and it was giving him plenty of
headaches because none of the window openings were uniform and
the rotted old frames were proving extremely hard to dislodge. John
was already exhausted from all he had done this year and he was
beginning to feel daunted and overwhelmed by what he had now
begun. Once he had pulled the frame out there was no turning
back.

*'Damn Myrkais for fucking leaving me in the lurch like this,'*
he muttered in exasperated rage as a chunk of wood chipped away
from the carved frame as it grazed into the rock wall. Even though
his guest had been long gone; John's rage had not yet followed him

off the island as every problematic situation he had met seemed to be an excuse to dredge up old feelings of injustice and blame. John could not move on and let go of the fact that the risk he had taken a year ago had not, financially, paid off for him in the end. He had long since let the expanded allotment fall fallow and now it had sadly become a haven for weeds. Every time his eyes turned towards it; the depressing thought arose that developments on the island had badly regressed this year.

It was already past eight o'clock in the evening and John was battling against the fading light at the end of another long and tiring day of work. It had been like this for weeks as he spent most of his time carrying out all his regular day-to-day chores around the property and only dived on into his carpentry projects when these were finished. Tiredness and a lack of aptitude for the job had long since turned these projects into a nightmare as John struggled gamely to translate the drawings he had made on paper into something real and solid. All too often though he had attacked the task in a state of rage; and it was not uncommon to see John furiously throwing bits of timber around the yard every time he made a mistake. He made so many mistakes in fact that he eventually had to go out and buy an extra boat load of wood. His face had been full of thunder for days after having been forced to take that decision.

Although it was too late in the season now, the thought had often crossed John's mind to bring in a second pair of hands; just for the summer period until the harvest had been gathered and the first autumn storm had rolled in. Putting that deadline in place seemed a logical and practical solution to avoid what had happened previously with Myrkais and the way his stay had turned sour. But John was in no mood to entertain such a solution for long and in truth he was not ready to open his island home again so soon. The idea was simply postponed until the spring along with his long list of projects for next year. Right now he would rather work a solid fifteen hour day than have that extra pair of hands helping him on the island.

John would have perhaps been surprised if he had been told

that he was not the first man to have declared war against the mainland and to have fought hard for his livelihood here. In modern times it was first purchased to create a new lighthouse station on this dangerous stretch of coastline and John's stone cottage was the original keeper's cottage that was built just shy of one-hundred years ago. The now abandoned lighthouse also remains standing; protruded on a rock that stands across a causeway on the other side of the island and that is only accessible at low tide.

Sadly, it wasn't put to use for much more than fifteen years as new technological advancements saw a powerful lighthouse emerge on the coast thirty miles south; a lighthouse so powerful that the one on Diarra was no longer required. The keeper was made redundant by the company; but he was so angry at the sharp way he was treated after such lengthy devoted service that he decided to remain here with his family and claimed the island as his own. A bitter dispute then took place as his previous employers tried and failed to evict him from the island. Eventually they gave up wasting their money on legal wrangling for a piece of land that now had little worth to them.

The keeper, his wife, and their two children stayed on in the cottage for a further five years and in that time they had added a couple of extra timber framed homes as they welcomed their extended family to join them. The keeper became the first man to establish the allotment on the island because no longer were his supplies given to him by the company from the mainland. John may not have known it but he had chosen a place that already had the history of a bitter exiled man setting camp there and saying 'fuck you' to the world.

However, that family eventually had to pay their dues as a vengeful fire saw those timber framed homes burn to the ground and the family was forced back onto the mainland. The stone cottage remained untouched.

For a long time after that Diarra remained empty and unused as locals felt the place offered a foreboding inhospitality; and word soon got around about the trials and tribulations of the previous tenants to put off any potential buyers who passed through. The cottage and lighthouse fell into a state of neglect. That continued until a real estate boom swept through the country twenty years ago and reached these parts. With life expectancy increasing, there was a growing demand from those wanting to retire out of the city and who were still healthy enough to create a new life for themselves in a remote part of the country. The island lifestyle also became fashionable and a raft of owners passed through this cottage over the intervening years.

However, none made it through to a second winter; all found the conditions here too harsh. Only the previous owner invested in improvements by splurging on the wind turbine and solar panels to replace an old generator that had guzzled fuel. Despite the difficulties, demand for Diarra remained high, and with every sale the price was raised until eventually John had to pay nearly all he had for it. After more than three years living here he had comfortably become the longest serving occupant of the stone cottage since that first family had vacated it.

After having successfully sealed in that first window frame; John somehow managed to complete the remaining seven over the next couple of months. When that first winter storm of the year rolled in at the beginning of October he was proud to see the success of his work as the cold draft that had constantly whipped through this cottage in the past had totally disappeared. Sat by the fire that evening; John couldn't believe how cosy and quiet it now was inside his home when compared to the wind and rain that lashed the cottage on the outside. For the first time in three years it felt as if he was able to retreat from the outside world and enter his own private sanctuary. There was a brief moment then when all the trials to reach this point were forgotten as he savoured the fruits of his labour. Not only had he completed what he had set out to do; but it had also been another bountiful year on his shrunken allotment. John had an abundance of produce in storage that would see him right through the winter.

By the force of sheer will it had turned into a prosperous year;

but if John thought that this would bring him lasting rewards then he was to be sadly disappointed. This year may have been challenging for him to endure in order to reach this point; but the coming months were going to take him down to depths that he could not yet possibly imagine.

## Chapter VII

*Wednesday, 29th December 2032*

It was mid-morning but John had yet to raise himself from his bed. Beyond closed curtains heavy rain clouds had gathered across the island and the light of day was swiftly turning once more to the blackness of night. Even though he had the heater running and had blankets wrapped around him; John shivered involuntarily and then coughed and sneezed. His body ached incessantly; and his back was especially sore from all the bending and heavy lifting he had done this year. Chopping up blocks of wood in early autumn had nearly tipped John completely over the edge. Today he was feeling very sorry for himself.

This was the third flu virus John had picked up in the space of a month and barely had he recovered from one before the next wave hit upon him. For weeks now he had been feeling fatigued and run down but this latest bout had taken him down to new depths. Nausea came upon him and John retched over a bowl; but there was nothing solid in him to bring up. John hadn't had the energy to make the journey across to the mainland in six weeks and so he had been reliant on his food stores to sustain himself. His diet had become bland and simple as John only had the strength to cobble together a large pot of root vegetable broth that would invariably last him a few days. He did not know what he needed to do in order to rebuild his immunity and his strength; and for the first time in years he felt a longing for his mother's hand and care.

His home may now have closed itself from the wintry winds;

but John's chilly mood permanently followed him like a draught anyway. Fleeting moments of frustrated short-temperedness were followed by long bouts of sagging depression. In scratching beneath the surface of all he had achieved this year; it was clear that no love had been etched in the wood John had carved and that a smile had not lit his face in months. Diarra had begun to turn upon him and to gnaw away at his flagging spirits.

Not only was John crippled low by his poor immunity and susceptibility to illness; he had also been struggling with sharp abdominal pains that came upon him suddenly and bent him over double; before slowly receding from whence they had come. Often they came at night and the pain would keep him awake for hours. He had run out of painkillers now; and in any case the ones he'd been taking had stopped having any effect on him.

These symptoms continued to have John in their hold for the next couple of weeks or so; but in his independence he stubbornly refused to admit that he needed to seek help. All he could try and do was to eat and rest. But then, on a crisp early January morning, John had an alarming wake-up call that he could not ignore. After a couple of day's respite he had woken up early and felt another wave of nausea come over him. What shocked him this morning was that when vomiting he also coughed up a small clot of blood. Later on he also noticed that spots of blood were also in his stools and that his urine had turned an unusual darker shade of green. Upon seeing all of this, John could no longer stubbornly pretend that this was nothing to worry about. In his isolation he began to panic and came close to suffering another hyperventilation attack as his breathing accelerated. After managing to calm himself; John lay there and felt very vulnerable and alone on his island.

But even in the midst of great pain John still retained his long-held mistrust of the system and any of those who worked within it. He had avoided medical institutions in his life for he firmly believed that doctors had no morals or ethics and were nothing more than pimps who took their cut for pushing the latest fancy drug on the market regardless of whether it helped or not. In fierce

41

defiance he refused to reach out to one for help. Instead the idea came the next morning to turn to the directory for those who were listed as being a part of the exchange network. To his surprise, John discovered that there was a woman on the list who advertised herself as a naturopath and a healer. And according to the directory she also lived not too far away in the major regional city of Wagsale. It was about an hour's journey south by train from Nabotan; the village where John moored his boat. Realising he had no time to waste he forced himself out of the house and onto his boat in order that he could telephone her. It would also be an opportunity to collect some much needed supplies for the home.

It was a freezing cold morning with a bitter wind blowing across the channel. John tightly wrapped his scarf around his neck and face. As he sat on the boat guiding the tiller towards the mainland; the irony was not lost on him that despite his best efforts to seal shut the fortress of his island home; right now he was weak and vulnerable and needing to reach out to another human hand. The shock of what had happened yesterday, on top of his ongoing pain, had humbled John to meekness. On the telephone, Mary-Helen said she would be delighted to see him and they agreed to meet at her home at midday on the following day. She was more than happy to accept a box of vegetables as payment.

# Chapter VIII

Tuesday, 18<sup>th</sup> January, 2033

After many weeks when John had barely left his home; it felt a long and arduous journey south for him by boat and train into the city of Wagsale. It was at least a fine, but crisp, morning and he had woken up feeling like it was one of his better days. He'd forced himself into eating a hearty breakfast of oats to sustain him through what he knew was going to be a stern test of his health. John was grateful that the feelings of nausea had retreated to the background.

Once at Wagsale station, John had to work his way out of the centre on foot and through to one of the older estates on the eastern edge of town. From the directions he'd been given; her house was less than a mile out of town. Having arrived in plenty of time John decided to test his constitution by walking there. It was slow progress but even in his delicate state he still had the wherewithal to look around at his environment with disapproving eyes.

*'My, my, I'd forgotten how fucking ugly city life can be. What a dump this place is. Look at all these rows and rows of squalid terraced housing all joined together. The way some folks choose to live; lying squashed on top of each other like that. Oh and look at that. Talk about the weeds taking over that garden. What a complete disgrace. Do the people living there not care about the filth they are living in? You have to wonder what weeds are going to be growing inside there head too. Yeah millions were spent jazzing up the city centre for the tourists but what are they doing about razing*

*this horrible shit hole to the ground!'*

John picked up his pace for he sensed a heavy and icky vibe around here that he didn't particularly like. The naturopath, Mary-Helen Thompson, apparently lived in the middle of all this squalor and he was immediately dubious as to what he would be receiving in exchange for the box of vegetables that he was struggling to carry under one arm. He mumbled to himself that he should have picked up a cab at the station; but despite these complaints he still had some stubborn pride left to plough on. It was quite enough to seek this woman's help today without asking for anymore. He was only dubious as to whether she would really have anything to give him that would get him back to health. The image of blood passed through his mind and made him wince.

John arrived and knocked hesitatingly at the door. The lady who opened was probably in her mid to late forties and was plump in nature with curly blonde hair floating down to her shoulders. John hesitated even more when he saw her because she had that noticeable motherly look which he instinctively detested because of his long estrangement from his own mother.

*'I surely can't trust someone like this*,' he thought to himself. To his mind she was one of those motherly looking women who like to get their claws into a man so that he can give them the children she wants; and then when he has he will promptly toss him out in the trash. Not that his own mother had been like that of course. She had tossed him out with his father too.

'You must be John. Please come inside,' she said opening the door wide.

'Thank you,' he answered; straining to be polite, as he followed her in. John shut the door behind him before placing his box on the empty table in the hallway. He was though already half looking around for an easy way out having already reached the conclusion that this had all been a very bad idea.

The house looked small and cramped and John assumed she must be living here alone as he was led through to the lounge area

44

and directed to take a seat on the couch. John was feeling breathless from his walk and was grateful to sit down. Nevertheless in doing so he felt a little uncomfortable that she hadn't set up a separate treatment room away from her home. It was unnerving for him to see a couple of framed family pictures above the empty fireplace and some personal papers and a woman's magazine strewn across the table before him. To him the whole set-up just seemed so unprofessional. He asked her why she worked from here and her answer was both blunt and honest.

'Because there are very few people who are interested in alternative treatments; so it is not worth setting up an empty room in such a small house or renting somewhere in town.'

'How do you make ends meet then?' John asked intrudingly.

'I work like everyone else does. I've just come back from a cleaning job for an extended lunch break. I have another job to go back to when you've gone.'

Her depressive manner left John feeling even more uncomfortable at having travelled all this way for someone who apparently had very little vitality to offer.

'Oh I never realised that you only did this as a hobby,' he said without tact.

'Don't think that the work I do is not important just because it is not valued by our society,' she reacted defensively with her hackles becoming raised. 'I thought you would at least understand that…being a part of this network as you are,' she added forcefully. John continued to fidget uncomfortably on the edge of his seat and she realised that a sore nerve had been touched and that she had lost her composure. It had been a long time since she had had a visitor, let alone a patient, in the house and she hadn't realised how much she had lost her confidence in the interlude.

Mary-Helen began to wonder quietly where her all conviction had gone to and was saddened that she was now so touchy to any criticism coming her way for the work she did. A couple of years ago all of her friends and family had thought her crazy to walk away from a secure comfortable job as a nurse in order to pursue a grander vision of healing work that she had long dreamed of and prepared herself for. They had turned their backs on her but in the beginning she had been strong enough to shrug off all those voices of worry and doubt because she had been so certain in what she was doing. However, whilst it is easy to feel vindicated when the rains come to water the tender seed you have planted and it shoots forth to life; it is tough to persist when there is nothing but drought that follows and the seed remains dormant and an un-manifested potential. Many months of effort had met with nothing more than uncooperative resistance. This drought had eroded away all of her conviction and faith in the niche she was so hopelessly trying to carve for herself in this world. And now the first drop of rain was falling and Mary-Helen could not help but see how insecure she was feeling as she desperately reached for it in the hope that it would not pass her by.

'Can I take your jacket?' she asked in a fluster as she tried to change the subject quickly before John could draw her into a discussion that would only cause things to deteriorate further.

'I'm fine with it on,' John replied sharply as if ready to get this over with.

'Well would you like a drink?' she pleaded.

'I'm fine,' John replied firmly.

'So perhaps we can start then. Do you want to tell me a little bit about the problem you'd like my help with?' she asked, whilst hesitantly taking a seat and trying to turn the attention over to him. She had been thrown by his abrupt manner and was desperately trying to rebalance.

John almost said there and then that he didn't and that this had been a terrible mistake. But then his abdomen started cramping and he winced a little at the pain which gave him the impetus to go on. He at least wanted to get something in return for his efforts in coming here…and for his box of vegetables.

'I've been under the weather for a few weeks with a virus and

I'm also having these abdominal pains for the last couple of months. I thought it might be indigestion but they haven't gone away.'

'Can I take a look John?' she asked moving in closer.

He lifted up his jacket; albeit with a great resistance

She leaned in closer, touched around his abdomen cautiously and gave a nod.

'Yes it feels a little tender and very swollen beneath your right ribs in particular; suggesting to me that there may be some strain on your liver. I also noticed your skin is looking a little pale and jaundiced as well. Do you have any other symptoms?'

'Not really.' John answered pulling his jacket down quickly. He did not enjoy a woman's hand touching his skin. An image passed through his mind of the blood that he had seen and for a brief moment he wobbled and was about to open up and reveal his hand. But a voice of doubt forced his lips shut; John simply could not trust her with the whole truth.

'What about feelings of extra tiredness or fatigue?'

'Well maybe a little. But that's probably due to these cold viruses I've picked up over the winter.'

'Has that included nausea and vomiting?'

'Yes, occasionally.'

'And have you lost your appetite at all?'

'Yes. But only because I haven't the energy to put food in front of me.'

'So you have been losing some weight since the pain began.'

'I don't know.'

'Well do your clothes fit more loosely?'

'Yeah I guess they do. But like I say I've been living off nothing more than a vegetable broth for weeks.'

'And have these abdominal pains gotten worse over time or do they just come and go?'

'They tend to come for a few hours then go. I can't say if they have gotten worse.'

'Does it affect your sleep at night?'

'Well it mostly happens through the night so yes.'

'How much alcohol would you say you drink each week?'

'I don't touch alcohol; I never have.'

'How was your diet before you were ill? Your body still appears unhealthily overweight for your age and size.'

'As I say I mainly eat the vegetables I grow on the island. There's nothing wrong with my diet...or my weight,' he answered defiantly.

'And how are you feeling emotionally John? Are there any particular stresses or strains you are under?'

'Nothing new.'

'So do you have any stresses or strains that have been around a long time?'

'Not really. Life is pretty good generally,' he said; brushing over the facts that could have surely told a different tale. John definitely did not want to go where this conversation was heading.

'Well tell me a bit about your family history? Is your mother still alive?'

'I wouldn't have a clue. She walked out on me and my father when I was seven and I haven't heard from her since.'

'Oh dear, John; I'm sorry. Do you know what her reasoning was?'

'I was never told. But knowing the reason doesn't make a difference; her walking out is inexcusable anyway.'

'I see. So you were brought up alone by your father after that?'

'Yes. However, he was very busy with the business so I had a nanny looking after me a lot of the time until I got to senior school and my father thought I was old enough to manage without one.'

'And is your father still alive?'

'No he committed suicide when I was thirteen.'

'That must have been very tough for you to deal with John,' she replied and took a deep exhalation. 'I'm sorry for your loss. Who looked after you from then?' she added.

'An uncle took me in although he soon packed me off to boarding school and then on to university. After that I went and worked in the city for a few years before coming out to an island north of here about four years ago.'

'You feel you've coped well then from your challenging childhood?'

'Challenging?'

'Well was not the untimely disappearance of your two parents from your life challenging for you John?'

'I guess,' he answered shrugging his shoulders nonchalantly.

'But you soon get used to fighting your own battles.'

'And you haven't felt the need for any help and support before now?'

'Look here, I didn't come here for a counselling session. I just thought you might have something that could help take the pain away without me having to go and visit a damn doctor. Do you have anything or not?' he answered abruptly bringing the discussion to a close. Clearly John's patience with these nagging questions had snapped and there was no chance now for Mary-Helen to wedge open the door that had just been slammed shut.

'I am only trying to get a handle on what is happening with you John. If you're not willing to help me then I can't possibly help you,' she answered weakly and defensively.

'Well this has been a complete waste of time hasn't it! I'm not surprised that people don't come to you for help. It looks to me as if you need to stick to your cleaning and to forget about your hobby.'

'There's no need to get angry and offensive John. I spent many years working as a nurse and on top of that have many years training in naturopathy and as a healer. I am simply here to offer and share with you what I've learnt.'

'So you're willing to share your words but where's the hard stuff to back it up? Don't you have any herbs or something tucked away somewhere that you give out to your patients? Or do you simply like to sit down and have a *chat*?'

John was almost shocked to hear himself saying these bitter words aloud. But he was sick and didn't want to leave without getting something in return for his vegetables. Mary-Helen simply felt jarred by his insolence.

'I can give you herbs if that is what you want but there is so much more that we could do together to help improve your situation.'

'Well thanks for the offer but the herbs are all that I want.'

'As you wish,' she replied, unconsciously raising her eyebrows at his stubbornness. 'From what I've seen I would suggest you take some herbs that will help give your liver a detox. This may make your symptoms worse to begin with but if you take them regularly they will hopefully ease a touch. I can also give you something to help rebuild your immunity. I will just go and check if I have these to give to you.'

She soon came back carrying two separate glass jars containing some dried herbs.

'You are in luck that these are two of the few jars I have remaining in my supplies. If you make a tea two or three times a day with both then you will hopefully find your symptoms easing. If you use just a small teaspoon per serving then this supply should last for about a month.'

John took the jars from her politely but was not gracious enough to thank her for her time as he stood up to leave. It was only as John walked through the gate and onto the street that Mary-Helen called out after him.

'Even if your symptoms should ease in the next couple of weeks I would urge you to visit a doctor and get them to take some tests for your liver.'

John did not turn around or reply.

Mary-Helen shut the door and loudly cursed herself for the way the session had gone. She tore her hands through her hair in abject frustration and despair before crumpling to the ground in tears. In that moment she was certain that the promise of rain had just slipped on past before it had even touched the seed and that it would never return. After yesterday's sudden glimmer of hope, given by John's surprising phone call, she had allowed herself to dream again that things would pick up for her. However, it had been dashed onto the rocks as quickly as it had arisen and she felt worse than if the call had never come. The mere thought of that left her utterly depressed. But with great effort she wiped her eyes, rose to her feet, and collected her things for her afternoon's work. With slumped shoulders she trudged out of the house to return to a cleaning job that did nothing to lift her spirits. To Mary-Helen this was insipid work. And though she was a humble woman who did not think it beneath her; she still knew deep down in her soul that she was standing in shoes that she had never been destined to fill. But bills had to be paid and so what else could be done?

## Chapter IX

John arrived home and he was feeling thoroughly wiped out from the long journey south and from his second boat trip to the mainland and back in as many days. He spent the next day recuperating in bed. John did as Mary-Helen had told him by brewing three cups of tea a day from each of the jars of herbs. However, despite noticing some overall gradual improvement over the next week or so; the symptoms still persisted. Because the pain felt so intense John remained highly dubious as to whether a few herbs could really help him and Mary-Helen's final words were still ringing in his ears to go and get medical opinion on it. John finally walked down to the jetty and prepared to go to the mainland in order to make the dreaded call. He got as far as the water's edge before stopping and holding his head in his hands.

'What the fuck am I doing? Am I so fucking weak and hypocritical just because I can't bear a little bit of pain? Yeah how everyone would look and laugh at me if they could see me now. John the lone warrior who went to fight the world; and who is now down on his knees begging for help. How the fuck has it come down to this. To think of all the money that I screwed out of the city to buy this place and to give the world the finger…and yet here I am now sticking that finger back up my own arse. Oh how those people would mock me if they saw me looking so weak and pathetic like this. Oh how my mother would rub her hands in glee at having washed her hands of me…and oh how my father would be ashamed that I couldn't be any stronger than him.'

John shook his bowed head before turning back around. He dug in his heels through the weekend before finally surrendering to the inevitable. Once more he took the walk and this time he followed through in making the crossing and giving the call to the nearest surgery; which was also back down in Wagsale. He had hoped in phoning that the surgery would have a locum working in Nabotan; but he was told disappointingly that everything had been centralised to cut costs and that he would indeed have to travel all the way south into the city. *Bloody economic lunacy*, he thought to himself whilst the receptionist spoke. He pushed for a better option but was told in reply that doctor's didn't even do call outs from the surgery anymore. If it was an emergency he could get an ambulance sent out to take him to the hospital there…but he would have to pay for the privilege. Ignoring his bitter complaints; the receptionist finally booked John in for an appointment for Monday the following week.

*Monday, 7th February, 2033*

When the day of his appointment arrived; John forced himself out of bed despite a sleepless night. It was not one of his better morning's and it was with a feeling of great strain that he made the journey south on the first train of the day. At least the doctor's surgery was located around the corner from the railway station and he did not have far to travel on foot. He was well ahead of time as he registered and waited in the reception area to be seen.

When John's name was called he steeled himself and took a firm walk down the corridor and into the open door at the far end. The doctor was wearing his white clinical attire and looked to be portraying an image of authority; even though it appeared to John as if he was barely out of grad school with his boyish features. He had his head down and was busy scribbling something on paper.

'Take a seat Mr Waideman,' he stated coldly after hearing the door close. He didn't even lift up his head from his writing as he spoke and John sat down opposite feeling ill at ease to be in this unwelcoming, cold and sterile environment. Finally, after a long uncomfortable period for John, the doctor put down his pen and looked up in acknowledgment of the person sat across from him. John noticed though that the doctor didn't even try to catch his eye.

'Now what's the problem?' he asked directly. The doctor made it clear to John that his time was precious and that he had no space in his diary for pleasantries.

'I've been getting some severe abdominal pains these past few months. It is almost as if...'

The doctor didn't let John finish and interrupted rudely:

'Okay. Come up and lie down on this bed and I'll check you over.' John did as he was told. 'Now lift your top up for me,' the doctor added brusquely.

John did as he asked and the doctor began to prod around to see where it felt sore. When he touched the same spot as Mary-Helen the doctor merely gave an 'ahh-humm' sound that did little to reassure him. John was told to sit up and pull his top on again.

'We are going to need to take a blood test and we will contact you to book you an appointment when we get the results,' he suggested matter-of-factly.

'Do you have any idea what it might be? I had some advice that it may be a problem with my liver. Can you tell if it is something to worry about?'

'We will know more when we get the results. I can prescribe you some stronger painkillers in the meantime if the pain is unbearable?'

'So you can't tell me anything else?'

'Not at this stage. We will know more when we get the results,' he repeated.

John rolled his eyes and gave a sigh at this unresponsive clinician before him. The red mist of anger was beginning to simmer.

'So you are saying that I have travelled all the way here for this?'

'Mr Waideman, my next appointment is due,' he answered looking at the clock on the wall. John had barely been here five minutes and couldn't believe that after a journey of nearly two hours to get here that this was all that he was entitled to. Loathe as he was to admit it; at least Mary-Helen had shown some interest and concern in his suffering. 'The nurse will come and take you for the test. Do you want me to prescribe you any painkillers?'

John shook his head in mock indignation before standing up to go.

'How long will the results take to come through?' John asked more coolly.

'A few days; we will give you a call to book your next appointment when they are ready.'

'I live on an island and have no way of being contacted. Can I book the appointment now?'

'I see. Arrange an appointment then for next Monday with the receptionist on your way out,' he replied as he buzzed for the nurse to come and lead John away.

*Monday, 14th February, 2033*

When the following Monday arrived; John was hesitant about going because he had barely recovered from the exertions of his last trip. The feelings of fatigue and exhaustion had not eased at all over the winter and he had forgotten what it was like to wake up and feel in good health and spirits. He was also feeling nervous as to what awaited him at the end of that long arduous journey today and he was not holding out for any positive news. He just hoped that the doctor would show him a pathway back to health again because the list of jobs that needing doing around the home was growing by the day.

It had been another early start so as to catch the first train into

Wagsale. As it was still wintertime, the first light of day was only beginning to catch the land as he left the home. There were though small glimmers of spring appearing as he walked to the jetty. After four years on the island he had become more attuned to the rhythms of nature and the signs she communicated; even though it gave him little cheer today. The first train was a commuter train and John felt out of place amongst the men and women crammed on board in their office attire ready for another day in the city. He found it disconcerting that the tentacles of the rat race had spread this far north beyond the major cities of the south. He did not miss those days one bit and felt grateful that being exposed to those past memories was such a rare event. On Diarra he could remain oblivious to what was happing in the outside world; he was no longer a part of this daily death march.

John arrived at the surgery ahead of his appointment; but he was grateful to have a seat and to catch his breath. He glimpsed the doctor popping out of his office momentarily and couldn't help but wonder if he would be in a better mood today. John certainly hoped for something more than what he'd got last week.

Even though it was early morning; the doctor was already running behind schedule and John waited impatiently. He feared that this delay would not help matters at all. Finally when his name was called he walked down to his surgery room and knocked on the door. If anything, the doctor showed an even more cold and grim facial manner as John turned to look at him sat firmly behind his desk. At least he did seem more present and attentive this time and not off in the past writing up notes from the last patient and shooing him out the door in a hurry so that he could get on with the next. The doctor held out his hand for John to take a seat without a word after John had shut the door behind him. However, rather than his attention being a comfort, the gravity of his stare was unnerving and left John feeling more fearful. He could tell instinctively that the doctor had something weighing more heavily on his shoulders and that he wouldn't be able to just boot John out of the door with painkillers this time.

'Well, what do the results say?' John blurted out anxiously before he had even sat down. He needed to break this moment of tense anticipation before it lingered on.

'We have found some anomalies in your blood test and we need to carry out a scan to understand what could be causing the anomaly. We have booked you to see a radiologist at the hospital this afternoon.'

'Anomalies? What sort of anomalies?'

'We will know more once we have carried out these further tests.'

The fear John was feeling rolled into anger at the doctor's non responsiveness. Suddenly his temperature rose at the powerlessness he felt in the situation and the lack of anything secure to grab hold of. The desk between the two of them felt like a wall and John was just desperate to smash it down. He was begging for some intimate contact but didn't have a clue how to ask for it.

'Well you're a fucking clinician aren't you? What did they teach you all those years? Don't hide behind your mask of fucking anomalies and I can't fucking say anything till I get some more fucking test results. What's your hunch doc? Is it the fucking liver? Oh don't just sit there hiding behind your desk like you're about to fucking cry. Have you never had to deal with a real fucking patient before? I'm over these fucking systems and procedures and stiff upper lips. Can you stop fucking hiding behind them and come out and get real with me? I am a human being you know who is fucking afraid of what on earth is going on with me. That's right I'm fucking afraid that there might be something serious to worry about here and all you can do is palm me off with your cool professional mask of 'I don't really give a shit if you are sick or not and I'm not going to fucking tell you what I really know about it'.'

John was standing now with his hands placed provocatively on the desk. As a man who'd spent his life avoiding conflict he found it strange to be postured like this after a bitter spoken outburst. But if you push someone hard enough into a corner eventually they will snap. And John hated anyone who held a position of authority over him; he had clearly hit his tolerance threshold with this man. And though he was not a violent person who had never laid a finger on another person in his life; the doctor did not know this and he was certainly feeling threatened by this show of aggression. Instinctively he placed one hand down close to the buzzer on the side of his desk that was there to attract a nurse or receptionist; but he chose to hold off from pressing it just yet.

A long silence fell between them as John waited wide-eyed for an answer and the doctor grappled inwardly for something that could diffuse the situation. It was soon obvious to both of them that his mental search for the right words was unfolding without success and it was as if he had no skill in how to deal with a patient who needed something more than a pile of drugs handed over the impenetrable wall between them. John was beginning to conclude rather dryly that this man had probably spent far too much time fingering dead bodies in his training and not enough on talking to living ones.

'I think you need to calm down Mr Waideman. I am here to help you,' he finally spoke. 'Now take this appointment card to Wagsale General Hospital. Your appointment is due at midday… and they may want to keep you in until we receive the results,' the doctor eventually stuttered and with nervousness in his pitch of voice. He said all of this with averted eyes.

John scowled menacingly at him but he knew there was nothing more to say. The doctor was clearly too well scripted in his professional monologue to get pulled into a dialogue of conversation with his patients. John might as well be talking to the female voice who gives directions in those navigation devices they have in motor cars; and who would just keep on saying '*take the next left*' over and over in mechanical response, if, with tears streaming down your face, you demanded her to give some compassion in answer to your suffering.

'Well thanks for your fucking time doctor,' was all John could say sarcastically; as he snatched the appointment card out of the man's hand and turned to go.

# Chapter X

John walked briskly and breathlessly to the hospital after having been given directions by the receptionist. Not that he really needed them because one look across the city and the grey concrete leviathan could quite easily be seen rising up above the flat landscape. He ignored the exhaustion and nausea he felt as anger coursed through his veins. John was fuming with this whole charade, and once he had arrived at the entrance, he was soon overwhelmed by the monstrous size of the building that spanned out before him. According to the sign at the entrance it was a building that could house more people than a small town.

*'Fuck these inhumane institutions,'* he muttered to himself as he bumbled his way around the maze of corridors looking for the radiology department. When he finally arrived at the right place a nurse came out and met John and told him to take a seat. As he had arrived well before his appointment time he had to wait sometime…but this wait did nothing to chill his mood. The radiologist eventually came and took him through for a scan. John tried to pry him for further information on what was happening, what the anomalies were with his blood test, and what he was looking for in the scan. But the radiologist was not at all forthcoming and simply told John to relax.

*'Well that's fucking helpful advice,'* he muttered to himself sarcastically under his breath as he went through the machine. After the scan John met with the hospital doctor who said that, depending on the results, he may have to come back in for further

tests in the next couple of days. This news only left John feeling more worried.

'Is it not possible to stay in the hospital and wait for the results?' John asked. He suddenly felt insecure and not at all looking forward to travelling home.

'I'm afraid we are short of beds at the moment and don't have the space to accommodate patients who don't require treatment,' he replied. His words felt cold and dismissive to John's ears. John was clearly unwanted and unloved here and that feeling almost brought forth tears to his eyes.

'But I live far away from here on an island just off the coastal village of Nabotan and I am just too tired and exhausted to travel back and forth again so soon,' he pleaded weakly.

'Can you find accommodation in the city until your results come?' the doctor answered clinically; somehow missing the cue for him to respond with a more compassionate offering.

'I can't afford that,' John answered decisively as if to push the doctor for a better alternative.

The doctor sat quietly for a moment to consider the options.

'I can't give you a bed that I don't have but what I can do is take a biopsy now as a precaution before sending you home to rest.'

'What does a biopsy involve?'

'Well we would apply a local anaesthetic to the area we want to look at and would insert a small needle into your skin to collect some tissue that we would then examine under the microscope to get a clear diagnosis. We generally only take this measure though if the scan confirms there is a problem; but I can do it now if you insist.'

'Well yes go ahead and do it now. But will it take long as my last train home leaves before five and so I will have to leave here at four-thirty at the latest.'

'Oh, that's going to be a problem,' he said looking at his wristwatch. 'The biopsy itself only takes a few minutes but we will need

61

to keep you in a few hours for observation. Four-thirty will be pushing it. Are you sure you can't find accommodation tonight?'

'Positive,' John answered refusing to budge.

'Well at the very least you have to promise that you will take a taxi back to the station because I don't want you overexerting yourself for at least the next twenty-four hours.'

'Are you going to pay for that taxi?' John asked sarcastically; still desperately trying to push the doctor to relent and give him a bed here for the night. He wasn't especially keen on going back to an empty home now; let alone in a few hours after this biopsy.

'Will you promise me?' the doctor repeated sternly as he completely ignored John's pleas for even a small act of kindness.

'Very well,' John lied through gritted teeth. Inwardly he thought to himself that he had no intention of paying for a fucking taxi and that now he just wanted to get this shit over with. He also knew that the doctor didn't care if he was lying or not and that he was only asking because he didn't want it resting on his conscience if John was found collapsed on the street one or two blocks down the road. '*Then again, if that happens he will have to give me a bed,*' John suddenly thought mischievously to himself.

'But how long will I have to wait for the results?' he added

'Usually a week or two depending on our workload. Your doctor's surgery will contact you to make an appointment when they are ready.'

'As I've just said I live on an island and so cannot be contacted,' John answered coldly.

'I see,' the doctor answered scratching his head and, to John's mind, he was probably thinking that he had more important things to be getting on with than dealing with these petty logistics. 'Let me see if I can pencil in an appointment for you with the surgery now and I will try and make sure the results are ready by then.' After checking his diary he picked up the phone and arranged an appointment for John for a fortnight Monday at eleven o'clock in the morning. After that he stood up to go but John persisted by trying to get some information a third time.

'Oh I know you are too busy to care but could you humour me a little by telling me what this scan and biopsy are for?' John asked rudely. He was beyond caring that this man would walk away thinking that this patient was being a real pain in the ass.

'There are anomalies in your blood test Mr Waideman and we need to carry out these tests to ascertain what is going on,' the doctor answered as he completely ignored the barbs thrown at him.

'That doesn't fucking tell me anything doctor! Now why can't you answer the fucking question?'

'We don't wish to cause you any unnecessary worry or alarm Mr Waideman until we have a clear diagnosis.'

'Well I have to tell you that the whole fucking mystery is not leaving me any less worried or alarmed. You're just being a fucking control freak by playing these games with me.'

'Calm down Mr Waideman. I am here to help you.'

John said nothing more and simply shook his head again. He was resigned to the blank wall of silence that was once again placed before him. The doctor stood up and nonchalantly brushed away any lingering discharge from this conversation by pretending to himself that he had fulfilled his professional duty and could now move on to the next patient. He simply asked John to wait in reception for a nurse to come and take him when a bed was free.

As John walked out and sat in reception he could not help muttering to himself:

*There it was again; the whole 'I am here to help you' line that clearly must be drummed into all these fucking doctors in grad school. They could be sticking a knife in my back and yet that is all they would be able to say to me whilst they are doing it. Seven years of study into patient care and they only have one fucking line to show for it! What a fucking joke!'*

It was pushing past four thirty before John managed to get out of this monstrous building. He'd had to wait sometime for a bed to be vacated and so he had only received two of the recommended four hours of recovery time after the biopsy. He was feeling tired and overwhelmed from all that had happened but stubbornly he refused to jump into one of the long line of waiting taxi cabs at the front. After he'd walked past the first cab in the line, John turned around and angrily raised his middle finger at the hospital building that was behind him. This was a last show of defiance; a desperate attempt to show the world that no-one could tell him what he could or could not do.

The light was fading and the sun was beginning to set behind the thick grey clouds that hung across the sky. It was an anxious breathless dash across the city to meet the train and John arrived with barely a couple of minutes to spare. He was fortunate not to have triggered one of his hyperventilation attacks in this foolish gesture of bravado. He was also starving and feeling woozy from not having eaten since breakfast; but there would be no possibility of food for another hour and a half or so until he got home.

Although it was now getting on to late winter and the nights were drawing out, it was almost dark when the train pulled out of the city and so it was a long and gloomy journey home. On his arrival at Nabotan, light drizzle was falling as he walked the short distance to the water's edge and pulled himself wearily into the boat. John started the motor and cast the torch down onto the water to help guide him safely to the eastern shore.

# Chapter XI

## Monday, 28<sup>th</sup> February, 2033

After two long weeks of waiting for his next appointment; John had done nothing more than stew in his own worry. The scan and biopsy sounded serious and it was hard to stop his mind from unravelling with worst-case scenarios. The anger from that conversation with the doctor at the surgery, as well as the one with the doctor at the hospital, was still alive in him and there had been no-one to listen to his airing of the problems with the healthcare system in this country. Their measly words of *'I'm here to help'* had remained firmly stuck in John's throat like a broken record. He was certain that his condition had only gotten worse since visiting those places.

On top of that there was a lot of weeding to do and his job list was still piling up on him. Luckily his supplies were still plentiful to keep him going; although some days it remained hard for John to even put a meal together and on the table. On those occasions the pain made it difficult for him to even sit up and to get out of bed; although he did have to think of his goat and his chickens. In fact, it was because these animals were relying on him that they helped pull John through each day and kept him going. Nevertheless, he knew that he was in a downward spiral and that his poor diet was not helping him regain his strength. Mary-Helen's jars of herbs had all been used up and a new stronger dose of painkiller had also run its course. And all this while, he knew that the doctor was holding on to a piece of information that could surely help him and his worsening condition.

When the day of the appointment finally arrived John was so fed up that he longed to stick two fingers up at the system and to say *'fuck you'*, like he'd done before in quitting his job and buying this island all those years before. But in truth he was now a pale imitation of that feisty young man and he no longer had the strength to be so petulant. Meekly he took the long journey south once more.

When his name was called it felt to him as if he was back in some horrible nightmare déjà vu loop as he walked that corridor into the doctor's surgery room. John noticed that the doctor didn't have the same authoritative poise after what'd happened during their last tête-à-tête and he looked across at John with a certain wary trepidation as if he'd been dreading this appointment in his schedule all night long. John simply smiled sarcastically at the doctor as if to mock any smug sense of him being in charge here. In that smile John was sending out the message that yes you may hold a secret piece of information over me that you don't want to give out easily but I am not going to come here and give you the satisfaction of begging for it. Instead he sat down firmly, crossed his arms, and waited for the doctor to speak first. He had in his hands John's results and John watched him look down at them nervously. The doctor was hesitant and John wasn't sure if that was caused by what he was looking at or by his fear of the man sat opposite him. Finally the doctor spoke to break the silence.

'We have had the results of the scan and biopsy through Mr Waideman. I don't know how to break this to you gently but the results reveal the worst possible diagnosis. I am sad to tell you that you are in the advanced stages of liver cancer.'

The unmentionable 'c' word hit John like a lightning bolt from the sky. Cancer? Could it really be true? Not even in his worst wildest thoughts had he considered cancer a possibility. Surely he was too young to have got cancer?

'Liver cancer?' John repeated; hoping that somehow he'd misheard.

'That's right Mr Waideman. Liver cancer.'

'But it's only alcoholics that get fucking liver cancer...and I've never fucking touched a drop of that shit in my whole life!'

'Alcohol is only one of a number of factors that may contribute to the condition. From the results of these tests we can detect that there has been some heavy scarring of your liver tissue which has led to cirrhosis of the liver. Because your liver cells have not been performing healthily they have become susceptible to attack from new cancerous cells which have created a large tumour.'

'Can you be so certain of that?'

'Yes the results are conclusive.'

'But I've only had problems for the last couple of months. Surely it can't happen so quickly?'

'One of the challenges we have with detecting liver damage early enough is that the symptoms often don't show in patients until it's too late. The scarring of the tissue may have been building up for many months or even years without affecting the functioning of the liver.'

'So what can you do to get this cancer out of my system?'

'Unfortunately there is nothing we can do.'

'What the fuck! There's nothing you can do?' John answered disbelievingly and in a state of complete shock at the man's cold impotence and directness of manner. 'What about surgery or chemotherapy...or something else for fuck's sake?'

'The problem with your liver cancer is that it is very advanced and will continue to spread very rapidly. On a scale yours is rated one of the worst diagnoses. If we could have detected it earlier then yes these may have been options for us. It is true that we could still try and give you a course of chemotherapy but the authorities are cutting back funds and have determined that it is not an efficient investment of resources for the return we get from this treatment in terms of positive results.'

John received his harsh words like poison and it almost made him choke with anger to hear them.

'I'm not a fucking digit on your calculator you know. I have rights as a human being here, so don't talk of me as just another fucking statistic that isn't worth the risk to try and heal from this shit.'

'It is out of my hands Mr Waideman,' he said limply, in a tone that held no power.

'Well how much money do you need to give me that treatment? I can sell my island if you want,' John pleaded desperately.

'The system doesn't work like that Mr Waideman. It is administered by regulations based on who would receive the most benefit from the treatment and not who would pay the most. Even if you could sell your island to cover the cost; chemotherapy would probably not have any real effect on an advanced condition that we would consider incurable. You can try and get legal advice to fight for it if you want…but I wouldn't advise you to take that road.'

'So what would you advise then? What can you do?'

'All we can do is to try and manage your pain whilst the cancer runs its course.'

'Manage my fucking pain. Is that the best you can do? After all your years of training, and with all the fucking research and technology you have in your hands; the best you can offer is to manage my fucking pain.'

'That is the best we can do Mr Waideman.'

John fell quiet at the hopelessness of wasting his time with this boy before him and the systems he was a part of. John suddenly felt very tired at the prospect of fighting him and the institutions behind him just to get his voice heard and listened to.

'How long do you think I've got?' was all he could say in a hushed whisper as the angry tone blew itself out in the hopeless air.

'Judging from the results of your biopsy and the amount of scarring of your liver we detected on the scan; you are probably looking at three to six months…maybe a year at best.'

The death sentence the doctor gave came heavily upon his shoulders and John felt utterly weak and alone as it sank through.

'Do you have friends and family around you to give you some support with regards this news?' the doctor asked as he tried to show some kindness and concern.

John shook his head and stood up to go. He didn't want this boy's pity and his contrived words of concern felt empty and meaningless. John knew then, as somehow he'd always known, that the system had abandoned him and that he couldn't come here again looking for something that was never going to be given to him.

'Well we at least need to talk about moving you into a hospice then. It says in my notes that you live alone on an island and I really don't think it is a good idea for you to go back there like this.'

'Fucking leave me alone will you,' John answered back coldly. 'I don't want your fucking pity.'

'Please Mr Waideman you must listen to me. If you are not yet ready to consider a hospice then at the very least you must let me prescribe you with some morphine to help ease the pain until you are ready to discuss this,' the doctor added urgently as if he was suddenly struck by a desire to try and do something helpful. He was fearful that he may well be the last person that this man before him would ever speak to if he left the surgery like this. John was almost surprised to hear his begging pleas of concern. But then again, he thought, the doctor was probably just thinking of himself and was worried of how it might look on his own performance review if he was discovered dead on the island alone. Because something like that certainly wouldn't look good for the doctor at any inquest.

'Fucking leave me alone,' John repeated again more firmly this time. 'And I don't want your fucking morphine either,' he said both defiantly and definitively; before leaning over and snatching the results from the doctor's hand on his way out.

John left the surgery in a daze. He was in no shape to return back to the island and went instead to a nearby coffee shop. He rarely drank coffee but he took a double shot of espresso to soothe

the shock. Yet there was surely no substance in this world that could ease the conversation that had just taken place. Three to six months was what he'd been told; just like that. John thought that he should have a good fifty years of life stretching out ahead of him…not a few weeks. And although John was not especially enamoured to be here on this planet; he definitely wanted to leave on his terms and when he was ready. And right now he was not ready to go because he did not feel at peace that he had achieved all that he had set out to achieve. And he definitely didn't want to leave in pain.

Deep down John knew that the doctor was right and that if he went back to the island like this; that he could quite easily curl up into a ball and fall away unnoticed in a pool of filth. After what he'd been through the past few months it didn't seem an attractive or pleasant way to go. But at the same time he had no desire to go to a hospice where he would be surrounded by the smell of sickly death at every turn and with his body pumped high with toxic drugs. Naturally his thoughts then turned to just bringing it to an end here and now and follow the way of his father by taking his own life. Surely that would be a lot swifter and a less painless way to go. And no-one would miss him. But somehow that thought depressed him just as much as any other option. John put his head in his hands:

*'Oh father; I know now how you felt when the institutions you relied on abandoned you, took away your livelihood, and left you to die. And here is your only son going down the same road despite all I've done to stop it. Oh what a tragic and cursed family we are from to have two of its men taken in their prime.'*

John ordered and knocked back another double shot of espresso and tears began to fall down his cheek. He was resigned and seemed too fatigued to look for any other way out of this tragic fate that was befalling him. All that fierce bluster of defiant omnipotence that he had wrapped around himself this past decade had finally been unravelled and it had taken barely a matter of minutes to pull away that mask. Without any defences he was forced into sitting here feeling naked, vulnerable and exposed. He was utterly alone.

But then a young waitress came over to take away John's two empty cups and as she reached out her hand she stopped for a moment, lifted her focused gaze, and looked at him. He wanted to turn away and cover up the fact that tears were still welling in those eyes because it was a honed instinct to be distrusting. But John had no will left to fight and that little boy inside was captivated by the warm glow that she emanated in that simple moment of eye contact. Without any shield of defence it was a piercing glance that went straight through into his soul. It was uncomfortable to bear but that little boy so wanted to be seen, to be held, to be loved and she was giving all of that in a way that no words can convey. She smiled compassionately and all the depression that hung from the doctor's cold touch of hand was momentarily washed away by its power. As she turned away again it was as if both of them knew that no words of sympathy would suffice and that they would have only ruined the tender moment they had just shared. And in those eyes, and in that smile, he saw a way through. John had to go and visit Mary-Helen again; and he knew he had to go immediately.

# THE SEPARATION

## Chapter XII

Mary-Helen had already returned home as she had only been required to work for a few hours that morning. She was surprised to hear the sound of knocking at her door. As she opened it she saw that the man standing before her looked far different from the one who had visited a month or so before. She immediately felt anguished to see him in this vulnerable state. John stood there awkwardly and blushed as he remembered his rudeness the last time he had walked away from her. He felt as desperate as he surely looked.

'I'm sorry to turn up here unannounced,' he finally mumbled. 'Can I please come in for a moment?'

'I was expecting you John,' was all that Mary-Helen mysteriously replied. For her this was more a welcoming affirmation of faith than what she truly felt in that moment. Since his departure she had fallen into a deep trough of depression and it was only her book of positive affirmations that had helped her to endure it.

Mary-Helen had been hard on herself for she soon realised that on John's first visit that she had behaved like a victim who was entitled to receive the reward of a patient to heal after all that she had sacrificed for it. John hadn't played along with that script and had simply shone a light on something ugly in her that she had not wanted to see before. She still struggled to face it now; but nevertheless the experience had strengthened her with humility and she was ready to give herself fully into service.

John thought it was an odd thing to say; but her words were at least reassuring and helped him to relax. She opened the door wide and allowed John to pass her by before she shut the door behind them and began to follow him into her lounge. A loud crash stopped her in her tracks as she had knocked into an empty glass resting on the side table; where it fell and shattered. John jumped in shock at the noise behind him. Mary-Helen, however, did not react for she knew instinctively that it was a sure sign of energy beginning to shift.

'Please go in and take a seat; I will clear this up first,' she spoke reassuringly.

John had taken the same seat as before and when Mary-Helen came in she sat down adjacent to him.

'How have you been?' was her first natural question to ask; although he was sure that his appearance would have revealed as much as any words.

'Not well. I've just come from the doctor's with a shitty diagnosis.' John said grimly whilst holding out the results that were still firmly wedged into his hand. He took a moment's pause. It was hard to say the next sentence aloud. 'It's cancer in my liver,' he finally spat the words out.

She reached across to touch his hand and looked at him softly in the eyes. She now had that same warm glow of light that the waitress had had. Gone was that sad and depressed woman who John had seen before and who'd had no vitality in her veins.

'I felt it might have been something like that. Can they offer you treatment?'

'No. They won't do shit apart from offering a few painkillers and a bed to die in.'

Uttering the death word aloud brought a huge lump into John's throat and more tears rose up inside and threatened to engulf him. He fought them back whilst Mary-Helen paused as if to find the right words in reply.

'I understand what you are feeling John because that's exactly

76

why I left the profession myself. I saw many people like you who needed healing but who could not receive that healing from the people they expected it from. But I'm afraid that there are no magic herbs I can give to you to take the cancer away at this stage.'

'So why did you give me the herbs before? If they could have worked a month ago then surely they could have worked now?'

'I gave you the herbs because that is what you asked for; but it was not what I thought would work for you...not by itself anyway.'

'Does that mean you can't help me?' John asked with deflation as if he'd hoped for something more from her.

'I didn't say that John but the last time you came here you were only interested in taking herbs and I need to know if you are more open to the other avenues of healing I can offer alongside them.'

'I am ready to try anything if it helps me to get rid of this,' he said waving his prognosis in the air.

'Do you still believe you can be healed John?' she asked; almost provocatively.

'Well I certainly don't want to believe in those fucking medical institutions and what they've just told me,' he answered instinctively with anger flaring again.

'No John. Go beyond this rebellious fighter who thinks he can conquer anything and anyone. He has no lasting substance to him. Deep down beneath that mask do you have faith in your power to heal yourself?'

John went silent for some time before laying down his defences and saying quietly and vulnerably;

'In truth I don't know.'

'That's good John. Now go beyond what you do or don't know in your mind. Do you have faith in your heart that you can be healed of this?'

John went silent again before he surprised himself by the bright words that came suddenly from his mouth.

'It was my heart that led me here.'

'Then that's a perfect start we can work with,' she said emphatically with a smile.

'Now then John; the first thing I learnt in my training is that there is only one reason why people don't heal…and it has nothing to do with their medical diagnosis. Some will have received a better diagnosis than you and died; whilst others will have received a worse diagnosis…as impossible as that sounds right now…and lived. Incredible as it may appear, the only decisive factor that prevents a healing is when the person chooses to hold on and keep the very thing that is destroying them. It sounds crazy that a person wants to hold on to this pain doesn't it; but if you look around you, you will see many people attached to poisons that are only destroying them. Some are just more noticeable than others. So what I've learnt over the years is that you can have medical surgery or treatment to clear the weeds but as long as you are still holding on it will come back as sure as night follows day. You can also go for therapy to talk about and get to know your pain. Your cancer then becomes like a whodunit as you try to figure out who is to blame for your problems and you can spend the rest of your lifetime diving into your past and trying to solve the mystery. But this only feeds the beast and will not help you let go of it. It sounds simple, because it only takes a second to do it, but the only lasting way to heal yourself is to start by cutting that cord completely. Genuine healing must begin as an act of faith from the heart and not an act of reason from the mind.

'So before we can go forward together I need to know if you are ready and willing to completely surrender and let go whatever story you are holding onto that is causing this illness; because if you are not your situation will remain incurable.'

'And if I let go?' John asked incredulously in response to her bold and outlandish statement.

'Then your journey of healing is truly ready to begin.'

She paused for a moment before continuing.

'Okay John. If that is clear to you then the next step is for us to bring this right out of the shadows and into the light for at the moment your choice to hold on to this in your body is largely unconscious. Now is the moment for us to look at it together so that you can see what it is you are truly holding onto. In seeing it clearly before your eyes it then becomes a conscious choice whether you wish to keep on holding on to that or not. Is that clear?'

'I guess so,' John answered with both intrigue and uncertainty at this line of approach she was showing to him.

'Then shall we begin by looking at this?'

John hesitated as if unsure whether to dive into this right now. It had been a momentous and exhausting day for him so far and he didn't know how much more he could expose himself to. Part of him just wanted to run away and hide. Mary-Helen picked up on his hesitation.

'Please John it is safe for you to go into this right here and right now and you have to trust me if you want me to help you. If at any time it gets too much for you then you can always call time out on the process.'

John nodded his head; albeit with some lingering reluctance. As he softened into the chair Mary-Helen got up and went to the kitchen before coming back with some notepaper and a pen to take notes.

'Okay I want you to close your eyes for a moment and just connect with your breathing. Feel the energy coming into the body on the in breath and then releasing on the out breath. Very good John. Now I want you to feel that energy moving through the body; starting with the feet. Wiggle your toes John and feel the aliveness in your feet. Now feel that aliveness coming up through the legs to the spine running through your back and then on up to your neck and shoulders. Feel it through your skull and your arms and hands. Yes very good John. Now come down to the heart and feel your heartbeat and the blood pumping in and through. Then slowly let your attention drop down to your lungs, your stomach, your kidneys, and finally let it rest on your liver.' At this point

Mary-Helen leaned forward and placed her hand on John's body to indicate to him where the liver could be found. 'Just hold your attention right there John where my hand is and feel whatever is going on in that part of your body. Now John does it have a name, a face, a memory? Does it have a voice that you can give to it John. Ask into your liver; ask whether there is anything to be spoken?'

John went quiet for quite some time as he tried to imagine what it felt like and what it looked like in that place where her hand rested. His mind was trying to make sense of what she wanted him to say in answer to her question but he couldn't think of anything. His mind went blank. Then in the silent gap, and without warning, John felt this tidal surge of energy rising up from within and the energy began to tumble out of his mouth through a stream of words.

*'From now on you have to keep far away from me Mamma you poisonous bitch! Get your hands off my fucking balls and stop manipulating me with your bullshit. I fucking mean it. Do not cross that line ever again. You do not have my permission to play those games with me; how dare you fucking drag me out into this fucked up world. I didn't want this. First you fucking suffocated me in your toxic womb and then you spat me out into a living hell. I want to go home. I want to be left alone. Take this oxygen away from me. I no longer want to breathe.*

*'I was your only son. Was I too much to love? And why did you bring me here to this fucked up place only to abandon me like that? I am nothing here; just another in a long sorry line of boys who have been fucked about by manipulative feminine bitches and discarded in the trash. Well I say fuck you and fuck off. If I had of been a nice sweet little girl would it have been any fucking differ-ent. I sure bet it would you bitch. This is their world not mine for men are nothing but extinct dinosaurs on this fucked up planet. And Papa surely agrees with me. I bet you have fucking read this note and tried to stop me from seeing it too because I know you fucking can't deal with the truth. You can't deal with the truth that you were never a fucking mother to me. A mother nurtures, cares,*

and lifts her children up high to be all they can be. They welcome, they bless, and they generously offer all of their fertile abundance. They don't fucking run off and abandon their responsibilities at the first opportunity. But that is the fate for all us boys down here isn't it. The first sight of a couple of balls and you grab them, slit them off with a knife, and try and stuff them back into the fucking womb before anyone notices so that you can be left holding a sweet bundle of fluff. What a loving way to welcome a boy into the world! And the result is that we fucking call that bundle of fluff a man. Why are you so fucking afraid of what men can be in this world? Why do you seduce us in and then try and devour us barely after taking our first breath?

'Not only that. Except for a token few of us you no longer need us on this planet to hunt, to farm, to fish, or even to manufacture with our brains and our brawn. You have got your ranks of machines to play that role now. Soon you will even find a way to manufacture artificial sperm so that you won't even need us to procreate. Where does all that leave a man today now that you have served us with our redundancy notice and told us to fuck off? But then of course I can't quietly fuck off can I, because you conveniently forget that you fucking set me up by inviting me to your lair in the first place. How fucking humiliating is that! Well knowing what I do now I wish I had never been born in this fucked up place; and especially not to you.

'And I am not alone in having my balls grabbed and slit by a manipulative bitch. Everywhere I look I see boys, boys, boys who spend their day pretending to be fucking men. Pathetic specimens they are with their squeaky high voices. Do you know how fucking embarrassing they are to me; and yet you probably had high hopes of me joining their fucking ranks so that you could hold dominion over me. Is that what you wanted me to fucking do? I know the road they are heading; the road to oblivion and yet you just sit back and laugh. Down that shadowy road is a maze filled with boyish tricksters who spend their days busily conjuring up new problems just to give themselves a fucking job in trying to solve them again; not

*realising that they have turned our planet into a fucking ugly waste-*
*land in the process. They are the evil product of your creation and*
*what else can they do but try and make the best of a bad deal. These*
*specimens are charming, highly intelligent, even sophisticated, but*
*yet at the same time completely fucking insane in the head. These*
*are the boys who have created schools that churn out robots rather*
*than humans; hospitals that churn out disease rather than healing;*
*ideologies that churns out violence rather than unity; government's*
*that churn out chaos rather than order; banks turning into casinos;*
*law courts filled with hypocrisy; factories turning into slave boats;*
*marketing turning into propaganda; marriages breaking down into*
*divorce; clear waters polluted; wilderness concreted over; beautiful*
*landscapes raped of its jewels; starry skies fogged; big trucks*
*rumbling down the multi-lane highways that tear up the country;*
*nature's foods laced with poison.*

*'Look at the list of outcasts. Murderers, rapists, abusers, alcohol-*
*ics, thugs, gamblers, drug dealers, war lords, shady businessmen,*
*corrupt politicians. These are always men; or if not they are women*
*foolishly imitating these boyish ways of men. Fuck knows why*
*women would want to imitate all that shit. And what else can I do*
*but sit back helplessly and wait for these insane little boys to sud-*
*denly wake up one day and realise what the fuck they are doing!*

*'And then you have the gall to point the finger of blame in our*
*direction and say that men are the fucked up problem on this*
*planet. You protest by serving a backlash by sending the whole*
*fucking planet into a wobbly spin and changing the fucking cli-*
*mate; and then you turn around and say that it is all down to the*
*hands of men who are so out of touch with nature. How can it be*
*though that you say we are to blame with the left hand whilst your*
*right pushes us further over the abyss? How can men be accused of*
*being out of touch with nature at large when they are not given a*
*single fucking chance to get in touch with their own nature.*

*'But not only that you bitch. One day a real man shows up; a*
*man who has great fucking ideas to do something fucking brilliant*
*on this planet. Papa was a genius and now his blood is firmly on*

*your hands. Because what did you do to him? Like every other man you reel him in, seduce him, and then without any loyalty you fucking turn your back on him and leave him to his fate. Afterwards you then send in the vultures to plot against him; to undermine him; anything to get him to fucking stop achieving the success that you know he deserves. Because you can't let a man get on top by sewing his balls back on can you? Well yes you may have fucking succeeded in killing that genius and getting your way; but know right now that your not going to fucking kill me too. Oh you may have taken away from me the one person who could have shown me how to be a real fucking man; but hey who wants to try and be one of those anyway when all you get is a bombardment of abuse for it. This world only wants sweet little girls and I don't want to play that fucking role either.*

*'So from here on in I am on my fucking own. I refuse to go along with this game any more so just fuck right off. I am battening down the hatches, closing the door, and giving you the finger. For I know that as long as the female bitch is wandering around pulling the strings that there is no-one on this fucked up earth who can be trusted to give you a cent without charging you interest and to not screw you around when your back is turned. You lie to my face, you throw rocks at my open bleeding heart, and you say whatever keeps you feeling superior on your fucking high horse. And so what we are left with is a world where everyone is just in it for themselves and what they can fucking 'take take take'.'*

John stopped as the energy subsided as quickly as it had emerged. He was feeling breathless and his eyes opened with shock at what had just poured out of him. He'd never voiced anything like this before to anyone and suddenly he was feeling uncomfortable and awkwardly embarrassed at what had happened. But Mary-Helen simply held eye contact to try and reassure him that he had not lost her from this vicious outpouring of emotion. It left John thinking that he was safe to speak openly and freely in her presence.

These words took John right back to his twentieth year and to his uncle's study. John had been on his summer break from university and rebelliousness had led him to walk in to a room he'd been strictly forbidden to enter by his uncle. He'd rummaged through a few papers absentmindedly; not searching for anything in particular. He remembered flicking through some bank statements as a letter fell to the floor and John could see quite clearly his father's handwriting upon it. He'd picked it up and in reading it discovered that this was his suicide note. This had been fresh news for him. For the previous seven years since his death he had been told that his father had died in a car accident on his way home from work; John hadn't even been allowed to attend the funeral. In discovering the truth John had realised why his uncle had wished to keep him away.

'Well John can you feel that this story has a lot of power and passion within it? Believe it or not; this energy you've expressed is something you've been holding in your liver for some time.'

Her words lifted John out of his reverie and in hearing them he took a long deep breath into his belly. It felt as if there was finally space for him to take oxygen into lungs that had been compressed for as long as he could remember.

From her training Mary-Helen had been told to halt at this point and complete the session. But as she observed her patient; she had the feeling that something was awry and that there was more there to discover.

## Chapter XIII

**M**ary-Helen sat in a very uncomfortable place as she weighed up how to proceed from this feeling of incompleteness that had stirred itself within her. She had been warned many times against unpicking the story by opening a dialogue with the patient and letting the conscious mind take over the process. In her training she had been told vehemently that an illness was not something to be figured out and with loose ends to be tied up.

Tentatively she leant forwards and placed her hand again on the same spot that she had touched before.

'But this isn't the core story you are holding there is it John,' she said firmly. 'What lies beneath what you've told me? What else needs to be revealed to the light?'

Mary-Helen noticed as she said these words that a look of apprehension washed across John's face. He looked vulnerable and like a small child again and his fearful expression revealed the message; *'please don't take me to that place.'*

'It is safe for you to drop into this John. You are being held here in a loving embrace.'

After speaking these reassuring words John closed his eyes and, after some resistance, Mary-Helen finally felt him yield to her touch and to soften into the love that was saturating the atmosphere. Suddenly the words came quietly forth on an exhalation of breath:

*'Mommy, come back. Please come back. Please, please come*

back. *Why did you have to leave? Please tell me what the use is of me being here without your solid earth beneath my feet? I cannot stand, I cannot move, I have no air to breathe without you. Who will come to take my hand to lead me through this place if not yours? There are so many unanswered questions. I am nothing but an empty vessel without you; my life has become a note that will never be sung. I am so afraid now that you have left me behind; I feel I've been abandoned here in a place that makes no sense to me and to a fate I now have to endure. I feel a foreigner on strange soil. The words I speak make no sense; the rules they play by befuddle me. Apart from you there is no-one else here I have found in whom I can place my trust. What am I to do to make my way? I feel so alone.*

*'All that is left for me is to wait and dream in the hope that one day you may have pity and return to me. I will look out for your kindness amongst those whose cold hearts are made of stone. Until that day comes there is nothing more for me to do than protect myself from the ravages of time and from those strangers who hide in the shadows to steal what is left of me. One day, will you return? Will you remember what I once was to you? Will you even recognise my face?'*

John fell into a deep silence after the last of these words emerged from within. His head was bowed and he was huddled into himself like a frightened child. Her inner sense told her that these were not only his words from his own experiences; she saw his long line of fathers standing behind him and stretching out across the history of time. She felt that these were men who had carried that story down the line as their unresolved legacy. Deep into that history Mary-Helen also sensed that this line also contained great strength and power within it. She saw what was possible if John could only break his attachment to his mother and create space for them in his world. She felt touched to see this support emerging and it gave her an injection of warmth and optimism of what lay ahead for John on this road of healing.

Slowly John returned his awareness back to the room and

gingerly opened his eyes. Mary-Helen smiled warmly as he did so.

'Thank you John for revealing this to the light.'

John's mind though was already wandering back in time to when he was nine or ten. He lifted his eyes to meet with Mary-Helen's and spoke soberly:

'I am reminded of an evening when I was a child. I was at the dinner table and my father was home to join me. I remember that feeling of excitement to have him home; it was a rare occasion for he was always so busy. No matter how much I'd misbehaved or how hard I tried to impress him after my mother left I just couldn't get his attention. But that night he was home and it just felt so good having him there. I remember asking him why he couldn't do this more often. I don't know why but his answer comes to me now.'

'What did he tell you John?'

'Well he picked up a piece of cheese off his plate with his knife and said something like; "Do you see this John. This is our livelihood here and I have to keep constant watch over it. You see son there are lots of bad little mice out there who would not think twice of sneaking up and taking a little nibble here and a little nibble there. And before we know it the cheese will be gone and we will be left with nothing. So I am protecting it because one day this cheese will be yours. And I don't want to just give you this small piece as I want to work hard to give you one that's even bigger for you to enjoy." After hearing this I understood him a lot more and just accepted that this was what being a good father meant. Immediately I stopped asking for attention and I quietly sat back and waited patiently for the cheese to come to me. That all changed when he died but strangely that is what I think of when I think of my father.'

'And it has also shaped your life since too. Is that what you've been trying to do on your island; protecting that cheese until the day your mother returns?'

'Yes; I think you're probably right.'

'I can understand how these two stories are pulling you in different directions and are tearing you apart. The question you have to face John now is whether you are willing to release both onto the fire and to take a risk of seeing and living a different way.'

Mary-Helen noticed that this statement immediately triggered something in John and it was as if a door had slammed shut again over his open heart.

'You can't tell me that it would have turned out better if I'd of gone down the road my uncle was trying to groom me down and to play the game the masses play so well. If putting this on the fire means going back to a life like that then I am not fucking interested. It's absolute bullshit to live an ignorant, falsely dutiful and superficial life like that where you spend your days busily wiping the arse of your superiors and mercilessly bullying your inferiors to get where you want. I would rather leave this fucking planet than to live such a pathetic life. You can't ask me to do that.'

'I am not asking you to do any of that John and to be honest I doubt that this life you so vehemently portray would be the end result of your healing journey. I simply don't believe your deepest creative self came to this world for a life like that. Right now I need you to forget about the world and its problems. I also need you to forget about the future and how things might turn out for you. Indeed there may be many, many more possibilities than you currently see. And hard as it sounds right now I need you to forget about your father and your mother and the choices they made in their life. Let me be blunt and say this is all about you John and your life. And right at this moment I need you to focus with all your might on the immediate choice before you; *do you want to live or do you want to die.* Don't respond to this question now John. I want you to go home and give yourself three full days to consider it. If this is too important for you to let go of then you will surely die as the doctor has predicted. If you want a chance of living then you must be willing to release it. Now I know you are not feeling suicidal because you would not have come here today if you were; and so for that reason it sounds a straightforward choice. But I can also see from all you have said to me today that this will be the hardest choice you have ever had to make.

'And let me say that if you don't want to release it then there is nothing more I can do than give you the herbs I have already given. But if you can; know that I will be here waiting to help bring you back to life by taking the next step.'

'Well say I do want to drop this; whatever this thing is. How do I go about doing it?' John answered with a little more openness and curiosity emerging again.

'I believe in the power of ritual acts John and how they carry an energy that causes a ripple effect through this seemingly solid material world. Fire is a good force for helping transmutation. So what I would do is encourage you to search for an object nearby that represents what you've been holding and then with clear intent release it into the flames. Fire is an element that carries the power to regenerate; destroying the old and paving the way for the new. You can use it to transmute this cancerous energy into something that can be used creatively and positively. That is how I would work to drop the story.'

John took in what she was saying so forcefully to him and once more began to breathe more deeply. He stayed silent for he did not know what he could possibly say in response to all of that. After everything that had happened today; it suddenly felt all too over-whelming to take in. Was it really only a couple of hours ago he was arriving at the doctor's surgery to be given his death sentence?

Finally, after a big drink of water, he was beginning to feel a little more calmed. John stood up and said that he was ready to leave and to return home to consider what she had said. John thanked her for her time this afternoon with a lot more gratitude than his first visit. This woman who he had once so rudely dismissed was now someone he looked up to in absolute awe. She gave him the notes she had taken from the session and followed him out. As she opened the door she said one final thing:

'Remember John, contrary to what your doctor told you, you now at least have a choice.'

# THE DESCENT

# Chapter XIV

## Mary-Helen

I stand at the door and watch as John walks away. He disappears out of sight and I cannot help myself but follow down to the bottom of my garden. I look up the street and watch as John strides confidently away. It fills my heart with warmth to see how courageous he is right now. He seems a completely different being to the man who showed up at my door barely an hour or so ago. He seems ready to wake up from a long sleep. And I am touched by the changes that have come over him in the short time that we have spent together. I even think back now to our first meeting and how closed and defensive he was. Tears begin to form in my eyes.

I turn away and return to my home and in doing so new mixed emotions begin to arise in me. I go into the living area and suddenly feel overwhelmingly lost and restless. I am not quite sure what to do now. I fall into a strange heavy and fuzzy state as I sit and drift as time passes with my mind wandering aimlessly. I feel frustrated at this cloud that is now hanging so heavy over me and which I am unable to shift. I light a candle and some incense; but the cloud lingers on. Sadness is pervading and fogging my awareness. I soon realised why as for the first time in my life I am utterly helpless in this situation. Typically I am so involved in my patients, so engaged, so hands-on. I like to be needed and right now I am missing all that attention I got in the hospital I worked where there had always been someone in need. And even though the healing master who'd trained me had made it clear that this is the way that the process must go; his words never touched me like they are touching me now. They seemed abstract at the time as they floated past by; but I am touched and struck by the fact that this three-day interlude is taking me in the opposite direction from the path I have always walked. I feel as if I am now standing on shaky ground, uncertain. Doubts are beginning to arise. What if John never comes back? What would I do then? How am I meant to spend the next three days? Am I meant to just wait for him or try and focus on other things? These are questions that had never crossed my mind in my training and had never been brought up by my master. I sensed now that this could be the longest three days that I might spend.

The next day I woke up after a fitful night's sleep. Everything seemed unclear in my world now. It was all spinning; and I was being shaken by it. I at least had my work to go to that day although it offered me very little comfort in that moment to use that familiar ground to regain my footing. In truth I cared not for it anymore. I could have happily stayed at home. But I went out and did what was required, although in truth I had little focus upon it and had to go over my work time and again. I returned to the office to pick up my roster of work for the coming week and it was only then that my employer took me to one side and told me very plainly that they were going to have to make cutbacks and that my pay was going to be cut by half with immediate effect. I received this news with detachment; it barely touched me. It felt like I was witnessing myself in some strange way as if it were not happening to me at all. The pieces of my life here in Wagsale were being moved around by a force that I could neither see nor compel. All I could do was go where the momentum was taking me.

That evening dragged into another long and restless period of uncertainty for me. I didn't quite feel myself. I didn't feel connected and aligned with any sense of what I was supposed to be doing here with this time on my hands. It all passed by in befuddlement.

Things took another turn the next morning as another piece of my life in Wagsale was changed upon me. I had been living here in this house on a week-by-week agreement ever since I had moved here a couple of years ago. But today a letter was hand delivered through the door. Our agreement was to change and rent was to increase. In quickly doing the sums I realised that my life here that I had forged and lived was no longer going to be viable to sustain. A huge change in my circumstances was imminent and yet I was betwixt and between as where the change would lead. I had imagined that I would continue to stay on here even if John did return. I envisaged him staying here and with me caring for him whilst continuing on with my duties. That idea was now quickly vanishing before my eyes.

But once again I received that news with detachment in awe at the invisible hand at work in my life and moving things into position. These events had sent a very clear message that I could not possibly ignore.

I went into my work that day with an air of resignation that this surely would not be continuing. Afterwards the rest of that afternoon once more passed me by in a strange daze of uncertainty and with apprehension as to what tomorrow might bring. I retired early to bed after being unable to force myself to eat and to find something to focus upon.

The next day I did not have to go to work and so I stayed home and waited. I waited and I waited and I waited. Time dragged on excruciatingly. Nothing I put my hand to occupied me but as the day passed John did not appear. Doubts and confusion stirred within and grew more furious as that day passed by. I felt myself beginning to fall into an even darker place of uncertainty. On more than one occasion I had the compelling desire to race out and to see what had happened to him. Was John coming? Was he even alive? Did he still have that fire of courage that he had left here with? I resisted the compulsion but felt helpless and without purpose as there seemed no possible course of action for me to take.

For two years it was true that I had been killing time like this in

Wagsale in pottering through each day and keeping my head above water. I had been waiting expectantly and patiently in persevering with my faith; believing that a patient would one day come to me and believing that all I had learnt would be put to use in the world. That faith had not left me completely in that time even though John's first visit had revealed my pride and arrogance on the matter. But now after his return I had been given what I'd always yearned for and yet right now this was not sustaining me one iota. The consequence was that my faith fell into a crisis that I had not tasted before. I felt teased; manipulated. This is because these forces that are moving my life now seem to only humiliate and depress me. As darkness fell I could no longer bear it and retired early to bed once more.

For three more days this continued. There was still hope I carried that John would come; that he was destined to come. I tried to hold onto that with all my might. But it was a tough period in my soul I can admit. Darkness had descended over me and I could barely rouse myself to go to work; to do the basics to sustain a functioning existence. It was clear now that I was leaving Wagsale so it was only natural for me to begin withdrawing my energy from this old life that was clearly not going to be supporting me. But what was to come next? I was confused. I pleaded and begged for answers. I wanted to know if I had done something wrong in sending John away like that and was being punished for it. It all felt at odds inside of me for it went against the grain of all I believed and knew. It had been my training to nurture and care; not to let go and send away those in need. Not only that but I sent him away with the harsh words that it was now up to him to make the next move. I questioned it now. I questioned everything as those days passed by.

Then on the next day, a week after John had come back to my life, things took an unexpected turn as another letter landed on my doorstep. Out of the blue I received news that my old position in the hospital had become vacant and my ex-manager told me that they were desperately short staffed. She wrote that she had felt that it was worth contacting me on the off chance that I would consider returning into that world of nursing for I was deeply missed there. I was touched and amazed by the lengths she had gone to in order to contact me. It was a plea that threw me into another place of confusion. Partly I felt some relief from it as it gave me something solid to place beneath my feet if I turned myself towards it. It felt good to know that I was needed and missed. With one phone call I could put an end to this tortuous life in Wagsale and go back to what was familiar and made sense to me. Helping people, nurturing people, looking after people to health and wellbeing; that was my life.

But still there was that insistent voice that reminded me that this was what had been comfortable; but that I had left that behind for a reason. If I went back would the same feeling arise again? And would I be able to forget the man who was so prominent in my mind everywhere I turned.

And so with the letter in front of me I continued to sit and to try and fathom what this invisible hand was trying to convey with the pieces that had been moving over this week. The mixed messages only served to confuse me. John had surely come back to me for some purpose other than what had merely transpired here those few days ago. Surely this was not it! Surely not! I had not given up everything and pursued wholeheartedly this path to just have this one precious hour with him. That experience helped quench a thirst but it had not satisfied the deepest longing within me.

Two more days passed painfully by with no guidance to move me. The letter continued to capture my attention on the living room table and I continued to hold off giving my reply. I had jacked in my cleaning job because I could not give away another ounce of energy to it. I hadn't left my home, but with each day it felt like John was drifting further away from me. The likelihood that he would turn up now was becoming more and more remote. I was beginning to waver irrevocably and I did not feel like I could hold out much longer. I had few savings and they would not sustain me for long without a decision. And if I did not respond soon to this tempting offer before me; my ex-manager would perhaps turn elsewhere.

I was beginning to teeter in that direction and I told myself a reassuring tale that maybe it would be different this time because I was not the same person who had left there. Perhaps there were patients that I could find time to work with now using what I had learnt in the interim as a naturopath and as a healer. Perhaps I could find more space to bring the creative soul work that now drove me, into that stressed hospital environment? Maybe this letter has come to me now to tell me that it won't be the same as it was?

But as I reflected further and really felt into it; in truth I knew that this tale was mere wishful thinking and that I had no passion or enthusiasm to follow down that road. That seemed to leave me with the option of either waiting here for John or chasing after him. Neither of these options felt good either and so nothing made sense to me. All roads were closed in that direction. I was over waiting. I could not chase.

The next morning I woke and felt the pressure hanging on my shoulders for a decision. I could not hold out any longer. By lunchtime, I meekly surrendered to the inevitable and picked up the telephone with the letter in my hand.

I began to dial and, as I pressed the fifth number, I heard a knock at the door.

# Chapter XV

## *John*

I walked away from Mary-Helen's home that afternoon but my mind was distracted and unfocused on my surroundings. It felt like I was walking that single winding path into the centre of the labyrinth as on autopilot I navigated my way through the streets back to the city centre and the railway station. In truth I could not tell you how I found myself sitting on that train for I felt somewhat disconnected from my physical body and its surroundings. The world around me now carried a surreal and distorted hue to it and my legs moved separately from where my attention had gone. I was falling deep into a sea of emotion; a whole gamut of them in fact that I had journeyed through this day and which remained within me. The pot had been stirred; but right now I was numb because I had surely hit my saturation point of what I could feel. It had truly been a tumultuous passage of time that had unfolded; beginning with fierce defiance, then submerging with the ravages of despair, and then finally lifted out of a harsh desert by a precious oasis of hope. I had been buffeted through it all and now all I wanted was to slip away into gentle retreat.

Even though I walked in a daze; at least I felt in a more stable state than the place I had been in after leaving the doctor's surgery. The diagnosis was still heavy and imposing but Mary-Helen had at least lifted it a little off me. She had hauled me back from the exit gate I was plummeting towards; and although my feet were not yet fully grounded back in this world, it did at least feel good to have that breathing space open in my chest after all these years of tight constriction.

It was a lengthy wait in the station for the last northbound service of the day. Finally it pulled in and I sat in a largely unoccupied carriage at the rear of the train. I took a seat on the left side with my head pressed against the window and dozed off to sleep; lulled into unconsciousness by the rhythmic movement of the carriage. My attention was brought back to this world momentarily as I watched the illusory scene of the sun plunging into the ocean out to the west. The sky was painted with vibrant colours of pink and orange in its wake and it was a scene of real beauty that touched me with a poignant message. It mirrored to me that I too had witnessed the fire of my soul submerging into an ocean of the darkest grief and I intuited that even after the golden glow of hope that came in the aftermath; I had still yet to reach the bottom of my depths. Dawn was still far away from me. The colours began to fade as dusk fell upon the land and I knew with tears welling in my eyes that I too was entering the dark night of my own soul.

It was pitch black by the time the train pulled into Nabotan station. Sleepily I dragged myself out of the carriage and onto the deserted platform. I was the only one to depart here and a chill and bitter wind whistled down that station platform and snuck in to touch me deep in my bones. I moved quickly but speed could not keep at bay the feeling of loneliness that subtly crept over me as I walked. There wasn't a soul in sight that evening and the whole place seemed bereft of light and life. I felt vulnerable and my steps began to falter as I was pressed down by a wave of resistance against my return home. I had the sudden desperate urge for company. I wanted to be touched, to be held, and for someone to tell me that everything was going to be okay. I was scared to go back to this cold dark world where only my demons lived alongside me and I knew that they might not ever let me return again. I began to have doubts and questioned why Mary-Helen had not kept me close to her bosom after having given me the breath of life and had instead sent me back to this land of the dead. I had no answers but it all suddenly felt so horribly wrong to me. Once more tears began to fall as I dragged my feet slowly down to the water's edge.

Weakly, and with sagging spirits, I descended into my well worn motor boat and turned the headlamp on to offer me light across the blackened waters. I knew well enough by now the right course across to Diarra and I soon saw her silhouetted against a waning moon that was rising behind her and casting a small amount of natural light in my world. The waters were choppy tonight and another chill breeze seeped right through me on these exposed waters and deflated me into exhaustion. Once I reached dry land I hauled myself up wearily from the landing deck and dragged my feet to a cold and unwelcoming home. Although I felt pangs of hunger; in truth I could not muster the enthusiasm to satisfy it and so I guided myself straight to my bedroom. I did not even undress as I slid down under the covers and tears continued to fall as I eventually fell away into a deep dark sleep. My dreams were not comforting ones that night.

I awoke late the next day and felt as if a forceful weight had come and pressed me down through the night. Oxygen no longer filled my recompressed lungs and my body ached throughout. I was in great pain. I tried to lift myself from the bed but felt dizzy as I rose and could go no further. My whole world seemed engulfed with a new wave of darkness and I could not bring myself to open the curtains in search of light. I regretted my refusal of the doctor's offer of morphine and chided myself for my stubborn pride. I at least knew I needed to eat and so I finally forced myself downstairs to grab a bowlful of vegetable stew from a large pot that I had fortunately prepared the other day and which should at least last me many more days if required. Afterwards I did nothing more than return to bed.

The next day continued in the same vein. It felt as if a dense fog had cast itself over me and I could do nothing to shake it. Lethargy took over and Mary-Helen's invitation seemed as far away from me now as it had before I had received my diagnosis. Any possibility of putting stories on a fire and letting go of the past seemed beyond me. It was simply an apple that was not yet ripe to pick and I only frustrated myself whenever I tried to force myself to rip it from the branch. This wound was no longer buried deep in my subconscious; but it was sitting there in my system like a heavy meal waiting to be digested. I could feel it. It was right there but it was too big right now to even try and move through it; to let it flow; to let it shift. All I could do again this day was rest and try to let nature take its own course.

That night I had the strangest dreams come over me; recurring dreams of a little boy trying to make his way up a mountain of ice. And every step he took up that mountain he slipped back down because there was nothing to grip onto. Each time the dream ended with that little boy collapsed in exhaustion after many attempts to overcome what lay before him. I too woke up more tired and exhausted than when I went to bed. I felt drained by these dreams and it was as if I had lived them.

The next day was no different. Time passed by. I did all I could to function. I ate from my pot of stewed vegetables along with stale bread. I showered; I went out for fresh air; I slept; I huddled by a warm fire; I pissed; I shat. But still this thing inside of me was not moving. Time began to lose all relevance. My dream world and my day world was blurring into one. I could no longer say who I was or what my life meant. It felt like I was under water and Mary-Helen's call, her rallying cry, was coming from dry land above. I could hear something but it was coming all garbled; it wasn't penetrating through to reach me. I knew her bold invitation was passing me by.

The next day I felt even more frustrated; angry even. I was angry that I was alone. I was angry that Mary-Helen had not done more for me. She had stirred this shit up inside of me then cast me back out into the world with nothing more than a piece of advice that was proving as evasive to hold onto as a wisp of smoke. I felt very sorry for myself today. I felt powerless, alone, and disconnected. I tried to find something to distract me from my despair, isolation and abandonment. But today it was still too much. Nothing could lift me out of the hole.

After that the days began to blur and I lost count. I resigned myself to the fact that Mary-Helen was not going to come for me and I was submerged by the weight of my emotion, my pain, and my suffering. I felt helpless. I got the sense that I was now beginning to fall apart at the seams. I felt like I was slowly leaving a world that held nothing left for me. I was numb to it all. Thoughts of suicide naturally came up as it seemed the only way to take the weight off my shoulders and this burden off my back. I didn't know how to shift it any other way than to end it.

My anger at Mary-Helen for teasing me and taunting me with that carrot she had dangled subsided; the flame of passion was smothered. Pushing away the temptation of resignation I tried to let unconsciousness whisk me away as I buried myself beneath the sheets. Yet the pressure kept building. Each moment punished me in my vulnerable, raw and exposed state. Oxygen was becoming a rare commodity. Symptoms of nausea persisted as the toxicity ran riot in my system. I was a dying man and I had no choice but to face and accept the fact as I dwelled in this hole and drowned in my grief, my sadness, my anger, and my despair.

# THE ORDEAL

## Chapter XVI

## John

Mary-Helen placed the phone back down on the receiver and walked towards the sound with a new wave of hope welling up out of the ashes within her. She did not want to be disappointed and to find something of no significance waiting there. But surely it had to be John. She opened the door and there he stood before her. Mary-Helen was taken aback though for he looked even more withered than even that desperate figure who had walked away a week or so before. He truly looked at death's door in his body; but yet as he stood there he beamed out a radiant smile that immediately transformed his features. Looking beyond the physical appearance Mary-Helen knew instinctively that he was now ready.

'The story is in the fire,' he spoke proudly to affirm what she knew to be true.

Mary-Helen could not help herself but rush forwards to give him a huge warm hug of welcome. He did not resist in the slightest and instead melted at the touch that he had been longing for. She finally let him go and guided him inside first with a hand on his shoulder as she followed behind. This felt so right to her and it was clear that the telephone call she had been ready to make only a moment ago had been so wrong.

'How has it been John?' she asked politely as they took a seat.

'As soon as I left here my health deteriorated quite markedly and there was no energy to even consider your proposition let alone think of travelling all the way back here again. Physically I was in too much pain to look beyond it to the prospect of healing.'

'Maybe I should have let you stay here John rather than send you back home alone...' she replied meekly. 'But I did what I believed was right,' she said to come back into her power and to honour her decision.

'I admit at times I was angry at you for doing that. But now I can see that perhaps it had to go that way as you had been trained,' he answered as if to reassure her that he now held no qualms about it. He then continued. 'Well the days passed by and normally the pain eases a little to give me a respite but this time it was there constantly. To be honest I was beat and could see no way through. I was getting ready to put an end to it all. I don't need to talk anymore about those depths I went to.

'But then early yesterday morning with the sun having barely risen over the land; I headed down in the kitchen to get myself a fresh glass of water. I had felt parched all night but had struggled to move to satisfy it. You probably can't imagine how hard it was to just get myself moving out of bed. I remember having to put my hands on something solid as I walked for I felt light headed and dizzy. I know I've been unable to eat enough to sustain me and have spent too long lying flat in bed; but I also know I chose to isolate myself by living in that place. Well when I got to the kitchen I began to pour the water into the glass from a jug. Then I felt this sharp pang of unbelievable pain in my side; nothing like I had ever experienced before, nor wish to experience again. I collapsed to the ground taking the jug and glass down with me. I was lying there amongst shattered glass. I was sure my time had come then and even though what happened next seems all blurry now I do recall screaming at one point to be taken away. My body felt paralysed to the ground but I don't feel like I was fully there with it. The pain was too much to dwell in it. I am not sure how long passed by but suddenly the blurriness vanished and everything became crystal clear and focused. I saw and felt a warm glow of light enveloping me; though I do not feel it came from the light of the sun coming through a window. It was something else. And as if by an act of grace the pain stopped. It must have only been for a few seconds… maybe a minute or more; but in that time it was as if I'd left the agony of my body and had been freed from its imprisonment. All the weight and burden of my existence fell away. I felt liberated. You will perhaps think I am crazy but my only thought at the time was that I must have died.

'But then in the same breath I knew I had in fact come back more into my own body. The experience didn't last and as soon as that grace came it went again. The pain returned and though it wasn't as sharp as before it was still intense. Yet it was somehow different now; it was somehow more spacious and less overwhelming. I could coexist with it; by that I mean that we had come to some agreement that it could stay over there and I could stay over here…for the moment at least. That sounds weird to say it like that; but it is the best way I can explain it. I knew that I had the choice to walk fully towards it into my death; but in that moment I realised that I do want to deal with this now for if I don't I will surely have to come back and grow through it again.

'I soon realised that in making this choice that the stories I had been holding onto had made their own way onto the fire. The pain was still there…but the roots that held it there, and that had suffocated me, had gone.

'Afterwards I thought about what you said and the positive results that could come from a symbolic ritualised release into a fire. But as I reflected on it I realised that this experience had been the fire. That warm light of grace, whatever that was, was the force that came to break the chains that were shackled between me and my wounded self. I needed no other ritual act to create that separation.'

Mary-Helen listened quietly in awe before replying;

'Thank you John; I am deeply touched by your story. I think you are truly ready to embark on the next step in your journey of healing.'

## Chapter XVII

### Mary-Helen

'John; I need some time to reflect on how best to proceed from here. Perhaps it would be a good idea for you to take a lie down and get some rest. You can use my spare room. The bed is already made up in there.'

After sharing his story, and after both of them had taken a long pause of reverential silence, John seemed surprised that Mary-Helen was now all a fluster and he wondered what he had said that had clearly unbalanced her. Sensitively he did not pry and instead reassured her that a rest would indeed be most welcome right now. He respected her too much now to question her judgment.

Mary-Helen was sat in the sanctuary of her bedroom and had a candle lit at her desk after having closed her curtains. She was feeling troubled. It was early afternoon and as she sat she knew that the troubled feeling was not to do with the next step she wished to take into the unknown with John; and nor was it to do with the swiftness that it had come about. Deep down, she had been ready in anticipation for the call…she had in fact been waiting for this for years. No instead the troubled feeling was that she had not been able to tell the full truth to John that afternoon.

She took out her journal and began to write.

*My dear one, you know that I am willing to do anything for you but what you asked of me today was truly a great burden for me to bear. For why did you reveal to me that you have already* given John his healing on his kitchen floor and then in the next breath tell me that John was not yet ready to hear this most powerful truth I was given. How can I withhold from him this secret when it would do so much to ease his suffering right now? How can I not assure him that it is has been done? And how can I speak to him these hollow words about the power of all the healing gifts I have learnt over the years when I know that it is impotent in comparison to the power of the instantaneous healing of your divine light?

So why, dear one, why do you ask me to help John when you have already given him the only help that he needs? Your mysterious cosmic dance strikes me as truly absurd. Do you not know that I have given my whole life to be a healer; that I have made so many sacrifices to get to where I am today? And then when you finally give me a patient, you go and heal him first! Are you trying to soften my pride by toying with me in this way? Are you telling me that I may be good…but not that good?

And please tell me; if I am not needed to help John on his healing journey then what part am I, and what part is anything I have to offer, to play in the remainder of this script?

She fell silent for a moment as if to allow the question to reverberate deep within her being and to give the deity she was addressing space to respond. Such was the depth of sincerity in her prayer that the response was soon forthcoming. She recorded:

'My child; although John has received the divine light of healing he is not yet ready to absorb it deep into the core of his being. It is as if he opened the door for me to enter but he is not yet home to receive me. He is like a fragile newborn who needs to receive your care and attention so that he may grow strong enough to accept what has been given. Without your help he will not make it through for he needs to have faith in you as a healer before he can return home and find faith in himself as his healer through me. If you send him back to the island alone with news that he has been healed then he will only sabotage and block the infiltration of my light that is being poured down into him right now. We need you to be the bridge that connects John and I.

111

*You have the gift of being able to hold this truth and to know how and when to feed it to him in small digestible chunks. You will be there to witness the unfolding miracle as what has been revealed to you today will be slowly revealed to him over the coming weeks. Trust that all of your training as a nurse, as a naturopath, and as a healer will serve to help you nurture John back to a place of wholeness.*

*You must understand too my child that it is my divine light that is the source of the healing process and everything else flows down from that place. You have gone through your training in the belief that the reverse is true; that you are the source of the healing and that my divine light is but a finishing touch that can only flow through once your work has been completed. You have long believed that I am the capstone that rests as the summit upon your magnificent creation. Yet, you must know now, without any doubt, that I am the foundation upon which everything must stand.*

*Please understand now that you are the one who serves my will and that I am not the one who serves yours. Your part is most precious; but come to me humble, and honour me as the healing source. Please understand that this time will be about your healing as much as it is about John's.*

As she stopped her writing she paused to give thanks for the revelations as given. In re-reading she felt the words sting; as words of truth inevitably do. She realised then that deep down in her gut that part of her reason for having dedicated her life to this work was indeed to be the rescue figure in someone's life. Her healing master had never told her so directly and so bluntly what she had just written and it was true that she had never quite understood the instruction that the patient must be willing to put the story on the fire before she can step in and take their hand. Now for the first time she did and it was going to be an ultimately valuable softening of her pride to know that she was only a bit-part actor and not the director of this unfolding script.

Although it was painful now, facing the truth did at least help ease her troubled mind. Mary-Helen uttered a final prayer for the strength to bear the burden of this knowledge that she was being asked to carry. A plan then began to form in her mind of how best to proceed. She closed her journal, blew out the candle, and felt ready to talk with John.

# Chapter XVIII

**M**ary-Helen quietly knocked and opened the door of the spare room and found John resting, but awake. He turned to face her and beckoned her inside.

'How are you feeling John?' she asked.

'Well rested now after my long travels here.'

'I will get you something to eat, but first, are you ready to hear my suggestion of how we could proceed from this place?'

John nodded keenly; encouraging her to continue. She took a seat at the end of the bed whilst he sat upright.

'When you spoke during our last session I had the thought of trying something which I think may help you. A couple of years ago I travelled across the ocean to Adanac where I learnt a healing modality called *mythos healing* by an elderly healing master. I'll admit that I have never had chance to work with someone who I thought could benefit from this; but my sense is that this modality could be perfect for your situation. Are you willing to trust me on this?'

'I am willing to trust your judgment Mary-Helen.'

'Thank you John. Now let me explain a little bit more to you of what this *mythos healing* is. At its heart lies the idea that deep in your subconscious are the answers to your healing dilemma and that all we need to do is to tease these out. Now we all carry deep within us a mythological story that symbolises the nature of our quest through this life; it is what we might call our founding archetypal story of who we are and what we are doing here. This is what we call the *mythos*.

'Now you've already completed the first stage of that process by releasing what we could call the *anti-mythos* from your system; and now there is an opportunity to fill the space by bringing the true *mythos* out of the shadows and back into the light. So through the healing sessions, the aim is to establish this reconnection. The idea is that this will help re-establish order right throughout the psyche. According to this healing master; all the problems we suffer with in our life, be they physical, emotional, mental or spiritual, are a consequence of our disconnection from our founding archetypal story of who we are and why we are here having this particular life experience. I feel this could help you John because from what you've told me I have a very strong feeling that your experiences as a child severed you from your *mythos*; you lost sense of how these served to fit into the grander plan for your life.

'So illness, any illness, can be seen as nothing more than an alarm bell which is warning us that something needs to be righted in our character and warning us to reconnect with our *mythos* more deeply than ever before. Through whatever cause, we have become disconnected and knocked off balance from the very centre of our Kingdom and we suffer heavily for it. This fundamental flaw, what we call our *hamartia,* is what we are trying to correct through the *mythos healing* journey.

'So the way we reconnect the patient with their *mythos* is through a process of gentle hypnosis that helps the healer lead you down into your subconscious where your *hamartia* is revealed and where you can remind yourself of what you have forgotten. Now the *mythos* is typically revealed gradually across many volumes that are all interlinked. Although each constellation is personal there is one constellation, with a wheel containing thirteen volumes, which most commonly appears from the limited research that has been undertaken into this field.

'Now much study has been done into these constellations and it needs to be understood that each volume represents a voice and perspective on different sides of a multi-faceted diamond that we might call your soul. Each is a voice in the psyche that needs to be heard and absorbed before you can get a sense of the *hamartia* that relates to them all. Although all of these messengers are contained within you at all times; there are certain moments of your life when each message comes through very strongly. Therefore the set of volumes that we go through in the mythos healing can also be seen as a chronological timeline in your past when messages were given; but were probably not heard and absorbed into the psyche.

'Often the final volume comes from the one who can see all sides of the diamond. He is the one who holds the voice of the court and who connects all the threads together into one coherent story; into one central *mythos* that is personal to you. In the classical wheel his is the story in the centre with the twelve pieces around him on the outside. He brings all the volumes together to form a conclusion from the *mythos* and this conclusion reveals the core error and flaw in the person's being that it has entered this life to learn from. This is the jewel of insight that needs to be unlocked and brought forth to bear on the rest of the psyche.

'Once that process has been completed, and let me warn you that it will take us as many weeks as there are volumes to complete that process, you will be ready for the final act of sealing your healing by bringing the *mythos story* into your conscious mind. It is critical that this is done only at the very end for if it is done before the whole *mythos* has been reheard then the conscious mind will only take, and ultimately destroy, the pieces it has. Let me remind you again that your healing journey is not a whodunit to be solved by the reasoning of your conscious mind and healing can only happen when we bypass it completely until the very end. The final jewel of insight must be recognised and honoured completely within the subconscious before all of it can be brought out into the light of the conscious mind.'

John was quiet for a moment as he tried to absorb and make sense in his mind what he was being told.

'So you are saying that throughout my life I've had certain experiences which carried a message which could have helped me understand why I've been born and why I've had to go through these circumstances?'

'That's exactly right John. You might call it the school of life. Often we think that things happen to us at random, especially those painful and traumatic events in our lives, but the truth is that they are all part of our curriculum. Believe it or not we have these experiences because if we learn from them, then they help move us forward and help us to fulfil our contract and mission for being on this earth.'

'So you are saying that by looking at the curriculum that I can rediscover what my contract is, see where I have gone astray, and to then get back on track to fulfil it?'

'That's right. Now for a lot of people this only happens at the moment of their death. With mythos healing we are trying to intervene before that particular alarm bell rings.'

'I see. And you are also saying that because I haven't grasped my contract before that I've now had to experience this cancer in order to help get me back on track?'

'Yes that's also true. In the beginning you were given little nudges to grab your attention…but as they haven't worked you clearly needed a real shake up; one of the greatest shake ups of all in fact. That is just how life works.'

'But is this really all you need to do to bring about healing? What about getting rid of the cancer in my body?'

'The beauty of *mythos healing* is that once the *hamartia* has been righted through your reconnection to the *mythos*; the alarm bell will no longer need to ring. The cancer will quite simply recede and disappear from you without a trace.'

'Can that really happen?'

'Yes John. Despite what medical science may tell you about this cancer being incurable, it is only incurable with the science they are working with. *Mythos healing* can and has cured seemingly incurable illnesses many times. Now it doesn't need you to believe in it but you must be willing to meet it with an open mind and heart. That is why you first had to go through the process you have already gone through to create this openness inside of you. We could not have proceeded without that.'

'But do we have enough time? If there are thirteen of these sessions to be held it will take us three months...and I simply don't have that time to play with? Can't we speed it along any more quickly?'

'John you need to let go of these fears, let the future take care of itself, and work with the immediate next step that lies before you now. At this precise moment you have two choices before you: you either honour and commit fully to the *mythos healing* programme as it has been conceived and developed...or you go it alone. I have nothing better to offer you and there are no short cuts in the process.'

John quickly understood that in coming here today that he'd wavered the option of going it alone and that yes he had to commit to this step before him.

'Okay Mary-Helen. I am willing to trust you.'

Hearing these words was like music to Mary-Helen's ears because it revealed how far John had already come in burning down these paranoid defences he had formed. But she had to exercise a word of caution.

'It is not only me you need to trust but the process of your healing programme. All has unfolded in perfect timing to bring you here to me today and all will continue to unfold in perfect timing on your journey to come. Although the process has healed many patients I can't offer any guarantees on the outcome of your healing. Maybe the process won't work out as you hope in removing the cancer and extending your lifespan. But what I can guarantee is that, in the grand scheme of things, the act of committing to your life now, and to your *mythos*, will ultimately stand you in firm stead. I say this regardless of what happens to you over the next few months. I tell you that this truly would be the greatest gift you can possibly give to yourself at this moment in your life regardless of whether it does heal the cancer in your liver or not. Do you understand that?'

John nodded his head slowly as he absorbed what she was telling him.

She paused for a moment in thought before accepting that John was comfortable with the pace of the session. She was so passionate about this work that she had to make a conscious effort to stop and check that she was not running away too fast ahead of her patient.

'Now the other thing I am thinking of is where we can hold these healing sessions. I don't think it is best for you to travel here once a week for a session in your state of health. Just before you knocked on my door this afternoon I was about to phone my ex-employer and to take the opportunity of returning south to my previous nursing position. I didn't know if you would return and could not wait any longer. You see I can no longer afford to stay on here and it is time to bring this chapter of my life in Wagsale to a close. But now you are here I feel strongly that I am meant to do this work with you and I am more than happy to postpone that decision until this work is complete. In return I would like to ask whether I can return with you back to your island home and to do the work with you there.'

Mary-Helen made this suggestion with mixed feelings. There was a part of her that wanted to immediately pull John away from this toxic place that she imagined he had barricaded himself upon. But there was also a part of her that knew that familiar surroundings would be important for his safety and that the island would indeed offer a secure container for him to dive deep into this process. It also seemed the most practical option available.

'You don't wish for anything more than a home over the next few weeks?' John asked, surprised by the kindness of her offer and suggestion.

'That is all I wish John.'

'Then of course you can come and stay! My goodness I am so tired and exhausted from all this travelling to and from Wagsale these past few weeks that I am grateful for your offer.' He paused for a moment as something struck him. 'Oh but my home has fallen into such a state these past few weeks that I fear you will be terribly uncomfortable there. And my supplies are running low and I'm not sure I am up to doing much on the allotment at the moment.'

'Don't worry about any of that John. I can put it right in no time I'm sure and I can do your planting in the garden too. I will hear no more of your concerns and I want you to focus all your energy on your own health. Have something to eat and then rest here overnight. I will pack and get ready to leave with you tomorrow.'

'Thank you Mary-Helen. I am humbled by your kindness to go out of your way to do all this just for me,' he answered quietly as if taken aback by the strength of her compassion. This was something he had never experienced before.

'I am not going out of my way John and as long as I have food and a bed I want for nothing more. And this is also for my benefit too. If only you knew how much I've put into this work over the years and yet there are few souls in this country who appear ready to receive the fruits of this training. Did you know that I've travelled across the ocean to the country of Adanac three times now to ready myself for this work with you? I poured all of my savings into this and walked away from a secure position in the belief that there is a real need for it here in Arasmas. So I am the one who is grateful that someone has come into my life to give me the opportunity to share my passion, my knowledge, and my skills. If it can help just one person in their life then all of this endeavour will have been truly worthwhile. Trust me on that.'

# Chapter XIX

## Friday, 11th March, 2033

Mary-Helen had few belongings to bring for her rented home had come furnished and she had only moved there with two large suitcases. She didn't have time to give the place a thorough clean and so would have to waiver some of her bond with this swift departure. As they left later that morning by taxi they were able to travel lightly and John was in good spirits having had a sound night's rest. There was an air of expectancy hanging over them both with what was to come on this bold journey of healing and neither seemed willing to break it with idle conversation.

Mary-Helen had never actually travelled any further north than Wagsale and so it was a new experience for her to look out over the rugged coastline of this part of the country as the tracks ran close to the cliff's edge. She was though grateful to observe from the comfort of the train as she could see fierce waves from a strong spring tide battering the shoreline below. Fortunately, once they had arrived at Nabotan and made their way down to the water's edge, the short crossing over to the island was on sheltered waters rather than on the exposed ocean. Sat on the boat Mary-Helen welcomed the gentle spring breeze that was blowing back her hair as she looked towards the imposing black rock of Diarra. On landing John politely led her to his home and showed her around. He seemed embarrassed that he had not had time to prepare for his guest and that she would easily see how far things had fallen into a state of neglect. Mary-Helen gently put him at ease and directed him to take a rest after their journey together. She was keen to be alone in order to get settled into her new temporary home.

Mary-Helen had brought a diary with her. After dinner she retired to her room to write. Little did she know then that this was to be the record of many sacred moments experienced over the one hundred days they would end up spending together on the island. Little did she know then that this was going to be the record of her healing as much as it was to be a record about John.

# THE INTEGRATION

## Friday 11<sup>th</sup> March

*Darkness has descended and the early spring air is beginning to chill. Looking through my bedroom window I can see a multitude of stars already flickering brightly in the clear night sky. A crescent moon is beginning to rise and its light is glistening upon the calm waters. The silence is deep and John has taken to bed early to rest from our travels.*

*Since landing on this distant shore I've been overwhelmed by the sheer vastness of a sky that fills the wide open spaces. I have been caged in a world of civilisation for so long that the remoteness strikes me as delightfully enchanting. The possibility of creating something anew here is utterly enticing and I simply cannot wait to begin to make my mark on this empty canvas before me.*

*This is though a beguiling place of paradox. All around I feel the light touch of nature's hand but at the same time the black rock of Diarra holds many dark secrets within it. I knew in an instant that this is not a place where man has prospered before and I have the sense that it too holds a cancer that must also be purged by the light of healing grace. But I am strangely not troubled by the heavy brooding atmosphere that clings to the damp mossy ground as I feel completely welcomed and at home here. I know there are protective forces at work who have paved the way for my safe arrival and who are assisting the part I have to play. My soul has been animated by this golden opportunity and there is no shadow force on this earth that can possibly overcome it.*

*But though I am confident I know too that all of my training is going to be put to the test in order to fulfil what I have been asked to do with this young man who has invited me here. Let me rest now so that I am ready for what the new day will bring.*

## Saturday 12ᵗʰ March

*By the light of the early morning sun I had taken a solitary walk to find my bearings. Seated on a sheltered rock on the far side of the island I'd begun to breathe deeply into the empty void I'd stepped into. In the world's view I'd left behind my security and had taken on something that offered no clear prospects. But to my mind I'd left behind a life that had no future and I was finally ready to start living the one I'd been born for.*

*The ocean was choppy, whipped up by the March winds, but inside I was in a state of complete calm. There was no past or future for me once I'd left the mainland behind and I was drawn down into the infinite depths of present time. Sat here looking out to the empty horizon I knew that there was nowhere else for me to be but here. A sweet serenity of surrender had taken place and now that destiny had finally brought me to this place I was not going to turn my back upon her.*

*In walking back across the soft ground I was mindful to walk with less haste. Given his past, I knew that I would have to tread carefully with John before he would give me his trust; so today it felt important to give him as much time at home alone in order to show my respect for his personal boundaries. However, whilst his welcome has been polite, and our conversations have been cordial, the distance between us must be bridged before the mythos sessions can begin. My intuition tells me that it will take a week, and though he offered impatient protest when I pencilled in the 17ᵗʰ as the date of the first session; I was firm in my instruction. For as I told him again; we must trust that all will unfold here in its own perfect timing.*

## Sunday 13<sup>th</sup> March

Yesterday I stood back and allowed John to play the role of host. Today, with him taken to bed to rest from his exertions, I was free to impose myself more firmly in his home and to start breaking through the formalities between us. I knew it was going to be a challenge for him to be vulnerable and to surrender his pride to my care but today at least he had little strength to protest against the flexing of my will.

I began by seeking to bring order back to his home. Rain drummed down on the heavy sash windows throughout the day so it was the perfect time for a deep spring clean. Methodically I worked through each room as silently as possible so as not to disturb the resting patient. It was obvious to me that John had had little strength to take care of his domestic duties in recent months and the dust and grime was thick and lacquered. I cared not though for my body was vibrating full of energy and I was grateful to put it to use as I worked briskly and diligently through the home. I knew that bringing order to his living environment was a symbolic act in John's healing journey for order in the outer truly does help to breed order within.

In the late afternoon John appeared and though he showed signs of embarrassment at what I had done for him; he at least expressed gratitude for my thoroughness. Although it pained him to see, I think he at least understands that he needs to accept this help and support now. His recognition leaves me with an impression of a man who at least knows and appreciates the virtues of a well ordered and clean home. I was even caught by surprise with his spirit of cooperation as he joined in by tidying through his stack of papers whilst I moved to clean his room. By the end of the day then, nothing had been left untouched; and I began to see this old cottage sparkling back into life.

### Monday 14ᵗʰ March

*The heavy rain had passed over by the time the morning light came and I had woken late to the sight of bright sunshine pouring through the window of my room. Outside a cool fresh breeze blew briskly throughout the day and it was a chance for me to open the windows and to clear out the stale sickly energy that had hung heavy in the atmosphere since my arrival. The smoke from sage that had been set alight helped to give the home the energetic cleansing to support the physical cleansing of yesterday. In clearing the past like this I was seeking to clean the slate in preparation for something new to emerge within the empty space. Once done the house felt so much lighter and welcoming and I was sure that the cleansing had helped to create a protective field around the house from the dark legacy that clung to this island. I was satisfied that I'd managed to create a safe container for John to now purge his cancer and to realise the truth of his healing.*

*John was still in need of rest and was playing the role of the good patient by not overdoing his exertions. I was still waiting for that first prickly reaction towards my presence in his home but he continued to remain placid and contained. Perhaps when he is feeling stronger I will get to see the rage that I know lurks just beneath his surface. It feels strange to have this longing for a reaction but I am not one for superficialities and we both need to be open and clear with each other in order for trust to build in our relationship. He needs to understand that I will not abandon him no matter what he says or does in my presence. He needs to feel held in the arms of unconditional love; a love which was not given by his mother and which I am certain he hasn't felt since.*

*But alas I cannot force him to play his hand; and I must bide my time as I inch ever closer over his boundaries. Patiently then I must wait for the next chapter of our story to unfold.*

## Tuesday 15th March

*It only took until the light of the morning before the script began to unravel before my eyes. Last night's call of surrender, and a deep restful sleep, had helped to set the scene and I knew intuitively, even before setting foot out of my room, that something was brewing in the atmosphere.*

*John was already downstairs preparing breakfast which I took as a sign of his growing strength after two days of rest. It was the first time I'd seen him awake at this hour and instinctively my awareness was raised a notch. For a short while we sat eating together in silence; although in truth I felt that it was not a shared time of peaceful communion. I felt John's agitation with me having stepped into his space quite intensely. I decided the time had come to test the waters even further by firing a few personal questions across the boundary that lay between us and to watch how they landed. The cordiality quickly dissolved when I managed to ask a question that overstepped his mark and that caused his hackles to rise. For a moment he opened just enough to allow his emotions to come up to the surface and to give a short and snappy remark. But that was as far as he would go as he shut up and simply left the room.*

*For the rest of the day the tension simmered between us as John stepped back and kept at a distance. He was at least revealing by his actions the difficult dilemma that he was now going to have to get off the fence and to deal with. For there was a voice in him that wanted me here to help him heal but there was also a voice in him that wanted me out of the way lest I humiliate him further. I will simply have to hang in there patiently whilst he decides which voice is the one worth listening to.*

### Wednesday 16<sup>th</sup> March

*John's inner saboteur became even more active today as he set out to prove that I was no better than the rest and to prove that I will abandon him at the first sight of trouble. Before he would get off the fence and trust me he needed to see whether I could first prove him wrong.*

*I had to tread carefully today and to give him no reason to doubt my willingness to give this gift of unconditional love. One false step and he would have jumped upon me and put me at the back of a long line of people who had failed him over the years. One false step today and our work together would have finished before it had even begun. I simply could not afford to let John down through the weight of my own pride.*

*It was in the evening that he set up my test for the day. After an afternoon spent lavishing over a hot stove to prepare a hearty vegetable broth for supper, I lay it before him as an offering of love. However, he took barely a mouthful before looking at me in disgust at what I had dared to serve him with. John angrily swiped the bowl off the table sending it crashing down to the tiled floor where it broke into pieces and demanded something appetising. I felt the hurt inside but could not express it. Breathing calmly I simply cleaned up the mess and did as he said without showing any sign of emotion at his childishness. Such behaviour was not new to me for in my nursing days these were events I witnessed often as weak patients strived for energy through power struggles with their carers. I had learnt to become immune to it then and fortunately I could draw on this detachment at the moment I most needed it.*

*It was truly a sharp lesson in humility and was one I had to respond to instantly. Did I pass today's trial? I will simply have to wait and see what tomorrow will bring.*

### Thursday 17<sup>th</sup> March

As I had expected, a third and final test was given before the healing session we are to begin tonight. As also expected, John took his actions a step further as he tried again to provoke a reaction that would justify his negative beliefs about women and about humanity at large.

The day itself passed by benignly as John kept his distance, and his defences raised, whilst I patiently skirted around his ego and kept busy with household jobs. He had buried inside all memory of last night's drama and it was clear that he was not yet willing to let go and to open to a mature dialogue. He was still not quite ready to let me in.

But there was a flicker of movement. A couple of times his eyes did turn towards me with a look of bewilderment as if he couldn't quite believe that not only was I still here but that I continued to be immovably present in my power and in the moment. I had not yet wavered from my commitment and I could tell that he was slowly teetering off the fence and preparing himself for a big step into the unknown. It is remarkable to see how swiftly these long held grievances can begin to dissolve in the presence of a deep abiding grace.

His ego's last stand with me came in the early evening. This time he was not content with the speed of my response to his request of receiving dinner in bed. Coming downstairs in a fury he spotted the book I'd been reading and tossed it angrily onto the fire; where it took hold and burned. Impassively I stood there and simply spoke aloud that I would not abandon him. These powerful words, spoken at the right moment, served to reach right through his deepest fears and cut through his resistance. He was broken open into silence and as I sat there with him afterwards I felt deeply blessed by this precious moment of openness and his wordless sweet offering of trust.

I know now that he is truly ready to begin the mythos journey that is planned within the hour.

# Chapter XX

*Thursday, 17th March, 2033*

John and Mary-Helen walked outside together towards the garden shed; and to the sanctuary she had created for these sessions. He could see the flicker of a candle burning through the glass and as he opened the door he got a whiff of incense that was perfuming the atmosphere. Taking a look inside, John was surprised to see that she had transformed it into far more of a welcoming space; having moved all of his garden tools out and stored them under the cover of the wood shed. Two old plastic garden chairs had been covered with woollen blankets and she had taken one of the side tables from the living area and placed it between them with the candle in the centre. Also on the table was a voice recorder she had brought with her and which she would use to record each session. It was her intention to write up each session in an unused leather bound notebook that John had given to her and which was also now placed on the table between them.

It was a cool evening; but after Mary-Helen had wrapped an extra blanket around his shoulders he was not uncomfortable. In truth John felt calm and ready to begin. It was as if the flash of anger had never been; and he now submitted himself fully into Mary-Helen's care. It was her task to remain present and to hold this as a safe and sacred space for them both. She began by inviting John to join her in closing the eyes and to take a moment of silence. This lingered until Mary-Helen pierced the stillness by speaking John's intention to heal aloud into the atmosphere. These words rippled and created a tingling sensation inside both of them. With a sudden whoosh of clarity Mary-Helen felt everything in the space come together and fall in line behind those noble words she uttered. Any lingering discord fell away to nothing in its midst. This was truly a time of healing. Nothing else mattered here.

After opening their eyes again she sent across a warm smile of recognition and with her eyes she flashed John the question: *can you feel this grace too?* Reluctantly, Mary-Helen broke the spell that had been cast by asking John to get comfortable before giving a few brief instructions as to what he could expect. John offered no questions and merely followed her cue as she invited him to close his eyes once more.

Mary-Helen began the session by lifting herself up from her chair and picked up the frame drum that she had lovingly created as a core part of her mythos training in Adanac and which she had carried with her. She began to pound; and it was through the rhythmic sounding of the sheep's wool drum stick against the deer skin that she gently coaxed John into an altered state of consciousness that would help lead him out beyond his rationally dominant conscious mind. This was a vitally important step in the journey. Once she sensed that John had drifted into a dreamlike hypnotic state; Mary-Helen began to slow down the drumming until silence returned. She quietly returned to her seat and after a lengthy pause she spoke:

'John, I want you to imagine that you are walking through a vast field of barley that is radiating goldenly in the light of the late summer sun. Feel the warmth of that sun on your shoulders and feel the sense of complete freedom and peace as you walk. Can you feel it?'

'I can,' he said after a long gap of silence.

'Now I want you to look across to a forest that lies on the other side of this field and to see the path that leads you safely towards it. Follow this path John and enter into this forest.' She waited before adding: 'Are you there yet?'

'I am there,' he answered softly.

'Now there is a narrow path that winds its way safely through the tall trees that are around and ahead of you. Find and follow that path and feel the cool damp atmosphere of the forest as you walk. Know that these trees are protecting you as you pass through this sacred place. It is safe for you to be here…'

After speaking this; Mary-Helen came to a sudden pause in her flow because she intuitively sensed John's resistance from walking any further down the path ahead of him.

'Why have you come to a halt John?'

'Because there's a man standing on the path in front of me.'

In hearing these words Mary-Helen was momentarily knocked off balance. Not once through her training had a figure appeared on the journey to the vault of the deep subconscious. Mary-Helen needed to adjust fast and to throw out her training manual in order to respond.

'What does this man want John?'

'He tells me that he is the one who has to lead me down this path; not you.'

'Do you trust this man John to take you?'

'I am hesitant for he is unlike any man I've seen before. He has this manner of wildness about him that is intimidating and which I dislike intensely. He does not appear to be a gentle figure. He is cold, wet, dirty, and with hair covering all parts of his naked body. I would say from the look of him that he has been hiding out in these woods for a long, long time. I am afraid of him and yet there is also something strangely familiar and reassuring about his presence here. I think I must have known him once…' John spoke tailing off at the end.

'So do you trust this man to take you John?' she repeated the question again.

'If I want to go any further then I have no choice. He has made it clear that this is his territory not mine.'

'Do you choose to go further into the forest with him John or do you wish to turn back?'

'Yes. I need to go on with him. It is clear.'

'Well if ever you need to stop and turn back then please give me a signal. I will not abandon you in here,' she said insistently.

After these words were spoken Mary-Helen noticed the same discomforting feelings stir in her as when she had been waiting for John's return back at her home in Wagsale. She was trained to facilitate and lead and so it was strange and discomforting for her to be taking this back seat role once more. All Mary-Helen could do was quietly turn her focus to her breathing whilst she waited for John to give further instruction.

'I have reached a simple mud hut that sits in a clearing,' John said finally.

Mary-Helen knew that this building was the vault that she had expected to be there.

'I am being led inside,' John added.

'What do you see John?'

'It feels beautiful in here: so ordered and fresh; so warm and welcoming. There are two chairs and a huge cabinet to the side that looks like an old fashioned cart wheel. I can count twelve open slots in the cabinet; placed like the hands of a clock and with an open circular hole in the centre.'

With this information Mary-Helen knew that John's wheel of mythos tales was indeed classical in nature and that they would be returning here a further twelve times to complete the journey.

'And what is happening now John?'

'My guide is beckoning me over towards this incredible piece of carpentry. I can see now there is a book held in each open slot and that he is pulling one out for me. From the image of a clock; the slot he has taken it from would be placed between the hands of nine and ten.'

'Can you take a seat and read aloud to me the mythos story he is holding John?'

'That is what my guide has already gestured for me to do.'

## The First Mythos

Once upon a time, in a land not so far away, there were the cries of a newborn, an *Econimus*, ringing out across the barren wilderness. Sheltered beneath a lone tree next to him, his mother lay unmoved as her spirit had already flown free. Oh what despair it was that had driven her here to give birth alone!

The burden of despair rested on her shoulders for it was she who had broken the timeless laws of her tribe by going with a passing stranger and conceiving a child who would be impure in blood. And the law was clear on the matter. This child would have to be taken away and killed at birth. As the months passed this woman became torn apart by the tribal duties she was bound to and her love of this fleeting life growing inside of her. No longer caring for her own fate she decided to take a chance and fled by cover of night before the moment of birth arrived. She believed this was the only way she could possibly save her child. And though she did die; by a miracle that *Econimus* did live.

But his father did not come as she had dreamed that he might. Nevertheless, it so happened that another tribe was passing by at the time; and one of the women who was languishing at the back heard the distant cries of the child. Drawn by the sound she slipped away from the group to discover a sight that no-one should ever have to see. But amongst the bloody scene lay the sweetest most innocent child and her heart ached for it. In bringing the child back with her she returned triumphant; and yet she only found the cold eyes of her kin upon her. But a bond had been formed and she refused to leave this bastard child to its fate.

It was though never easy for the *Econimus* to be raised amongst those who he did not naturally belong. Life here was treacherous as he was shunned and teased by both young and old alike. He came to know quite early on that he was not one of the tribe; and in his despair he had no idea of the sacrifices these two women had made so that he could at least feel the breath of life in his bones. Instead he sulked and blamed them for taking him away from his true home and abandoning him to this impossible destiny.

As the years passed he realised that his only salvation would be the rites of passage that all boys go through upon reaching their eleventh birthday. He hoped this would help him take his rightful place here.

But the time of his eleventh year came, and then it passed by with no invitation forthcoming. The elders had simply refused to integrate the *Economius* into their fabric of community life for they too had their laws to follow. His surrogate wept with dismay for she knew without doubt that with no rite of passage that this child would wither and die if he stayed here. And this would not be a physical death; but the slow death of the spirit that dwelled within him. For it was longed deigned in lore that no-one can sustain a life of eternal adolescence upon this land.

And so it was that these two women who had given everything; had both fallen short because of the laws that had to be upheld. His sole hope of salvation now rested through reconciliation with a father whose identity and whereabouts were utterly unknown. It was surely an impossible quest; but it was now his only prospect. And so the surrogate began to prepare him for the journey and to educate him for the long road ahead that he must surely travel.

Seven years later the *Economius* was deemed ready and so he left behind this woman who had raised him all these years without praise or reward. He would never see her again and she would end up dying a lonely and painful death having isolated herself from the rest of her kin. But she did not quiver in the face of their rejection for she had loved and she knew that a life of love is always one that is worth any sacrifice.

As for the *Econimus*; the search proved fruitless but he did not mind that there was no swift resolution. For having been stunted by the merciless tribal politics of his youth; he now enjoyed the freedom of the open road. After all these years of being belittled, his confidence slowly blossomed as he felt the wind on his back guiding him on his way. New wings grew within to help lift him on that breeze and to carry him far above the mundane trappings of a domesticated life.

Yet his freedom came at a cost. For he now wandered in a fatherless world and remained stuck in the image of boyhood that others had created for him. The *Econimus* held no responsibility or conscience and brazenly he followed the path his own father once walked as he crossed into strange lands and seduced the women and fought the men who he met there. Everything that those two women had sacrificed to gift him his life, seemed to have been in vain.

Then, right towards the very end of his life, the now weary *Econimus* came upon a land that was very different to any he had seen before. The grass here was green and luscious and there were the most beautiful and exotic wildflowers in bloom. He finally felt as if he had come to a place that was strangely familiar and for the first time in his long life he felt as if he had come home. Was this finally the land where his father lived, he wondered? He walked and walked until a golden palace could be seen rising up in the far distance. It cast a spell over him for it was a building of such beauty in a world of such ugliness. A gentle breeze drew him closer.

The *Econimus* arrived at the entrance gate but there was no-one there to welcome him. Nevertheless he walked forwards and confidently pulled the bell himself. But alas it seemed as if the place was deserted for no-one came and opened the gates for him. He tried again, and then a third time, but all remained quiet inside.

But in truth the palace was not empty; for the *King* of this kingdom stood watching the *Econimus'* arrival from the window of a bedroom that was once his mother's and was then once his wife's. And now it had become the room where the *King* safely kept his son and heir. Placed behind the *King*, therefore, was a crib where his baby son lay gently sleeping. The *King* turned as if anxious that the noise below would disturb the resting infant; and indeed he did start to stir. The *King* quickly rushed over to soothe the infant back to the deepest possible sleep and he was delighted when he did so.

Having soothed his son back to rest, the *King* did not dare to leave this bedroom and to see who it was that had come to speak with him. From where he stood he could see that the figure was alone and carried nothing of threat; but he was wary in case it was a sign of change coming to his land. He had become fearful that dark times were looming for him and his kingdom; and so he was now paranoid about any strangers who now entered and came to his door without prior invitation.

But what the *King* did not see was that in the presence of the *Econimus* and the breeze that accompanied him; the landscape of his kingdom had been transformed from a place that had long been parched by drought to one that was now fertile, luscious and green. And because he did not see this he did nothing more than stand there hoping that this stranger would eventually return from where he had come.

And this is the path the *Econimus* was forced to follow; walking away with his head held low.

As he left, the land returned to its withered state behind him.

## Friday 18<sup>th</sup> March

*After last night's breakthrough the atmosphere in the house was noticeably calmer today and I finally felt that John's personality had caught up and surrendered to the earlier calling of his soul. It seemed as if I now had his full permission to be here and we sat comfortably together in the kitchen for a late breakfast; in an aroma of coffee and the sweet nectar of acceptance.*

*I could tell that he'd slept deeply and restfully; but for me alas I had not had a peaceful night. I had tossed uncomfortably as my mind busily ruminated over this strange and unique twist in John's journey. The presence of this wild man in the forest had caught me by surprise and again it was another stark reminder that I was not the one who was leading John's healing process here. I am continually humbled by these forces that are at work here and which are unfathomable to me.*

*My mind however did not stop trying to fathom the unfathomable. I wondered; was the wild man I'd brought him to the great father himself? I am in silent awe of this figure and I respect deeply the importance of his protective arm around John's shoulders. Even so my feminine pride has been clipped by the revelation that a male figure is needed to initiate John into his mythos. Though I've never mothered a child, I could today connect in and feel the pain of mourning from my distant female ancestors who have loved the sons they've carried through childhood but who cannot carry them any further beyond puberty. For it has long been deigned in lore that only men can turn boys into men and there is nothing I can do but respect this sacred order. I must now do what all mother's have done before me and that is to help nurture and to help bring him safely to this altar…and to then let him go.*

## Saturday 19th March

Another restless night followed as my mind continued to murmur with the voice of proud discontent. It feels as if the tale of the first mythos has stirred up the dredges of darkness within me as much as it is to do with John's tale. Deep down we are all as one here.

'Please understand that this time will be about your healing as much as it is about John's.'

These ominous last words of warning given to me on the mainland are ringing through and haunting me right now. I saw myself plainly as the surrogate of the tale who desires to raise this vulnerable infant as my own and it hurts to surrender my control over him. This over-protectiveness runs deep as a core wound in my breast and I must now clear it if my work here is to continue.

So I took a long walk across the island and watched as the waves crashed fearlessly upon the shore. It was a wet and wild day but I cared not for the force of the elements helped to cleanse and to soothe my aching heart. I was simply burning with this restless desire; wanting to do more, to say more, to help more. And all I can do is to lay it down upon the rocks below me and to let the waves wash them away. All I can do is to surrender my desires and come back home to the deepest truth that there is nothing here for me to fix.

I stood there and I let the tears fall freely as I released the heavy burden I'd carried for far too many years of needing to be the saviour of humanity's pain. I may have been warned that this healing was to come; but to feel that responsibility lift was something beyond comprehension. I had been cleaned out into a beautiful state of nothingness where I knew not who I was or what role I was here to play. In truth I was now just an empty channel that was surely ready to be filled again with the force of divine grace.

### Sunday 20<sup>th</sup> March

*A crystal clear morning followed yesterday's wet front and I heard the garden finally call my name. Our food supplies are already running low and I wonder whether I will be able to salvage a good enough harvest that will support us both until I leave.*

*It was a small plot of ground in a sheltered area at the front of the cottage but as I walked around it I could see that she was in a sorry and neglected state. Weeds had begun to take over and to drain vital nutrients from the seeds that John had somehow managed to plant earlier this year. I was no gardener, but I was at least willing, and I set to work in clearing the ground. The soil was soft and in good health and it was light work to pull away the old growth in order to create space for the new. Last week had been about bringing order to the home and now it was time to bring order into the garden.*

*The matured female goat came over with an unsteady gait and she looked in poor health trapped here in the grounds of the cottage. In my heart I was tempted to set her free to return to the wilds so that the light of her soul may be rekindled and brought back to peace. But I held back and let her be for now. Instead I simply laid my hands upon her back and poured my love forth into her body. She at least seemed to welcome the extra attention.*

*John came outside briefly later on to see how I was getting on and to show me what was planted where. But today he was looking pale and lacking in vigour and so he wisely did not stay for long before returning inside to rest and to keep his body warmed. Despite being off colour his spirits are noticeably in good health at present and he appears quite relaxed and content in his being. There is a softening taking place in him which leaves me feeling in good heart for the long road that still lies ahead of us both.*

### Monday 21st March

*It seems as if my preparations in the garden were not finished for she called my name again today. Physically there seemed nothing obvious left to do so I simply went and sat quietly in meditation upon the small stone bench that glowed in the light of the morning sun.*

*In the silence I received guidance that though the seeds that John had planted now had space to grow; they were severely lacking in vitality and strength. Strangely, I was told that it was not water or nutrition that they were lacking but love. This was a new revelation for me as I never had given consideration to the important part that human hands have to play in bringing health to nature's garden. It seemed then as if John had had nothing in his heart to give when planting these seeds and this gift of love was something that nature could not give to herself.*

*As I was guided through the garden I intuitively placed my hands upon the soil where I felt it was needed and sent my loving vibrations deep down into it. Though it was odd for me to do this here in this environment it was at least something I'd practiced before on humans and animals. As I did so I was struck by the revelation that we were now entering the time of the spring equinox where the forces of light and dark were becoming balanced. It is a time when nature's hand turns the world towards the light and as I worked I sensed deep within that I was playing a helping role in turning this garden towards the light too.*

*After this was done I sat quietly again for a while and basked in the knowing that the kingdom of nature was already responding to the vibrations of my loving intent. As time passed I became more certain that this was another critical piece in the puzzle that would help lift John, and this island, right out of their darkest night.*

## *Tuesday 22<sup>nd</sup> March*

*For a third morning the garden called my name and for a third time I could do nothing but respond. It felt as if the physical, and now the energetic, work had been completed and so once again I went and sat quietly in meditation to await guidance. Soft grey clouds moved swiftly across the horizon and there was a cool damp chill in the air.*

*In observing the garden beds I became increasingly puzzled as I sensed that my efforts were safely completed for now and so I was curious as to what else I was needed for. It was then that I became aware of a subtle presence around me. I could not see it nor feel it but I could sense there was something there from the atmosphere that had suddenly become infused by the grace of light and warmth. Many, many years ago I had stumbled upon a book that talked of nature spirits who work quietly to protect the natural world and to keep the rhythm of the seasons turning. Interestingly, this long forgotten book was the first thing that crossed my mind when this presence passed into my field of awareness. Though I am sure that there are few left in this world who would believe such a myth, I was at least open and sensitive to the possibility. Although I don't yet know why, in sensing it, I was left in no doubt that this contact was also significant to my work here on the island.*

*Alas though, this presence seemed to disappear as swiftly as it had come for the atmosphere turned noticeably cooler again. But I was not saddened by the departure for I felt that this being knew that it had found a willing listener in me and that it would surely return. Deep in my heart I knew that it wanted to help with the vision of healing that I was creating here on Diarra and I knew I could call upon it again and again. As I continued to sit in meditation I was left feeling utterly overjoyed to receive and to acknowledge this being's outstretched hand of protection.*

## Wednesday 23rd March

John's condition took a turn for the worse today as his liver continued its cleansing of the toxins deep within. As my work here serves to stir his pot and to get things shifting through, it is inevitable that his health will deteriorate further before it can improve. His temperature was on the rise and he was close to feverish as his body reacted to try and purge itself of its many burdens. All I can do today is to be on hand as his nursemaid when I am needed and to allow him space for rest when I am not.

I could not travel far from his room and so it was an opportune time for me to be in quiet contemplation and reflection within my bedroom. I listened to the tape I'd recorded from the first mythos session and began to write out the story in full. I planned to give him the completed set of stories to read once we had finished and so I was careful to present my words neatly. I find it fascinating that John has not felt the need to ask a single question about the session and that it appears to have given me more cause for reflection than he.

As the story became alive again in my mind whilst I wrote, I was aware that I still felt ill at ease with the fact that the session had not unfolded in accordance with my training; and I was not yet fully comfortable with this male figure who had taken over the lead. Afterwards, then, I decided to write my concerns down in a letter to my master in Adanac whilst it was still fresh and to seek out his counsel and advice on the matter. Whilst I could not hope to receive a reply before my time on Diarra is complete, the act of writing it down did help me to release and let go before our next session tomorrow night. I sealed the letter and will ask John to post it the next time he has to return to the mainland.

## Thursday 24ᵗʰ March

Darkness has fallen upon the island and the moment of delving into the second mythos is now coming close to hand. Fortunately his temperature has dropped throughout the day and so I have been able to give John the green light for the session to go ahead. There has been a sense of eager anticipation hanging over me throughout the day following the transformations that occurred after the first and I wonder what lies in store for John this coming hour. I can tell that he too has been impatient for his next session to take place this evening.

I have come out early to the garden shed in order to prepare a sacred space for his arrival. I have my rituals that I go through in order to create a safe and protective container for John to step into as we ready ourselves to dive deeper into the next layer of his mythos. There is a small table in the centre of the space; upon which a scented candle burns and around which two chairs sit. My drum rests against my chair. In the background I have soft harmonic music playing quietly to help lift the vibrations and a stick of incense burns by the doorway to cleanse the energy field of those who enter. Four glasses of water infused with four different flower essences are then placed reverently in the four corners of the room.

With the space prepared I have now sat to write this by the light of the candle. It burns with a beautiful glow and the flame flickers slightly under my gentle breathing as I sit close by on this cool evening. I am drawn in ever further by its spellbinding charm and the radiance of its light as I place these words upon the page in the stillness of this sacred hour. Glancing at the clock that ticks quietly on the table I see that I must soon slip into a place of meditation in order that I may come home to the core of my being and to the centre of my power. I know how vital it is for me to be fully present here in the moment so that John may feel safe to surrender within the arms of my loving intent when he enters into this sanctuary that I've created.

## The Second Mythos

*Drawn from between the hands of seven and eight.*

The *Econimus* was a child of sixteen years and he was seated in a place of honour by the side of his Father; the chief of the tribe. All looked upon the *Econimus* with respect and treated him kindly for they did not dare incur the wrath of the chieftain. But although the *Econimus* was in a place of privilege; the tribe were facing bleak times. A long drought had descended over the land leaving it withered and parched. All forms of life were dying or disappearing and there was pressure on the chief to uproot and to move his tribe on in search of fresh pastures. But he feared that they were not strong enough to travel and so he resisted. Instead he would disappear to his private place atop a mountain at the centre of his kingdom; where he spent hours looking upon his land and quietly dreaming the dream of an abundant spring.

And so whilst his eyes were turned longingly towards the stars; fear swept through the kingdom beneath his feet. That fear first took root in the minds of the men of knowledge in the community and in their doubt they lost faith in their leader to bring sustenance to the people. In desperation they met in secret and they plotted against him. To call forth the rain clouds that had forsaken them they believed a sacrifice had to be made; and as one they agreed that it was the chief who had to be taken and killed. And so they came by stealth at night to take him.

The chief was caught off guard by what was happening and cried out in his fear. He asked who will replace him as chief and was told that it is his eldest son who must be elevated. It was the *Econimus* who was being chosen to take on the role in his place. And so the chief was killed and burned at first light the following morning before the mourning and watchful eyes of the rest of the tribe.

147

The *Econimus* was elevated as promised but he was still young and had not yet been prepared for the role bestowed upon him. Despite his lack of knowledge; he stubbornly refused to seek the counsel of those who had killed his Father for he did not find them wise or trustworthy. So the *Econimus* bore the burden of responsibility alone.

But the days passed and the rains did not come. The *Econimus* knew that if he could not find a way to bring abundance to his people soon that he would surely suffer the same fate as his father.

He could not stay patient for long and so the *Econimus* decided to search for water. Against the elders' wishes; he called on those who were the fittest and together they began to dig deeper and deeper into the earth. They found no water but the *Econimus* did unearth a mineral that glinted in the light of the sun. Feeling this to be a positive sign he gathered all he could carry and then travelled alone towards the nearest place of civilisation. He walked for twenty days. Once there he finds a clever man who sees the value of the mineral and who asks him where it has come from.

In his naivety the *Econimus* tells him and then gives the man his treasure in return for a handful of silver coins. With this, the *Econimus* returned with rations that brought much needed relief for the tribe. Despite this, the men of knowledge still counselled otherwise when the *Econimus* made plans to dig more of the mineral from the ground. Once more he ignored their counsel.

But before the *Econimus* could begin; the clever man who had purchased the mineral arrived with an army of workers and stated his own intention to dig. As the chief, the *Econimus* challenged the man; but he was told in reply that he had no rights of ownership over the land or its treasures. But in seeing the chance for easy profit, the man did offer the *Econimus*, and those who were fit to work, the opportunity to join his team in return for basic sustenance. It was a poor deal but the *Econimus* was not skilled to barter for anything better for his people and weakly accepted the man's terms without question.

So the fittest men of the tribe worked in terrible conditions to clear the land; but at least their livelihood was sustained by their efforts. This continued for a few months until all the mineral had been taken from the earth. When it had, the man and his army of workers swiftly left to return back from where they had come. Having left; the rains then came for the first time in years.

But as was forewarned; the rain did nothing to sustain them for they had broken nature's timeless laws by emptying the land of its fertility. Instead the tribe were flooded from their homes and were forced to move on elsewhere.

They travelled to a place where the rains were being safely absorbed by the land and set up their new home here. The *Econimus* was counselled to draw on their remaining supplies and to wait for new life to return to the land. But once more he ignored the advice and gave out the order for the men to dig. This time another precious mineral was discovered and so the *Econimus* walked this time for thirty days back to the place of civilisation and to show the clever man his discovery.

A second time the man returned with his army of workers to clear the area of its value; and again employed the *Econimus* and the fittest men of the tribe. This time after they had finished the winds picked up and created a dust storm from the loose topsoil that had been left discarded. It was impossible to stay and the *Econimus* had to decide for the tribe to move on again.

Finally, having travelled on the back of the monsoon rains, they came to a fertile place that was already teeming with life. The others were keen to go out and hunt; but the *Econimus* knew not the ways of hunting and he was worried that he would be seen as weak for his lack of skill. Against their counsel for a third time; he gave the order for all the best men to start digging. Once more a mineral was discovered and this time the *Econimus* walked forty days back to the place of civilisation to the man who knows of these things. On the way he passed a stranger who seemed not to be from this place and who looked at him queerly. The stranger did not stop nor speak.

A third time the man came with his army of workers and cleared the land; leaving an empty and desolate place behind. Although he had provided food for his people, any life that had been here before had now gone. There was no reason to stay here for the *Econimus* was keen to uproot his people again in search of more precious minerals. But this time he was to lead them no further for he had to travel alone on his own journey.

He arrived once more into the familiar beautiful land that had the golden palace sitting in the distance. The *Econimus* walked again towards it and this time he was surprised to see that there was now a figure positioned at the entrance gate waiting to meet him.

'Pray tell me who lives in such a beautiful place?' the *Econimus* asked walking up boldly to him.
'This is where the *King* of this Kingdom dwells,' the *Gatekeeper* replied sternly with a deep imposing voice.
'Am I welcome to see him?' he asks nervously with his head now bowed.
'You are most welcome,' was the *Gatekeeper's* warm and surprising answer.

The heart of the *Econimus* leapt in glee at these words as the last time he had come here he had not been given a welcome like this.

'There is one condition though,' the *Gatekeeper* adds cautiously.

'Anything, anything,' the *Econimus* responds as if his spirits are not dampened by such a seemingly small request.

'You must first prove to me that you are free of *hamartia*,' the *Gatekeeper* says.

After saying these scripted words, the *Gatekeeper* steps forward and for the first time takes a closer look at the *Econimus*. In looking his face begins to redden and he starts to quiver uncomfortably in his bones. Without a further breath or word the *Gatekeeper* turns around and walks swiftly away back to the safety of his sentry box.

'Wait! Wait!' the *Econimus* calls after him. 'Am I not free of this *hamartia*?' he pleads desperately.

'You are most definitely not free of it! Now please just get out of my sight and only come back here again if you rid yourself of what you are crippled with.'

Astonished; the *Econimus* could do nothing more than what the *Gatekeeper* had asked of him.

## Friday 25ᵗʰ March

*For me, a long and sleepless night followed the reading of the second mythos and so a restful day was needed to restore the strength back to my weary body and mind. Though John's health had remained stable throughout the session it was not long after he had taken to his room that it deteriorated rapidly and I was called into action. Something in the session had clearly disturbed his soul and he began purging himself through an intense fever once more. The thermometer crept over one hundred and kept going and all the while he was drifting in and out of consciousness. He tossed and tossed all night like a rubber dinghy in an ocean and nightmares seemed to be flashing swiftly through him as he cried out in moments of terror before subsiding again into a whimpering simmer.*

*I could not do much but hold a cool flannel to his hot and sweating face and to be there to try and soothe his dark and troubled soul. In this longest of nights where I did not stray, and where there was only a candle flame that offered the solace of light, I simply gave all the care I could. But I knew I was not alone and that the angels were there by my side to help guide John through this hell he had plunged into.*

*I could see clearly this deep rage of grief from his father's passing that John had buried and had allowed to fester because he had simply been too young to handle it. But these things surely cannot be buried forever. Some may try to take it to their graves it is true but they will surely have to return and to deal with it again in another life. Though it is incredibly painful for John to uproot and remove this now; I could only see a beautiful field of grace surrounding him. As I sat I sensed that there was a tremendous cosmic 'yes' beginning uttered there; an answering cry that came in the hour that John has finally chosen to face down his demons. There was then a sense of destiny hanging over him that night.*

## Saturday 26<sup>th</sup> March

A more restful night followed as John's fever began to ease and he slept deeply for twelve hours or more. But during this day I felt his spirit was slowly losing its vitality much like the clouds overhead were blocking the light of the sun. His mood was as grey as the atmosphere as the grieving process continued to run its course. John had lost all sense of appetite and he was bringing up a lot of bile which made it hard for him to digest. Though it was tough for him to endure, the liver cleansing process was a good sign of progress and I did all I could to enthuse him with this news.

But he did not respond warmly to my rallying call and it took all my powers of persuasion to get him to take regular doses of a herbal broth that I'd prepared and which I knew would help speed the process along. With me he was like a little child who stubbornly refuses to take his medicine.

I knew that something was deeply troubling his mind which was a natural continuation from the troubled stirrings deep in his soul. As the soul purges itself in the dark of night; so the mind purges itself in the light of day. With this all unfolding then, John seemed distracted and wrapped up in his own world. All I could do was to leave him be and to let him work through the process in his own time.

In the evening he was sat down by the fireside and seemed to be lost in its flames as if drawn away to another time and place. I sat at a distance on the dining room table reading but keeping one eye alert. In slow motion I watched as he crumpled up into himself and finally began to shed some of his golden tears. Tenderly I came over and put my arm around his shoulder wondering if this was possibly the first time in his life that he had allowed himself to cry before another soul. Regardless, I knew that this release was truly a blessed moment.

### Sunday 27th March

Today the sun shone warmly upon the island and John was desperate to get outside and to receive its blessing. He had been cooped up inside for days now and so I gladly encouraged him to go. Having lost his appetite he was weak in body and quite unsteady upon his feet. So I led him by the arm into the garden where he was content to sit and be for an hour or more.

I would go for a walk later that day but I felt to stay close by in case I was needed. With an empty house at my disposal I relished the chance to play sweet sounds of music from my collection and to meditate in its vibrations. After the recent days of deep purging within the house these beautiful harmonies came forth to sound out a more uplifting note and tone. The words spoken were from a foreign ancient tongue but I cared not for they came straight through into my heart and gave rise to intense feelings of overwhelming joy.

But more than I felt its effect on my own heart; I felt its effect on the whole atmosphere around me. I could sense that celestial beings were gathering here on this glorious morn in response to the note that was being sounded out and they were truly gracing this home with their loving presence. Shafts of golden light poured through the window panes as the clouds of yesterday dissolved. John's tears that had fallen by the fireside had been truly transformed into a stream of gold.

Looking outside I could see that although the note was inaudible to his ears that John's aura was responding radiantly to the higher energies that were permeating right through the thick walls of this old cottage and right out across the black rock of Diarra. Both of us in our way had found in that moment the peace that surpasses all understanding and the peace that is always here.

## Monday 28<sup>th</sup> March

*As night follows day and day follows night in the dance of creation; so John's journey of healing too must follow the same pattern of changing cycles. After yesterday's uplift then came today's descent down into another deep and dark place. The sun was covered again and the island seemed to close its doors and to cut itself off from the rest of the world. Yesterday I have never felt so connected and today I have never felt so alone.*

*The few tears that John shed the other day were nothing compared to the tears that came forth today. There was a torrent that was coming right down the hillside and it was strong enough to rush right through the shallow stream of gold that had barely been formed. It was truly an almighty flood; this deep seated grief that was pouring right out of his body and which did not seem to stop and rest at all. After looking so peaceful yesterday it stung my heart to see him in such a state of deep distress today. I needed all of my strength to just sit by his bedside and to quietly witness this erupting volcano throughout the day.*

*How much further was there for John to fall before there would be nothing left for him to release, I wondered in amazement as I sat? Deep down, I knew the answer that he would both rise and fall again many times before our work would be finished here.*

*It was at dusk, however, that the day was transformed as I saw a tear shimmering as it ran softly down his face. It was only one more tear of many; but it was one that glowed as the colour of the sun and which illuminated brightly this darkened room. I watched in awe then as this toxin stained tear dropped down to his pillow. Ugliness had been transformed to beauty right there before my eyes and it simply filled my heart with wonder. What a gift then to grace this most lonely of days.*

## Tuesday 29<sup>th</sup> March

Today I sat and pondered reflectively in the aftermath of John's tremors. All was quiet in the house and he slept deeply for most of the day. A ceasefire had been called within his soul and I was grateful too for the chance to breathe again for myself. But in the midst of this spacious time, doubts arose as to whether I had taken on too much here. I was afraid of losing sight of who I was as I risked drowning deep within John's tears and his pain.

I called forth a prayer for the light of protection for I was losing sight of the path as the mist of unworthiness descended around me. For who was I to try and take on this task that had been asked of me with none to call upon? I had felt so sure before but now my footsteps were hesitant ones as I wandered down ever deeper into John's abyss. Would I get lost down here and was I really strong enough to bear the heat of this fiery place without being destroyed by it myself?

There were it seemed no angels who could descend this far down into the depths of the earth and so I had felt them step silently away from John's bedside yesterday whilst he lay grieving in my arms. They were clearly passing on the responsibility to hold John in love right onto my shoulders and the weight felt very heavy now that it was to be carried alone. I could rely on nothing here but my training and the goodness of my own heart.

I had also been aware that there was another presence in the room although I sensed that it was not his time yet to step forward and to relieve me of this duty that I must currently bear. Was this the man that John is destined to become when this impostor in his place is revealed for what he really is?

## Wednesday 30<sup>th</sup> March

Another long and sleepless night passed by as John continued to descend ever deeper down into his abyss. All I could do was to be present there by his side and to bear witness to his soul's latest torturous display of terror. Only at the light of dawn did these choppy waters begin to calm and only then was I feeling comfortable to step away from his bedside and to get some rest.

It was a most distressing sight to see John speaking wildly in tongues as he drifted in and out of consciousness through the night. Oh what nightmares he must have been having and the sweat just poured and poured down his face. I don't think I'd ever before seen a patient who had been carrying so much darkness within and who had so much anguish to let go of. But whilst I mopped his face tenderly, I knew I was at least feeling stronger to hold the love and to be his anchor after yesterday's moment of doubt. Fully here in the moment it had given me good heart to know that all the reserves of courage I could possibly need were here waiting to be brought forth. How arrogant had I been to think that our invisible helpers had stepped aside when in truth it had been my fear that had closed the door to them!

Today John was at least perky enough to roam free from his bed; although he was quietly withdrawn with me and did not know how to speak of what was taking place. He could not be fully conscious of what had been happening, but nevertheless I sensed his sheepish apprehension and his instinctive fear that these demons of his could destroy me if we were not careful. I was mindful then to be of good cheer and I constantly reassured him of my strength and my resolve to see this through right to the end. Surrendered here in this tender state, I knew that this was a critical moment in his journey and that he was now counting on me to pull him through. I longed to give him the good news that the gift of healing was already here waiting for him, but for now I must keep my tongue in check and to simply use that knowledge for myself in order to keep my spirits raised.

### Thursday 31st March

Tonight we must embark upon the third mythos, but as I sat to write up the recording from the second this morning, I could not help but reflect back on the fullness of the week that had just passed. So many rapid changes had been taking place within John's body, mind, spirit and soul that it is amazing to see that there is little left that is recognisable from the man who was speaking on this tape a week ago. Layers of skin had been shed and it was noticeable to me that he has been losing fast the excess weight he had been carrying for his protection. He is beginning to trust again and there is room now for him to breathe more easily and to claim his life anew. As I write this I wonder curiously what this next chapter in the story will be.

My enthusiasm to ride this rollercoaster is a continual surprise to me. Normally my reserves are sadly in short supply and it doesn't take much before I slip over into burnout. How odd I found it at the time that many of us who step into this nursing role to care for others; then lose the ability to care for ourselves. That loss of joy and passion became just one more reason to leave that sterile loveless world behind.

So how is it then that after three weeks of intense work that I still have this boundless love burning within my heart and this tremendous appetite for the task? I have such enthusiasm that a sleepless night can't even derail me off this track that I am racing down. With unbridled joy then I sat in the garden today basking in the warm sunlight and connecting with the nature spirits that dwell there. There is such magic and grace to be found and savoured here that it just brings me fully into life. Right now I simply don't want to miss a single beat of any of it.

## The Third Mythos

*Drawn from between the hands of three and four.*

In a place not so far away; loud bells began to ring and the villagers came swarming out of their homes and to the place of worship. The young *Econimus*, led by the hand of his mother, was among the congregation that gathered there. But he was not content and so whilst sat on the hard wooden benches the *Econimus* began to squirm restlessly; bored by the dry sermon of the man in robes who preached before him. His mother saw him and firmly told him to behave.

Outside of this time of worship, the *Econimus* was just as restless too and often got into boyish mischief with his friends. But despite his mother's complaints; in truth he was not a bad child for his heart was full of goodness and his mind was full of curiosity and wonder about the mysteries of life. The *Econimus* was, therefore, a willing learner and deep down was keen to do right in this world.

That goodness of heart drew him back to the place of worship at the centre of his village time and time again. And though he had little appreciation for the sermons; the *Econimus* did love this magnificent building and he marvelled at the skill of the craftsmen who had created it. As the years passed he came often to sit quietly alone in the walled garden directly outside where he could look upon the majestic building in peace. He knew that contained within these walls of the garden was a special atmosphere that offered him solace and reassurance from the busy world of village life that often agitated him. In sitting here he began to yearn for that most intimate and sacred contact with the source of all things.

It was a yearning that eventually led the *Econimus* to leave behind his worldly commitments and to enter into a life dedicated to prayer. Against his mother's wishes, he left his home and walked by beaten and unbeaten paths until he came to a city far away where he was invited to join a community of worshipers. He was sent to work in the kitchens by day; but early morning and the late evening were times where he dedicated himself in reverence to a higher power and to the one true source of all there is. He would come to spend many years here.

The *Econimus* believed he was pursuing a worthy calling; but all the while his mother remained displeased. She felt her son had abandoned her and her plans for him; and was simply pursuing his own folly. Sadly she became ill and passed away.

In his grief the *Econimus* felt guilty and blamed himself for her passing. Doubts began to enter his mind and his belief wavered.

Those doubts escalated in time because no matter how hard he tried; the *Econimus* was never given the moment of revelation to justify his committed devotion. Instead of light all the *Econimus* saw in the empty spaces was darkness as visions turned to dust and dreams to nightmares before his eyes. In this place he no longer felt the warmth of company when he sat in silence and so with each passing day the *Econimus* felt the source of all things drifting further and further away from him. The more he tried to reach out the worse it seemed to get. The *Econimus* lost weight and became anorexic for a time.

His frustration was only exacerbated when he listened to his fellow companions speak of what they were experiencing from their own time of contemplation. They would speak eloquently of healing, light and grace but these powerful words did not serve to bring the *Econimus* any warm cheer. In their company he came to feel like a dolt and so the poisonous fire of envy was stoked deep in his gut. That fire choked the goodness from his heart and slowly it turned cold. His faith was in crisis and so the *Econimus* began to question whether he truly belonged. For the first time here, he felt utterly disconnected and alone.

But his ties with the world outside had been broken and there was nowhere else for him to turn. In despair of his situation he began to weave a tale of lies. First he lied to himself by pretending that all was well when in truth he was beginning to give up on the harsh disciplines of this life and was no longer giving his full devotion to the rhythms and routines. He had begged to leave the kitchen so as to spend more time in solitude in his chamber; which in truth amounted to a greater period of time falling into a deep state of sleep.

But the *Econimus* did not stop there. He went even further by lying to his mentor and to his fellow brothers and sisters. He began to speak falsely of revelations given to him directly; revelations which he had only memorised from books he had read. However, this simple tale of deception began to spin beyond all his control. For the *Econimus* discovered as he said these things that others would listen keenly to what he had to say and would praise him to the hilt for his charisma.

In seeing an audience grow around him, his mentor advised the *Econimus* to take his teaching out into the world and to spread the good news beyond the cloistered walls. The *Econimus* had no hesitation in agreeing to the suggestion because he saw that this would earn him his place and purpose in this world.

And so like the priest of his childhood, the *Econimus* was given a place of worship to preach from and he became a popular figure amongst those who attended. For the *Econimus* had mastered how to say the things that people wanted to hear and which they approved of warmly when they heard them. He only wished his mother was alive to see what had become of her son in her absence.

There was only one moment of doubt that arose in his mind after that. One week there was a stranger who came and sat at the back and looked at him intently. In that look he felt as if his whole façade had been pierced and the *Econimus* blushed in embarrassment and looked away. When he looked back he saw the stranger running blindly out of the door in fearful panic and he was never to be seen in his congregation again. The *Econimus* tried to put it out of his mind.

Finally the time came for the *Econimus* to return to the Kingdom that was well known to him. He walked through and arrived at the gate where the *Gatekeeper* was awaiting him with a familiar question;
'Have you lived a life free of *hamartia*?'
'I have,' answered the *Econimus* confidently. 'I have dedicated my life in praise to the *King* of this Kingdom and not only that but I have showered that praise on others. I have put him first like you have asked me to. I have lived a blessed life as a result.'
'I am not interested in platitudes,' the *Gatekeeper* replied tersely. 'I can see that you are still riddled with *hamartia*,' he added bluntly.

The *Econimus* still admires the *Gatekeeper's* position of power and still longs to earn his permission to enter. So he is hurt by the accusations.

'I have done the best I could in the circumstances with the choices I made. I was failing to make a difference by pursuing a truthful path. This was the only sure way that I could bring some good to the lives of others and to help save their souls. You don't know what it is really like out there,' he finished lamely.
'You are not there to save the souls of others; and especially not when it causes you to sacrifice your own. What good can possibly come from a life of falsehood?'
'Please tell me what it was I was supposed to do!'
'To stay true in your devotion to the *King*! Such devotion may have

caused some hardship but you cannot come into his palace without paying some price. That is the way.'

'So why did I fall short?' the *Econimus* asks pleadingly.

'Because you let yourself be seduced by your feelings of guilt. That is my judgment of what happened.'

'How am I not supposed to feel these things?' the *Econimus* exclaimed in disappointment.

'I cannot help with that. All I know is that your mother cannot help you get through this gate. Her way is not your way.'

'So is that it then? Have I blown my chance to enter this gate?' the *Econimus* says with his head bowed in disappointment.

'This time you have; but I will give you another chance to right your *hamartia*,' the *Gatekeeper* offers kindly in return.

'You would do that for me? Well I will most definitely take that chance and right my *hamartia*,' he answers boldly.

With that the *Econimus* turned on his heels and walked back from where he had come.

## Friday 1st April

*Today, for the first time since my arrival, John began to confide in me and to voice aloud the dreams and nightmares that I have only been witnessing from the outside. Finally he is beginning to reconnect again with the riches of the kingdom within and is discovering a whole new landscape; one that he is now willing to share with me. For so long he has been numb to his heart's desire and his soul has been left lying dormant and untouched. Yet now it is becoming animated before my eyes and suddenly there is depth and meaning arising in our conversations that before were tinged with courteous superficiality. He is now becoming more fearlessly authentic and real to himself and it encourages me to speak openly and honestly in his company too.*

*I wonder if the reading of the third mythos has triggered something within and has opened up a cavern of secrets that have long been closed from view. I think that this mythos is one that many of us would surely relate to in a world where exposure of our true nature will often only lead us to humiliation and failure...even by the hand of those closest to us. Sadly there are few who can be trusted with the gift of our deepest truth and of our most inspired dreams. Having no -one to share them with; it is natural for us to lock them away for safekeeping and to simply wear the masks that our audience wish to see.*

*But I feel blessed to see John now willing to give me his trust and to let me look within to the depths of his soul. There are dark crevices but there are also beautiful jewels that I see glistening there and that are waiting to be revealed to the light. It is a sign of his growing strength and self esteem that he has given me this welcome invitation today and I am glad to receive it lovingly within the centre of my heart.*

### Saturday 2nd April

*A deep abiding calm had descended upon the house today as if we had found the still point between one breath ending and another beginning. That stillness was not empty and cold but was exceedingly rich and full. It was pregnant with possibility and with new life potential. I could feel it penetrate right through and illuminate my very essence.*

*Never had I seen John so content and at peace with himself and with his world as I saw him today. His aura was crystal clear and perfectly whole and there was nothing here to disturb the silence of this day. It was a gift of spacious refuge that we needed in order to draw breath on this rollercoaster ride that we are both on.*

*So spacious was this day that I had ample opportunity to be in solitude and to come home to myself. Although I am not tired by this work I could gladly savour the opportunity of rest that I was able to take advantage of.*

*So contained was John within himself that I could naturally step away from his story and energy field and back into the womb of my own life. John has needed my energy and care constantly since I have arrived here and so to be able to shut down my outer senses for just a few hours, and to retreat to that quiet place within where I was unavailable to the world, was so nourishing for my soul. It was truly a sweet time.*

*Today then he did not need me to be standing there by his side for even a moment and this is a positive sign of his progress back to independence and health. The road is of course still long and I am not getting carried away with false expectations that the end is nearly in sight. But that doesn't stop me from feeling the deepest gratitude within for the precious stillness and light of this day.*

## Sunday 3rd April

Over a plate of steaming vegetables and rice we sat together and joined hands and took a long moment of sweet silence. The food was simple but I felt this blessing nourish it with the love of our hearts. Surprisingly it was John who had initiated this new ritual into our daily rhythm and I felt truly grateful to be sharing this moment of communion between us. For the first time too in my company he has let his gorgeous long black hair flow down to his shoulders and he seems so much more open and freer because of it.

How remarkably easy it is then to transform what had been just another day into something clothed with splendour and magnificence. How easy it is to transform the mundane and everyday routines that we pass through with eyes shut into something that is sacred and meaningful. How easy it is to bring ourselves back to the glories of life. Truly John has taught me a valuable and humbling lesson on this day.

His hard shell is gradually softening, and though his hands were calloused as I held them, I could at least feel warmth and light return to them. John's openhearted gratitude reveals that he now has something to give back in return for what he has received and his generous spirit has helped to lift mine and to let it soar again.

We took that silence right through our meal as I savoured each and every mouthful that passed through my lips. The atmosphere was literally dripping with the power of the sacred during this early evening hour and it revealed its face to me in the rain that was drumming down softly on the windowsill outside. Drip by drip I was filled to the brim and beyond.

Both of us slowed right down to honour the moment and our mindfulness turned itself into sharp focus. Everything became magnified within its light and nothing was missed from its illumination. We dove deeper into the void beyond space and time and into the eternity of the moment. Once there, neither of us wanted to break that silence we shared on this golden night.

## Monday 4ᵗʰ April

Heavy rain lashed against the old cottage incessantly today and fierce winds blew in off the ocean as a storm front hung itself over the island and refused to budge. It was not the day to venture far outdoors and so it turned into another restful day within the home.

Without sunlight the house stayed dark and cold throughout the morning and so we lit the wood fire early in the afternoon and together we gathered around its enticing flame. John dozed peacefully on the couch whilst I sat and read quietly before drifting away into a state of sleepy reverie as I snuggled in to the fire's warm embrace. She lulled me softly within her comfortable and secure bosom and she sang sweetly into my heart. I was like a little baby cocooned up again in the mother's womb and I gladly feasted upon this restful hour as I melted away into the chair.

The sounds of the wind and the rain outside only left me feeling more comfortable here and it was just one of those days to make the most of this magical force that dances here before my eyes. The crackling sound of burning wood sent goose bumps tingling through my spine and they burst through into ripples of excitement within my heart. Oh how the smallest things can create such feelings of joy.

There were plenty of jobs to do around the home but I could not raise myself today for something that did not inspire or stir my soul. Instead my intuition guided me to relax deeply and fully into this moment for these jobs could wait another day. It was blissful to be in this illumined energy that was establishing itself here on the island and to not have to strive so hard to lift the vibrations. If life could be made this simple all of the time then how wonderful that life would be.

167

## Tuesday 5<sup>th</sup> April

Today I had the freedom to experiment and to put my naturopathic training to use. I'd had a vision a few days before of a concoction of native flower remedies that could usefully serve to support and stabilise John's improving emotional health and his opening heart. Beech would help him to see more good and beauty in his world. Cherry Plum would help reduce his need to stay in control. Walnut would give him protection from outside influences during this major upheaval, whilst Elm would ease the overwhelm and burden of responsibility that he carries on his shoulders. Finally some Rock Water added to the mixture would help ease the impossibly high standards he sets for himself.

I'd already scoured the island in search of these five ingredients a couple of days before and had easily found what I'd been searching for. I am continually surprised how nature offers us exactly what we need close at hand! The four flowers I spotted were blooming in good health and there was a small pool where water spirits danced and where the vibration was high to provide the fifth ingredient. So today with a large glass bowl in hand I went and filled it full with water from the fast flowing stream before collecting the four flowers that were bathed in sunshine on this fine spring day. I placed them reverently in the bowl before adding the additional Rock Water I'd collected in a glass jar. As it was not yet the season to draw on the light of the sun to complete the process, I returned to the cottage and had to boil the mixture down. I filtered it several times and then mixed it with an alcohol preservative that I'd brought as a part of my collection of treatments.

Having not lived close to nature before, this was the first time that I'd experimented with making the remedies myself and it was a delight to see how my knowledge had helped the vision come to fruition. I knew that this remedy was going to serve well as another piece in the puzzle and John was truly a willing patient to take what I put before him without question or hesitation.

## Wednesday 6th April

*Following yesterday's experimentations I am for the first time beginning to understand how my three distinct trainings dovetail together into a complete healing package. Before now I'd always seen my nursing, naturopathic and mythos training as distinct modalities but I have to admit that here on the island those distinctions are blending together right before my eyes. They are becoming all one.*

*So I see now that being here with John and doing this work gives me a clear revelation of how thirty years of training has been preparing me solely for this three month window of opportunity. With only one or two of these gifts at my disposal I know that I would be unable to give John the fullness of treatment that he needs and so my years of training truly allows me to work across the multi-layered and complex world that we humans inhabit. Come the end, nothing is going to be left untouched within the realms of his body, mind, spirit and soul.*

*I know then that the channel between him and the Divine runs deep and long and as the midwife here it is my duty to make sure that that channel is cleared of any remaining debris so that he may ultimately receive the gift of healing that is there waiting to rush right through. It could all happen at the speed of light but I know that together we must honour the process of removing every stone until there is nothing left to stop this flood of grace from descending fully into his life.*

*In receiving this revelation today I am tantalised by a vision of bringing the fullness of my training to bear on more souls in the world rather than prioritising and focusing on one skill alone. I don't yet know how such a vision can manifest, but as I hold it close to my heart, I am feeling truly excited by the possibilities that lie ahead.*

### Thursday 7<sup>th</sup> April

*Today I returned to the garden where the nature spirits were playing lightly in the breeze that blew gently through the illumined space. When I scanned my inner eye, I could feel the aliveness in the soil and knew that there was an abundant supply of her gifts that would soon manifest here. The vibrations of these playful spirits were truly a delight to behold and so I sat there quietly and lavished them with my loving attention. They simply love to respond to an audience that embraces them.*

*But these graceful beings were not the only ones playing here on the breeze. A variety of birds soon came as they descended here to join in the blessed dance. A wagtail and a robin hopped gleefully around my feet whilst a bonny blackbird sang out from the depths of its heart before plucking a worm out from the fertile ground. Two thrushes, a magpie, and a skylark came to add their own unique voices to the choir ensemble that was forming here.*

*I simply sat there and closed my eyes as I slipped into a peaceful state of meditation and ascended into a place of light that my words cannot possibly describe and that my mind cannot contain. Safe to say though that I merged into all of creation here; and I became one with its most subtle dance. Time stood still and the world of form dissolved into nothingness as I basked in this exalted state of mystical union.*

*But of course I could not stay indefinitely and at some point I had to return back to the earth and to feel my feet again on solid ground. Of course though I was not the same and the higher vibrations I glimpsed sustained me through the rest of this day and helped to fill my heart right to the brim and beyond.*

## The Fourth Mythos

*Drawn from between the hands of six and seven.*

In a bustling city not so far away there was an important public official who held authority over the governance of this place. He had risen slowly through the ranks; starting out as a mere office junior in these halls of power before expanding his influence over many, many years. He was now at the peak of his career and all his hard work and effort was being handsomely rewarded. He was a man who was a born leader and who relished being in this seat of power. His heart was big and generous in its intent, but like many others who have stepped in these shoes, he was easily corrupted. But under his care this city did prosper and so he happily excused his questionable behaviour.

Working as an advisor for this man was the *Econimus*; who too had worked hard over many years to earn a privileged place in the day-to-day running of the city. The *Econimus* was a respected man of knowledge whose advice was keenly sought after by this man. The *Econimus* though managed to remain completely detached from the political corruption that went on behind the scenes during these years and he enjoyed his position and the responsibility he carried. He was a pure idealist who blindly turned his eye away from how his wise advice was being manipulated and distorted by the man in whom he had placed his trust. This is because the *Econimus* would give clever advice in saying that this is what needs to be done to improve things; but took no interest in the methods that were employed to achieve his suggestions.

For this important public official was far more pragmatic in getting things done more and did not waste time following a due process. He was especially adept at manoeuvring people around in order to get his own way and this is exactly how he had risen through the ranks. In blatant and not so blatant ways he pressed against the weak spots of those who opposed him with both threats and promises; and so under his charge the city blossomed exactly according to his will.

But then one day the *Econimus* received an alarming wake up call as his eyes for the first time were opened to what was really going on in his house of work. In the corridor he came across that public official doing something that struck him as completely abhorrent. He was so shocked that he went and immediately gave in his resignation. The official was caught by surprise but did not probe further; and the *Econimus* gave no explanation.

In the empty days and weeks that followed the *Econimus* stewed over what he had seen and he felt angry and betrayed in seeing something so noble so horribly tarnished. He bit his nails down to the quick as he wondered what he should do about it.

Eventually he decided to become a whistleblower and sought an editor who would be willing to publish his story. He tried and tried but no-one seemed interested in taking the risk of publicly shaming this official for his *hamartia*. He even went to one place, and as he presented his story to the editor, a stranger in the corner sat there silently hanging his head in disappointment.

But driven on by his fanatical desire to clean up this man's dishonesty and to bring about justice to his city; he persisted by investigating this public official further. He was prepared to create and publish the story himself if he had to.

Unsurprisingly, it did not take long before he found people who had plenty to gossip about over this man's *hamartia*. Naively the *Econimus* never checked the truth of what he was being told for he had already condemned this man as guilty. His fury and indignation about this man he had once trusted was fast become a raging torrent.

Although he didn't know the real truth behind these tales; from what he had briefly seen in that corridor nothing he heard surprised him about this man. To the *Econimus* the evidence all linked together to form a clear conclusion and so with what he had gained he had enough material to bring shame on this man. And so he did publish the story and drew a lot of attention from what he wrote. It made such an impact that this official, who had given his life to serve this city, was forced into resignation. Ruined and disgraced, this man disappeared from the city and spent his remaining days in a much less prosperous place.

As for the *Econimus*; well he suddenly stepped into a new line of employment as an investigative journalist who dedicated the rest of his career to uncovering lies and deceit in the lives of others. Rather than hiding naively on the sidelines, he now actively fought for his ideals on the battlefield as he publicly damned others for their *hamartia* in order that they may clean up their act. The *Econimus* was a terrier who would not give up the chase for what he believed was going to be a more fair and just world when he was done.

Finally the time came for the *Econimus* to return to the Kingdom that was well known to him. However, before he even got close to the gate, he saw the *Gatekeeper* sprinting out purposely to meet him. Fear seemed to have gripped the *Gatekeeper* completely as if he didn't want the *Econimus* to come any closer. There was to be no polite greeting this time.

'King slayer get away from this place. King slayer get away from this place,' he shouted whilst waving his arms around frantically as he ran.

The *Econimus*, not understanding, turned around to see if there was someone else there behind him. Seeing no-one he replied in shock;
'What have I done now?'

'You are still riddled with *hamartia* that's what. Do not come any closer. I don't want the *King* to know that there is a troublemaker who has come even this close to the palace.'

'Well if you don't stop making that racket he may well notice,' the *Econimus* answered gruffly as he looked up hopefully towards the windows of the distant palace where the sun was glinting upon them. He was beginning to grow tiresome of this *Gatekeeper* and his criticisms.

'Tell me what I have done now?' he asked again.

'In your spite of the *King* you've exposed the Kingdom to attack; that's what.'

'I did not spite the King. I do not even know him. I saw *hamartia* and sought to clean it up. Isn't that what you told me to do?'

'You don't clean up *hamartia* by becoming a troublemaker! Keep your head down I tell you. Do you hear me? Keep your head down! Don't get involved in things that are none of your business. Don't rock the boat for people will react and come back at you if you fling arrows around like that. I simply cannot allow any of those arrows to follow you any further into this land.'

'Well how could I have done it differently!' the *Econimus* asks defensively in protest.

'The *King* is your guide here. He alone can stop you from behaving so petulantly and immaturely. One act of *hamartia* swiftly leads to another when you ignore him,' the *Gatekeeper* replies forcefully.
'When will you ever learn?' he adds crossly.

'I am sorry. I just thought I was following your orders from what you told me the last time I was here,' the *Econimus* begs quietly. He remains desperate to enter this gate and is fearful that he has run out of chances. He does not like to be admonished and he does not enjoy upsetting the *Gatekeeper* like this.

'I told you nothing of the sort! But regardless of your accusations I will give you another chance to return and I beg of you this time to go away and learn from your mistakes. I don't want you to come back having tossed away another chance to do something good. I want to welcome you back and to open the gate for you. Now go!'

'I will take that chance and show you my willingness to change,' the *Econimus* answers with greater humility before turning away.

## Friday 8th April

After the rediscovery of the fourth mythos last night, John had stirred earlier than normal and he had seemed keen to join me for an early morning walk over to the lighthouse at the far side of the island. The light of dawn gave a soft pinkish tone to the cloudless sky. The air was fresh and we both had our jackets zipped up to the neck whilst we awaited the sun's appearance above the far horizon and its warm orange glow.

The world around us was slowly beginning to stir into life to welcome this new day. Birds chirped eagerly to welcome the light and I was still reverberating excitedly with yesterday's fond memory alive and tucked safely within my heart.

We walked together that morning with a sacred silence whose peace ran true. John was clearly absorbing and processing the fresh insights he'd received into his blood and he walked gently in a beautifully contemplative gait. In glancing across I had for the first time seen through the youthful form to a wise and ancient soul who had surely trodden this earth for eons. He simply oozed with the light of timeless wisdom as he took each self-assured step up the steep slope before us.

With each additional piece of the mythos being put back in place, John was truly beginning to come home to himself and all those scattered and broken pieces were being brought back together into one integrated whole. In looking at him in that moment I was left dumbstruck as to how strong a powerhouse this soul will surely become by the time of our journey's end.

On this day then we walked together as equals and he was no longer my patient and I was no longer his healer. We were simply old souls whose paths had crossed for this short period of time and who had met to share their wisdom for a while. That wisdom penetrated deep then; right into the silence of that cool spring morn.

176

## Saturday 9th April

It is remarkable how quickly the light can fade and for the darkness to return. By day John had become a wise elder but by night he transformed swiftly into the childhood state of confusion. Once more then I was called to sit like a sentinel by his bedside as his night time terrors returned. Once more he had become my patient and I had become his healer. After a stable few days of peace the rollercoaster ride had returned.

I sat in a wakeful state right through until morning before grabbing some shuteye myself. He was not feverish this time and so did not need me to mop his brow or offer my touch whilst he tossed and turned. But nevertheless I felt that my supporting presence was needed in the room to help hold John in a safe container of light.

It was the simple miracle of my beingness that I gave freely to him that night as I sat unmoved in a state of deep meditation. Having peeked into the vast depths of his soul only that morning I was easily able to make and hold contact with John's eternal and deep abiding light and to look right through the tremors taking place at the surface. I knew that it was in being silently witnessed for who he truly is that John was able to stay afloat and to not disappear into the blackness of that night.

Gradually, ever so gradually, then the tremors began to subside back into the void from which they had come. Silently and gracefully they had been seen as nothing more than the illusion that they were and so there was no place left here for them to stay. Swiftly, and effort-lessly, the dark cloak around his soul dissolved and its precious face was revealed to me once more. Yes I can now recognise this innate and tender beauty that lies within and I know that nothing will ever cause me to forget that face. As I see it so John will soon see it too. This I know to be true.

## Sunday 10<sup>th</sup> April

*Today I took a long contemplative walk across the island having become re-energised by a full night's rest. John itched to join me but his body has been weakened in recent days and I insisted that he needed to stay home and to take time to rest.*

*Once outside I welcomed this precious time of solitude that I'd been granted and it gave me space for reflection on all the changes taking place. Life here on the island has been very full since my arrival and so I was grateful for the chance to give a long exhale of breath and to relax in the still point at that breath's end. There has in truth then been little time to step back and to take a look at the bigger picture of what is unfolding rapidly here and in the progress that has been made. In the midst of it all I have had to rely solely on the sharpness of my instincts in order to carry me through. It has purely been about responding fully to each and every moment of our time together.*

*But then again I know that I am only here to take care of the details and it is not my place to see where this grand adventure is ultimately leading us to. Despite this I cannot help today but be curious and to ask myself the questions that I cannot possibly answer. Ultimately though my meandering contemplations only lead me down empty dead-end streets.*

*Out of the heat of battle then my faith in this omnipresent force falls frustratingly short. On this spacious day I have watched and seen how my mind still seeks a foothold and still seeks to steer this vessel. I must be vigilant then; and as I write at this late evening hour I must release this subtle desire for control and to rest again in the lap of the divine. I must say to myself over and over then; not my will but thy will be done.*

178

### Monday 11<sup>th</sup> April

*For the first time today I became hopelessly overwhelmed by the intensity of the energy that rumbled and shook this old cottage to its foundations. Having momentarily stepped off the ride yesterday I surprisingly found it difficult to jump back on today and to get back into tune with the rhythm and flow of these higher vibrations. I think any stranger who would perchance pass by this land would definitely need some forewarning and preparation before stepping ashore. I had a glimpse today then of how shockingly dangerous this healing container can be for someone who touches it with ice cold hands. I can see today how it possesses the power to obliterate the human mind into madness. This business of healing is truly not a game to be played by those weak at heart.*

*I was submerging deep into an ocean of my own making and was struggling to breathe and to ease my way back into the fire. I shielded myself away from John for most of the day as I cried and cried in the safety of my room. Though he was progressing he was not yet ready for me to be so openly vulnerable and I knew that I must work through this deep cleansing alone.*

*Yesterday I had a crisis of faith and today I had to repair the holes in order to pull me through. At times the energy was simply too unbearable to be with and I twisted and turned whilst the waves came and pounded over me. Late in the afternoon I simply had to get out and I walked briskly across the island and sought the refuge of the lighthouse. Whilst I sat heavy clouds gathered ominously overhead and soon the heavens opened and the rain began to pour. Without hesitation I ran out to welcome this treasure with open arms. As the water soaked right through into my skin my soul was renewed and recharged for the challenges ahead. Right there in the eye of the storm she came and purified my resistance. She came to give me permission to dip my heart again deep into that never changing well of peace.*

## Tuesday 12<sup>th</sup> April

*My self imposed veil of silence on these matters of my heart was gloriously lifted today in a moment of enraptured delight. It was only brief it is true, but it was strong enough to wrench right through these steel bars that I'd put up yesterday for John's own protection. In that moment I felt safe to be utterly naked and free again before him. In that moment I felt I could be truly me.*

*It came with peals of sound as John burst unexpectedly into a state of uncontrolled laughter that cut right through my solemn and cautious mood. I know not what triggered his mirth but I knew that this was akin to the deep bellied laugh of the awakened one who had suddenly seen right through the illusions of his own mind.*

*It was the laughter of sanity that cut to the bone and wrestled me out of these roles and responsibilities that I'd allowed to fall heavy on my shoulders. It was the laugh of the divine reminding me to become childlike and innocent again and to take away this veil of silence I'd put in place. In that moment I knew that I was being invited to trust John with the truth that sat deep in my own wounded heart.*

*Beyond my pride I saw how being the strong one of the two is hindering the healing process for us both. I still needed to release my tight stranglehold on all that was unfolding and unravelling around me and I am forced to admit that he does need me to show my fears, my vulnerabilities and my flawed human fragility. So whilst he continued to laugh aloud, I cried away another river of tears. He was not taken aback and together we made the sweetest music with our feelings. It was such a blessed release to show to him these teardrops of mine and to blur these roles and responsibilities that rest between us into the dust.*

## Wednesday 13th April

*Whilst joy comes by day; terror comes by night and I was called to watch over John's soul again whilst he moaned and writhed in restless sleep. As I sit and write these words today I wonder how many more tortured nightmares he must endure before my watching eyes. Will he ever find that permanent safe haven of peace where torment has no place left to dwell?*

*It is as if he remains cast under a spell and the strings of this marionette rest out of his hands and are being pulled at will. How else could it be when this soul is so full of light one second and in deep despair the next? It seems as if the cards are dealt and they will land and fall where they will. There is simply no series of logical steps to this healing process and I must be ever alert and vigilant for when the momentum flips.*

*I never initiate a conversation with John about his nightmares; but I can feel their energy intently. Last night, whilst I sat, I saw his aura suddenly shatter into pieces before my eyes; much like a pane of glass being dropped to the ground. Like a surgeon I had to step in immediately and patch up the holes in his psychic field. Instinctively I laid my hands over his navel; a few inches away from his sleeping body and let them move outwards on their own course. The heat in my hands grew ever more intense as I worked and I saw that they'd begun to blister. I had tried this approach in hospitals before but never before had I experienced such noticeable and alarming effects. I was though not deterred from continuing. Gradually John's breathing returned to a normal steady rhythm and I felt that his energy field had returned to a place of wholeness. Despite the transformation, I was wary of leaving his side that night and so I stayed and kept my vigil right through until the first glimmer of morning light.*

### The Fifth Mythos

*Drawn from between the hands of ten and eleven.*

Whilst growing up in his small village the *Econimus* was always eager to please and in so doing he stayed well out of any mischief. And whenever his friends dared to roam into the deep cave systems outside the village, a place where he had been told not to venture, he always held back and refused to go. For he feared disapproval and he distrusted his friends who he thought would abandon him should he ever get lost in the labyrinth of passageways which led he did not know where.

The *Econimus* knew that his guardian was a man of strict loyalty who performed his duties without question and the *Econimus* keenly wanted to follow in his footsteps. This man toiled long and hard and often did so without any warm praise or recognition for his efforts. But nevertheless, to the *Econimus*, he maintained the image of holiness in his being and so he too wanted to follow a noble path of virtue by avoiding all temptation through his adolescence. He desperately wanted to believe that a life of virtue was worth living regardless of any sacrifice that may be asked of him. This time he was determined to stay vigilant in holding on to the memory of the Kingdom; which he knew was waiting for him should he keep his promise and not stray from the path.

As he approached adolescence the time came for the *Econimus* to be given his place in this tribal community. The elders rewarded his loyalty by assigning him the duty of night watchman. It was a tremendously powerful ritual they took him through to prepare him for these adult duties; or so he told himself anyway. For he had naively turned his eyes and ears away from the circle of elders when they had started giggling amongst themselves after having so solemnly given him this duty for the village. To the innocent

*Econimus* it seemed a tremendous honour for he was to be the sole watchman and so it appeared as if a lot of faith was being placed upon his shoulders to take on such a responsibility. He was told that he was to be the first ever night watchman as before now there were none who could be trusted with such a privileged position. Though they could hardly keep a straight face in telling him this; on hearing these words of praise he felt truly blessed.

So it was then that through the full length of night the *Econimus* worked alone and diligently kept watch over his village whilst the others slept soundly. This was to be his lifelong contribution to the community and it was undoubtedly a humble and noble sacrifice he made to his people. By day he slept and so he never got to taste the pleasures of communal life and its graceful rhythm of work and play. The other men and women used to tease the *Econimus* and they knocked on his door whilst he rested to invite him to come out and join them. But he always refused with the excuse that he needed to stay in bed so that he may be fully refreshed and awake in his work at night. Ringing in his ears was the reminder of how important it was to fulfil his duty and avoid all unnecessary distractions along the way. The *Econimus* was resolute in his desire to learn from his past mistakes and to make sure that he maintained due diligence. If keeping watch at night was to be his duty then he would make sure that he performed it to the best of his ability. He was not going to waste this chance lightly.

But he struggled against the natural laws of his body which could never be tamed into a nocturnal habit. No matter how much he slept by day he was always tired at night and so it became a real effort for the *Econimus* to stay awake and to keep guard. Not that anything ever happened on his watch; for there were no predators and there were no obvious threats for him to dispel. This occasionally troubled him, and so, in the shadows where his mind could easily roam unchecked, he sometimes quietly wondered why he had been given this task. This was not all. A few years later the elders of the tribe came and asked him to walk on the hour through the sleeping quarters of the village and to loudly bang a drum as he did so. They offered no valid reason for this but they asked the *Econimus* to do this every night from then on. Once more he obeyed blindly out of a sense of duty.

Even though he did not question it aloud; the *Econimus* always felt very uncomfortable when the clock struck the hour for he dreaded this task. But no-one else complained about it and so he continued doing it without further hesitation. However, he did notice that after this began that no-one came knocking on his door by day anymore.

And so the *Econimus* persisted in this strange task that was assigned to him and which he hoped would one day reap its handsome reward. In all the years he performed his duty; only once did something unusual happen. One night he glimpsed a stranger lurking in the shadows and who he sensed was trying to talk to him. The *Econimus* listened hard but could not understand what was being mouthed. He walked closer but every step he took forwards the stranger took two steps back. Eventually the stranger disappeared altogether and was never to be seen again.

Finally the time came for the *Econimus* to return back to a familiar Kingdom and he was confident that he had done enough to gain access. He had surely learnt his lessons from his previous visits here and had done what the *Gatekeeper* had asked of him.

He approaches and this time the *Gatekeeper* gives a smile and asks him the familiar question.
'Do you wish to enter the gate?'
'I do.'
'In order to gain access to the *King* you must first prove to me that you have lived a life free of *hamartia*.'
'I can prove that this time,' the *Econimus* answers keenly. 'I obeyed my calling without losing integrity or dishonouring my

agreement. I was devoted and I did what was asked humbly and without protest. I have learnt the error of my ways. I am ready to enter.'

'But the question is what were you devoted to? Were you devoted to the *King*…or were you devoted to something else.'

'To the *King* of course! If I had of been selfish I would not have followed through my tasks and would have spent my days mucking around with the people in the village and sleeping on the job at night. I would have wasted my opportunity to serve.'

'I do not see someone before me who is devoted to his *King*. I see someone who is weak and powerless and who is still riddled with *hamartia*. You clearly do not understand what a life of service entails and where to place your loyalty. You must have allowed yourself to be misled out there.'

The *Gatekeeper's* words are strong and forceful and on hearing them the *Econimus* is dismayed. The *Econimus* had put this Kingdom first; he had done the best he could and yet impossibly he is being told it is not enough! What had seemed a simple quest in the beginning; has become one he is now losing heart in. In reaching for a better feeling; the *Econimus* stumbles onto explosive rage.

'Fuck you; you impossible bastard! I am fucking trying my best here to meet your damn condition. Go on and send me back out to fail again. I don't fucking care anymore.'

The *Econimus* is now daring the *Gatekeeper* to react. He is testing the boundary the *Gatekeeper* holds because he wants to know if this man before him has any real power or influence over his destiny - or whether in fact he is just a meagre bureaucrat setting him up to fail through the weight of impossible inertia.

'I am only the messenger,' the *Gatekeeper* replies without flinching. 'Come to me free of *hamartia* and you are welcome to enter through this gate. If you don't you can't. This is the law I must uphold.'

'But you are fucking playing games with me here,' the *Econimus* answers in continued frustration. 'Way back in our first meeting you said I needed to take on board the wisdom of the elders in the tribe and to give *them* my trust. Now here on our fourth meeting; fuck me is it really our fourth meeting; you are telling me I've been misled for following this advice. And you expect me to fucking respect you? It's just bullshit.'

'There is no right or wrong; no one answer on which path to follow in life. The only enduring advice I give is to put your King first at all times. The rest only applies in the moment I give it because no two situations are exactly the same. The cost of not following advice that endures is the cost of *hamartia*; and no man with *hamartia* can enter this gate. This is the law.'

The *Econimus* doesn't know how to respond to the calm manner of the *Gatekeeper* before him. The *Gatekeeper's* condition sounded so straightforward in first hearing it but now it seems so far out of his reach. It now appears an impossible riddle to solve because he can't get in to meet the *King* unless he is free of *hamartia* and he can't rid his *hamartia* unless he first meets the *King*! The *Econimus* has reached a crossroads and the outcome is no longer guaranteed. This meeting has marked the end of his era of innocence.

'Very well; I will try again and I will find a way to master this,' the *Econimus* finally answers; but with tears welling in his eyes and without any confidence in these words he utters.

## Thursday 14ᵗʰ April

*The hour is late but there is simply too much adrenaline pulsing through for me to turn to sleep yet. We have just completed the fifth mythos session and a restful silence has fallen upon the house. When sleep finally does come to me I am sure I will be grateful for I have only catnapped throughout this day and my body feels weary and in need of a full night's rest.*

*I feel that tonight we have reached a point in the mythos where things are beginning to become clearer to my mind and I can now get a sense of where the story is going. It is beautiful to receive these rich insights that lie beneath John's past storyline of events and I cherish this gift of intimacy dearly. As a healer I know it is not necessary for me to piece the puzzle together; but as a friend, doing so does at least help me to feel personally more connected to this man I am currently sharing my life with. It helps me to be much more empathetic when I can go beyond the mask that separates him from me and to touch the heart of love that unites us as one.*

*Tonight turned out to be a truly beautiful session. Even though the story appeared heavy; I felt so much richness and light. When we stepped out of the vault together and back into the room I could see that John's aura was positively glowing from the precious jewel that he had discovered from within. He returned with an illumined radiance surrounding him and it felt almost as if there were a thousand angels that had descended to protect him. Or then again perhaps it was just the solitary influence of the wild man who guards the vault and who is becoming a stronger figure in his psyche with each passing week. But regardless of what name is put to this protective force; its presence here assures me that John will surely sleep soundly on this night. Blessed be.*

### Friday 15<sup>th</sup> April

*I too slept soundly last night but oddly I was wide awake before the first light of morning. So high is the energy vibration on the island right now that it seems as if sleep is not so important in my life as it was back on the mainland when I needed a regular nine hours of rest. Here I can be awake one night, have six or seven hours the next, and still feel full of life and vigour. In fact, coming fully into that vibrant wakeful state with eyes wide open is exactly what my journey here is all about. It is about extending that hand of gratitude for all that is here far and wide.*

*And my heart is so full of gratitude at the moment that I can just leap forth from my bed to welcome each new day that comes. I simply don't wish for any second of this life to miss my warm and tender offering of appreciation.*

*On this early morning, where the stars still shone in a moonless sky, I rose and stepped outside to embrace the cool spring air that greeted me. Wrapped up in layers, I walked down to the jetty where the water lapped calmly beneath my feet. Looking to the mainland, and beyond to the east, I could see the first slither of dawn appearing on the horizon. In time, tiny clouds that dotted across the sky turned pink and then orange as the light of the sun began to offer itself to this part of the world. Finally she revealed herself to me and I cast my eyes on this great ball of fire as if it was for the first time. In her presence everything turned golden and the water glistened as if fairies of light were dancing upon her surface. On this beautiful morning I was giving myself away to the light and the light was truly giving herself away to me.*

## Saturday 16th April

Today the garden called my name and I was eager to get my hands in the dirt and to ground all these higher energies I've been connecting with down into the earth. Casually I asked John if he wanted to join me and I was surprised by his willing enthusiasm for fresh air and physical exertion.

There was much there for us to do but to begin with I was horrified to see how insensitively John went about the task. Whilst to him the land was silent; all I could hear were the cries of my nature spirit friends who wept in lament at man's forcefulness. Quietly to myself I spoke to appease them with my apologies and to call them back as I felt them scatter towards the garden wall and beyond.

Having had such peaceful coexistence between us in the home it caught me by surprise to experience these issues of rank and responsibility here in the garden and I knew instinctively that I had to deal with this matter delicately. John certainly would not have welcomed a lecture on how to tend to his plot.

It was strange to see how strong my feelings were for the garden. As we worked I noticed how she'd now become my baby and I saw how tightly I wanted to cling to her and to protect her from John's exuberant assault. My clinging to these defenceless beings only served to build a ridge of separateness between me and John and I knew it would be wise to bite my tongue rather than react from this place of disunity.

On this day I began to see how John's re-emerging strength and power is going to shift the dynamics of our relationship. Change is necessary and I cannot dare halt her flow. I can only hope that John will learn in time to manage his power less boyishly than before and in these transient times of adolescence I must be willing to let him be and to let him find his own way. But whilst I worked as a peacemaker between the kingdoms of man and nature, I knew now how challenging it can be to love someone without conditions.

## Sunday 17ᵗʰ April

*Moments of transformation occur so swiftly here on the island and I am delightfully baffled by John's sudden change of mood today. He was keen to continue our work in the garden and I have to say sadly that my initial reaction was lukewarm. I only joined him so as to keep a watchful eye and to help maintain the peace.*

*But as we began I was amazed to see how the heavy hands and cold heart of yesterday had magically disappeared overnight. I'd done or said nothing to instigate it, but once I saw what was happening, my fears immediately subsided to let the momentum roll.*

*Where before we had been solemn and serious adults at work; now nature had become our playground and a mischievous childlike innocence had swept through John's soul. His light and playful spirit today helped bring those walls of separation tumbling down and he helped me to release another layer from the burden of responsibility that I'd been carrying. The shifting dynamics that had led me towards caution were blown apart as we blissfully shed those fears of stepping onto each other's toes and simply dived together into the cosmic dance.*

*I know not if our nature spirit friends were the ones leading the dance or whether they too simply came to join in with their iridescent delight. How rare it is to see an adult in this world who has the courage to come out and fan those flames of childhood magic and spontaneous joy. Especially John; who's soul, more than most, has long been carrying the heavy cloak of adulthood upon his shoulders. Like many he'd been forced to grow up too soon and this naïvely trusting and vulnerable infant had become entombed for his own protection.*

*So how enraptured I am then to see this dusty tomb prised open a little! Why today it should happen I know not, but I will cherish those few hours where he revealed and shared with me the innate simplicity of his being.*

## Monday 18<sup>th</sup> April

*After yesterday's time of open vulnerability I feel there has been a dramatic shift in John's relationship towards the feminine and I sense that a core wound has been healed within. His willingness to show me his trust is deeply touching and I am keen to respond with encouragement so that he may continue to flower and blossom here.*

*Today his attention turned towards the masculine, and over a mid-morning cuppa, he began to confide in me about the feelings of devoted love that he still felt for his father. For John, suicide had clearly not in any way lowered his standing upon the pedestal that he had placed him upon as in his eyes his father had not given his life away cheaply but had it taken from him by unjust circumstance.*

*I listened quietly to John's warm hearted admiration of his father's selfless generosity and observed how this was all dovetailing in with the theme of service and honour that ran through the tale of the fifth mythos. Clearly something was stirring deep within the recesses of John's psyche about his adolescent struggle to try and join his father upon the moral high ground. Today then he spoke to me of his guilt and his remorse for being unable to emulate the impossible standards he had set himself.*

*On this day I saw John's deep emotional attachment revealed to me and I saw that this is one of the key things that stands between him and grace. I could not speak it aloud; but through the mythos he will eventually have to make peace with the injustice of his father's death and move on to live his own life. For John to be healed he will have to pull his father down from that pedestal in order to step out of his shadow and his shattered legacy. John will have to learn to be mortally human and to see the beauty in the flaws of our mundane existence. He will have to learn to embrace the dark as well as the light and to taste the love in all.*

### Tuesday 19<sup>th</sup> April

*The reading of the fifth mythos has not only stirred something in John but in me too. Today I took with me the words and emotions he shared yesterday on a long walk around the island's edge; and I felt how they were animating some of my own attachments and beliefs. Like John, I too have had my moments of questioning the injustices of the world; and like his father I too have played the part of the innocent martyr.*

*Though I have never contemplated suicide I have at times struggled to stay on my own moral high ground and to not abandon myself and my calling. It has in truth been a thankless task to persevere with my soul's work and with my devotion to serve in the most exalted way. I now have no concern for second best and for these superficial platitudes of nursing care; even though these once brought me comfort and wealth.*

*I know what it takes then to make peace with a world that has no apparent concern or interest in the work I do and I know what it takes to no longer be their martyr. I've done so much letting go of my resentments over the years but still the energy remains present and it is so easily triggered when the right circumstances arise. At times like this I must remind myself that this is the path I chose to walk down and that these were necessary tests of my devotion to follow my soul's lead wherever it went.*

*As I reaffirmed my choice, I began to walk in more confidence and I reminded myself that suicide, or any other act of self-betrayal, would only have kept me bound in a dark place that cannot possibly be imagined. Right here and right now I am so grateful to have persevered through those bleakest nights of doubt.*

*I also believe that John too will make peace too so that he does not have to join his father there.*

## Wednesday 20<sup>th</sup> April

A surprise awaited me towards the end of this day as John insisted on reclaiming his kitchen in order to prepare us both a special evening meal. As he shooed me away for the afternoon I was heartened to see how improved his energy levels are today from having needed a recuperative couple of days after his weekend exertions in the garden.

I don't know if it is the effect of the flower essences I prepared, or the mythos journey itself, but John is certainly more emotionally connected nowadays and that thick insensitive skin of his has become far more translucent. The fifth mythos has stirred in him that innate longing of his to care and to share what he can give with others. I can see that he has this big heart that just needs a little coaxing to reveal itself and its glory.

When I was finally called downstairs I could not help but laugh warmly at the extraordinary lengths he had gone too. For the table had been set upon the finest cloth and there was a candle glowing in the centre. Two small vases of freshly plucked spring flowers were placed at either end and in the midst of it all was John who simply stood there in all his radiance holding out a chair for me to sit upon. In this light, this gentleman was barely recognisable to the angry adolescent who had first shown up on my doorstep with such fierce defensiveness and rage. Tears came to my eyes as I caught another glimpse of how far he has come in such a short space of time.

It was only a simple meal it is true but it is in the small things taken care of lovingly that I am always touched the most. Within each tiny mouthful of food I could feel the vibration of John's heartfelt appreciation and gratitude towards me and my efforts here. When one heart gives and receives to another over and over; the effect quickly multiplies until the whole atmosphere is simply saturated with love.

## Thursday 21ˢᵗ April

Tonight we will embark on the next instalment of the mythos and so at this time of the week John is always a little more restless in anticipation of what is to come. He still has plenty of energy left to burn even after yesterday's exertions and he was at times pacing around like a caged animal that is eager to break free.

It took all of my patience to hold a calming influence in the home but eventually by the afternoon I could not help but urge him to take a long walk over to the lighthouse. It was odd that he needed my permission before he could step out alone and alarm bells rang as I saw how he was giving me the authority over his health. Now that I could see it clearly, I realised why today had been so heavy and trying. How little does John know that I cannot possibly hold that responsibility over him for this is a matter that rests between him and his maker alone.

Having been graced with a rare slither of time in the house alone, I turned on my collection of songs to the beloved and ramped up the volume to send vibrations of love bursting throughout the house. If John is a caged animal then I have been a caged bird who'd finally heard that call of freedom which led me to sing out to my heart's content. I sung out to the divine and gladly released those expectations that I'd allowed John to put on my shoulders. I am no miracle worker and to finally admit that fact to myself gave rise to such a huge wave of blessed relief. When my arrogant belief that I was a healer had been pricked I had so wanted that power returned to me. But now I can honestly say that I have no cares for it and I just simply want to enjoy the dance and to let the story unfold. I am free now to just be me!

## The Sixth Mythos

*Drawn from between the hands of four and five*

The *Econimus* was scribbling furiously on a piece of scrap on a desk piled high with papers. It was early morning and he was not yet dressed or shaved for this was his first act of this new day. If anyone had of walked past this scene they would surely have been shocked by the apparent mess, with the floor covered with pieces of paper as well. But to the *Econimus* these papers contained all manner of pioneering ideas and inventions that came through him in times when he was feeling inspired. It had become an addictive pursuit, and though he struggled to get everything down on paper, dwelling in this creative fire gave him so much joy. He felt so connected, alive and passionate whilst sat at his desk and he found it hard to return to the rigours of day-to-day living so as to put bread on the table.

With the piles of paper stacked around him he had long sensed with resignation that if anyone saw him like this that they would surely think that they were nothing more than the scribbles of a madman. But he persisted because he believed they could be useful to the people in his community. His only problem was that he did not know what to do with all these ideas and inventions; he did not know where to begin in filing these papers together and working out how to transform them into gold. All he could do was cling on to a slim thread of hope that one day in the future someone would come and give him the help he so dearly required.

And then it seemed as if his prayer was being miraculously answered. For one day, at a later point in time, a stranger appeared in his life. And, after they had talked for a while, he asked permission to cast his eye over these ideas. The *Econimus*, who felt he had once met this man sometime before, agreed and invited him in. Immediately the stranger saw merit in a couple of things he saw and became very excited. Keenly he told the *Econimus* that he could help bring these particular inventions to life and into the marketplace. This stranger went on to explain that he was a businessman who ran a successful factory in a neighbouring community and that he was looking for new ideas. Within this factory he had ready access to all the labour and to all the machinery he needed to begin the process of creation. In return for his investment he asked for half of the profits and he promised the *Econimus* that if he agreed then he would soon become a very wealthy man.

It was an incredible offer and the *Econimus* thought that this could finally be the answer to all he had wished for. He was tempted to shake his hand there and then but something caused him to hesitate and so he asked for some time to give it thought. Sensing his doubt, the stranger kindly offered to show him around his factory and to explain his plans in more detail. He agreed and so they went together immediately.

On arrival the *Econimus* was instantly left awestruck by what this stranger had built for himself. The factory was a most beautiful creation and so the *Econimus* knew instinctively that his ideas would be in very safe hands here and that this was not a false promise he was being lured by. It was obvious to him that this stranger was more than worthy as a partner to go into business with.

But again something stopped him from going ahead and once more he asked for more time to give it thought. The stranger seemed genuinely surprised by the hesitation but said that he would return the following morning for a final answer.

The *Econimus* had a long and largely sleepless night. He did not know what was troubling him because this stranger coming into his life was exactly what he had desired. With him he would finally see the fruit of all those hours he had spent in the creative fire.

But then again he had only met this stranger that day and so the doubts remained as to whether this was a man in whom he could place his trust.

Finally the *Econimus* fell into a deep sleep and he had a dream where his father appeared in the distance. The *Econimus* tried to reach out to him but he found he couldn't move forwards. Looking down at his feet he saw the stranger's face and he saw how he had both arms wrapped tightly around his legs. No matter how much the *Econimus* squirmed he could not break free of his grasp. He was helpless as he watched a hooded figure walk up behind his father and drag him away like a rag doll into the dark abyss. The *Econimus* woke up with a scream.

Taking this dream as an omen; the *Econimus* decided to send this stranger on his way. The stranger arrived early next morning and he shook his head in mock disappointment after hearing this decision. But he said nothing more to try and change the mind of the *Econimus*.

However, after he had left, the *Econimus* could not come to a place of ease. He became paranoid because the man had seen his ideas and could easily bring them to market and take all of the profits as his own. To stop him the *Econimus* took the step of putting patents in place on all his ideas so that no-one could trade upon them without his permission. Then, in still not knowing how to take the ideas forth himself, the *Econimus* locked all his papers away in a secret vault. He promised himself that he would not show them to the world again.

The *Econimus* tried to forget what he had locked away as he now devoted all his time to putting bread on the table. The flood of inspiration dried up and no new ideas or inventions came to visit him ever again. Meanwhile, the ones he had kept were never brought to market and so the *Econimus* lived the rest of his days in a state of poverty he had long grown accustomed to.

The time came to return to a Kingdom that was familiar to him. The *Econimus* approached but without any hope or expectation of gaining entry this time. Once more the *Gatekeeper* appeared to meet him and he asked him the same questions as before;

'Do you wish to enter this Gate?'

'I do.'

'Have you lived a life free of *hamartia*?'

'No,' he answered; having grown tired of defending himself and his actions.

'And yet you want to enter this gate?' the *Gatekeeper* asks again; somewhat taken aback by this admission.

'I do,' the *Econimus* replies.

'Even though you know you have not met my condition?'

'Well I don't really know if I have or if I haven't. I just don't want you to think that you have any power to disappoint me anymore.'

'Well you were right. You are still riddled with *hamartia*.'

'You probably think I should have shook hands on that deal. But it was the *King* who told me not to. Of that I am confident,' the *Econimus* answers boldly.

'What I think is not of any importance. All I know is that you can't have put the *King* first in your life because you are standing here before me oozing with *hamartia*. That is the fact of the matter.'

'So can you give me some fucking details here because if you don't I can't possibly move forwards in this stupid game we are playing. Tell me straight. What should I do differently?' the *Econimus* retorted in evident frustration.

'That is not my place to tell you that. Only the *King* can give that advice.'

'So what are you fucking going to do about this situation? I am over playing this game with you because I'm never going to make it am

I? You say I am the one who is not making the right choices and that you are just a messenger. Yet you are the one calling the shots around here. So go on and tell me how you want this whole story to end. And, more to the point, what are you going to fucking do to make it so?'

'I will do what I have to do. That is, I will send you back out in the world until you learn to make wise choices.'

'And if I don't...'

'That is not a future you should wish to contemplate,' the Gatekeeper added gravely.

### Friday 22nd April

*During last night's session there was something that seemed oddly out of place; although I couldn't place my finger upon what at the time. There was nothing different in the way the session unfolded from the previous five, as I continued to play the role of silent witness; but I remember becoming suddenly perplexed as I sat in my otherworldly state of deep meditation.*

*Today I recalled that moment in the early morning light whilst I was tidying around the home and pondered what it might have been. Then it came to me in a revelatory flash; it was John's voice. Yes that's right. For suddenly in reading aloud the mythos his voice had changed tone completely from anything I'd heard before. Whereas John had always had a loud grating voice with lots of harsh disharmonic tremors within it; last night it became soft, sweet, deep and almost melodious in nature. How interesting it is that this shift has come about almost in opposition to where the mythos tale is heading and the harmonious voice did not really ring true with the words being spoken. Perhaps that is why it instantly struck me as odd.*

*I do remember having read before that the tone of one's voice often reveals how centred and contained an individual is within their power. The more harmonious the tone the more balanced and comfortable an individual is with their own inner authority. Apparently, when harmonised, the voice is no longer searching for something outside of itself.*

*After yesterday's drama of John acting so powerless, and with his voice chasing after me for permission, I was curious to see if something has indeed shifted overnight to bring about a lasting change. I did not have to wait long though before hearing those first welcome notes of quiet gentleness that now did not pierce the silence so harshly. As I was able to quickly spot the change, I wonder now if John notices it too.*

## Saturday 23rd April

*A cloudless sky endured throughout this day and John boldly took the opportunity to test his strength and to take a longer walk around the island. I was amazed to see him acting on his own intuition without me having to say a word of encouragement and to simply go off as he will. The swiftness in which things change here still has the power to surprise and catch me off guard. Even more surprising is that I don't have to say a word to help push things onto a different course whenever they go seemingly awry.*

*He was gone sometime and returned enthused by what he had discovered on his explorations. I had not realised before how little he knew of his own island and how shallow the distance he had only ventured before from the cottage. It is noticeable now to see that the work here is helping him to overcome his breathing difficulties that had once confined him. How odd it would seem to those peering from afar that in sickness he is now fitter than when he was in better health.*

*He spoke with a childlike freshness and it reminded me of my own discoveries of distant treasures on those first couple of days spent here. Though it is small in size the island does indeed have such a rich tapestry of beautiful rock formations with many little nooks and crevices to explore. Given its precarious location here on the edge of the wild and expansive ocean it is perhaps not surprising that the geology is so rich and varied on the island's far shore. Here in the sheltered waters on this side it is of course naturally less interesting for exploration and this is the bland island that John has only known until now. Today then is a sure and gentle sign that he is beginning to show renewed interest again in an outside world that he has shunned and closed himself from for so long. He is getting ready to join the ranks of the living.*

### Sunday 24<sup>th</sup> April

In the quiet of the early afternoon John was in bed resting and a deep peaceful silence has fallen upon the cottage. I have felt the chill within my bones today, a chill that seems to have this old cottage in its grip. On a day like today I simply cannot imagine what the winter would have been like here before John had replaced the windows. Our stock of firewood is running low now to indulge in stoking the fire and I've had to make do with the warm clothing that is wrapped around me in layers.

Ceremoniously I prepared myself a lavish afternoon tea that was fit for a queen and each detail in the preparation was taken care of reverently. A slice of fresh apple pie was carved out intricately and gently placed upon a piece of John's finest crockery. A pot was filled with loose herbal leaves that released their aroma when the boiling water was added. Everything was then placed gently upon a silver tray.

I took myself to the sanctuary of my bedroom where I continued to take care of each detail mindfully and giving it the utmost care and attention. Simply pouring the tea was to me a deeply spiritual act for it felt as if I was here making tea for the beloved herself. This was my own private time of intimate communion and I made sure that I relished each moment with the fullness of my conscious intent. Looking deeply I could see the light of divine grace pierce its way through to embrace this most sacred Sunday hour. It is tough to hold those eyes open for long but in truth one mere second is powerful enough to give the sustenance that will last me through this lifetime. I cannot help now but devote the rest of my life to this love I have so sweetly tasted.

## Monday 25ᵗʰ April

*A pleasant surprise lay in store for me this day as John was keen to take the boat across to the mainland in order to stock up on supplies for the larder. Although we live well here on the produce from the garden we are not able to be fully self-sufficient. So every months or two he has to purchase extra from his meagre savings. Sadly both of us have found it difficult to escape the world of commerce over the years; although John is freer from it than I ever managed. I can appreciate how living on an island really does give one the sense of separation from the herd of the collective consciousness.*

*It is interesting that our paths have been shifting in different directions as John has been learning to come back and to make peace with a world he has escaped from; whereas I have been revelling in the freedom that this separation brings.*

*Despite my contentment, I was at least curious to join John for the ride and to get a taste again of civilisation; even if it was only in the little village across the water. The water was calm and the crossing was smooth and John was feeling brightened to be out on open waters. Whilst he refused my offer to pay my share for the groceries, I insisted on treating us both to a drink from the neighbouring bakery. After six weeks it was though strange to have other people milling around us. And though I am sociable by nature, I was feeling a little jarred by the noise of conversations there. In truth my curiosity was short lived and I for one was glad to put my post in the mailbox and to beat a hasty retreat home.*

*By contrast, John surprisingly seemed to be feeling quite comfortable and at ease here as he chatted easily with the owner whilst I was hastily making my way to the door. This leaves me wondering now whether he will try to sustain his isolated way of living once our time together is complete. Is his soul getting ready to reconnect again with the wider world?*

## Tuesday 26th April

Before yesterday's trip to the mainland I had not given a single thought to the future that lies beyond my work with John. But today I could not help but ruminate a little on the possibilities and on the shifting directions we were heading in.

It is true that it had always been in my mind that it would not be healthy for John to stay any longer on the island beyond our time together; but I had easily let it all go because it really had been none of my concern. But now after feeling how my heart and soul had yearned to return 'home' to the island; I was suddenly feeling a little more entwined in John's future plans.

Before now I'd simply assumed that I would have to return back to the nursing world I know once our work had been complete. But now the seed of doubt had been sown although I know not what I would do here if I were to stay on...and it seemed unwise to delve too far into the possibilities. All I know is that after a lifetime of searching I finally feel as if I have found a place to call home. Here on Diarra there is something special that makes my soul sing and it is a protected place where I finally feel safe to open my heart wide and to share all that I am.

There truly is nowhere else I've been to, in my forty-eight years on this earthly plane, that has given me this feeling of being perfectly in the right place at the right time. Everywhere else I have had to adapt and change shape to squeeze into shoes that were truly not mine to fill.

But despite my yearning; strangely I am feeling at peace with the future and I can loosen my grip on that longing of mine to stay. Even if I do have to go back to those places, and to cage my heart again, I do know that my short blessed time here on Diarra will have at least made this life of mine worth living.

## Wednesday 27th April

Darkness descended again upon the island last night and the wind howled ferociously across the ocean and rattled against the windowpanes. After a couple of weeks of long and peaceful sleep I was called once more to John's side as another storm brewed within and keeled him over. It is astounding to see how the dreams of day can flip and turn into a completely different story through the dreams of night. He has gone from having been so calm and relaxed into being so restless and disturbed.

I sat there by his side and wondered what it is that is being stirred now within the murky recesses of his soul. What dross was being dredged up here from the depths to be transformed into the light? The answer is not mine to know and my part is simply to sit and to hold him in a loving vibration whilst the cleansing and purging takes place. If there is one thing that my nursing care taught me then it was the art of simply sitting there patiently by a patient's bedside through the night. It truly is a practice that requires a lot of discipline when body and mind are aching to drift off elsewhere.

Then suddenly from nowhere I felt this energy moving through my body and these softly soothing and coherent sounds emerged quietly from my lips whilst he passed through his nightmares. Ancient and long forgotten lullabies began to stream forth as if I was here tending to a baby child and not a fully grown man. For a moment I put the brakes on as if embarrassed by what was coming through; but the momentum was so strong that I truly could not halt it for long. I could only sense that the child within John was feeling frightened and needed to hear these songs in order to feel safe and protected again. Regardless of what I thought; these words had their effect for his body soon became still and his breathing returned to normal. Magically then, his soul had returned back to a place of rest.

## Thursday 28ᵗʰ April

As I sit and write at this early evening hour I can feel this incredible yearning bubbling away inside of me like a molten pool of lava. This fire is hot and insatiable and I know it will consume every last bit of resistance that stands in its way. That includes my mind which has fallen utterly silent by what is taking place by the flickering light of the candle. My mouth feels parched dry and in this moment I have this absolutely unquenchable thirst to be struck down in awe by the power of the sacred. Right now I just want to pull back that curtain of illusion and to finally see the face of my beloved before me. The promise of eternity is tantalisingly close now.

There is a momentum that has been building and building since I first set foot upon these shores and it is a force that is no longer in my hands to control. It is a force that has pulled me right down into the depths of the ocean and has consumed my identity. No longer am I distinct and no longer can I find the boundaries where I begin and end. Time stands still and there is absolutely nothing of me that is left within the cinders of this fire.

I am falling into the void but strangely perhaps it is in the emptiness that I feel most potent and alive in this world. I cannot put the brakes on this momentum although it still has the power to scare as well as excite me. For in losing my mind here I am at risk of sliding into madness as much as I am slipping into love.

Later tonight we will embark on the next mythos and yet here I am unravelling at the seams. As I dissolve into the light of my being I wonder what John will make of this translucent and ghostlike apparition that I am fast becoming?

# The Seventh Mythos

*Drawn from between the hands of one and two.*

The *Econimus* was lying awake after another sleepless night. Grief had been hanging heavy on his heart and he felt limp and had no zest for living. The plague had spread and death was a spectre that held this cursed place in its grasp. Even those who'd survived had not been left untouched by its twisted hand. Indeed, for the *Econimus*, death had come for all his family except for him.

Before death had come for his father; he had given the *Econimus* a single shilling from his pocket and he had urged his son to take it and to use it to redeem his name before death took it all from him. His father was desperate to ensure that his life and work was not spent in vain. The *Econimus* took that shilling from his hand and gave his promise that he would do his best to honour him.

Grief had caused him to forget this promise; but on this day he pulled himself up from his sleeping place and the shilling fell out of his pocket and onto the ground. The sound of it hitting the flagstone jogged his memory and he felt ashamed that he had not yet honoured his father's final words. In picking that shilling up from the floor the *Econimus* immediately took the decision to leave this place and to go in search of better luck and fortune.

He journeyed to a more prosperous land and oddly there were two doorways through which he could enter. On the doorway to the left there was a notice attached and it read that in return for a mere shilling he would receive all that he would need; his board, a chance to do an honest day's work for the benefit of the people here, and care for his good health. On the doorway to the right there was a notice attached and it read that in return for a mere shilling he would be given a place at a card table where he could earn a fortune or else leave with nothing.

The *Econimus* sensed this was a setup but he did not hesitate in choosing the doorway to the right and he placed his father's shilling in the slot. He did not hesitate because he had grown tired of trying to make the right choices in order that he may be accepted to see the *King*. The doorway to the left seemed too hard to navigate. At least going through the doorway to the right would bring him no disappointment. In truth he felt as if there was nothing more he could possibly lose.

So the *Econimus* went through and took his place at the gambler's table. He quickly surprised himself because having expected to crash and burn in an instant he discovered instead that he had a knack for the game and that luck was firmly on his side. His shilling began to grow and multiply quite rapidly. He did not seem to care that whilst his pile of money grew; others next to him had seen theirs diminish. If they wanted to play this game then that was their responsibility and not his. He was not going to cry over their losses.

In truth no-one liked the *Econimus*...and it was not just because he was on a hot winning streak. It was the way he laughed and mocked as he did so as if he didn't give a damn about the feelings of anyone else. He was not there to make friends; he was there to make money. People started to leave the gambler's table, or else sit far away from him. But the *Econimus* did not see it as a sign to slow down or stop. He kept on pushing and pushing for more.

Finally the *Econimus* decided that he had earned enough to have redeemed his father's name and that the time had come to walk away. So he stood up and asked to cash in his winnings. The stranger he spoke with nodded his head in agreement but then asked the question;

'What are you going to do with all this money you have acquired?'
'Make sure that no-one gets their grubby hands on it that's what!'
'Where will you go?'
'Far away from this place of losers; that's where. Now give me my money!'
'But I can help you spend it wisely,' the stranger offered kindly.
'I'm sure you can but I don't want to spend it! It's mine to hold so give it to me!'

And so the *Econimus* left that place and dug himself a big hole far away from preying eyes where he could put away his winnings. He decided he didn't want to spend it frivolously because he wanted to make sure he had some left at the end to throw in the *Gatekeeper*'s face and to mock him too. No, in fact, he wanted to hold on and throw *most* of it in his face.

And so the time came for the *Econimus* to return to a familiar Kingdom and he made sure that he collected his large sack of gold on the way. He walked slowly through the beautiful landscape dragging it behind him until he came to the gateway that was familiar to him. On hearing his arrival the *Gatekeeper* appeared and asked his usual questions.

'Do you wish to enter this gate?'
'I do,' the *Econimus* shouted loudly as he looked up at the Palace in hope that the noise would get the *King's* attention.
'Have you lived a life free of *hamartia*?'
'Probably not; but look at all the fucking money I got along the way!' the *Econimus* hollered as he pointed at the sack on the ground. He then dipped his hand in and showered the *Gatekeeper* with all the gold coins he had carried to this place. He stood provocatively with an aggressive stance that was goading the *Gatekeeper* to react.
'And yet you say you wish to enter the gate?' he answered without a tinge of emotion and with the look of utter bewilderment as to what

he could possibly do with this rogue *Econimus* who was now behaving so obnoxiously. 'I don't follow your reasoning as to why you think your actions deserve that kind of merit.'

'I trusted my fucking gut. I went out for it big style and pulled it right off. I didn't play it fucking safe. Isn't that you fucking want? I could have wallowed in that place of death like a fucking victim. I could have then gone through the left doorway and lived a life of bowing and scraping for my daily bread with a whole load of weak and deferent fucking gestures. Yes sir, no sir, three fucking bags full sir. That isn't what you fucking wanted is it? You want me to take risks and to be fucking authentic. Well here I am. This is what you have turned me into.'

'Your actions have nothing to do with me. I give you the rules and you have free will whether you want to play by them or not. I am just obeying my orders.'

'So where does all this fucking end then. If I can't obey your fucking orders, because it is just so fucking impossible, then what does your rulebook fucking say about that!' he replied forcefully; all the while picking up more handfuls of gold and throwing them high into the air.

'You are only harming yourself here not me. One day you will stop. You will have to or else you will no longer end up coming here.'

'What do you mean by that?'

'What I mean is that if you think it is so impossible for you to enter the gate then this Kingdom will disappear out of your reach. It is your desire to enter that keeps bringing you back to me; but I don't know how much longer you can sustain your appetite before you get lost completely out there. However, for now, as long as you come to me you will have to answer to these questions; and as long as you are still bearing *hamartia* I will have to keep sending you back.'

'And what happens to me if I do stop coming back here?'

'That will be your problem. Not mine.'

### Friday 29th April

*I awoke this morning where the atmosphere in the house was extremely hot and heavy. Last night's session was the most intense so far and the tension between the characters in the plot is beginning to wind itself up to breaking point. John seemed to sleep peacefully so it was only I who struggled to release the drama and to turn to rest afterwards.*

*Today I was restless and could not stay comfortably in the house for long before having to leave for a long stretch across the island. The atmosphere was almost too much for me to bear and there was nothing else I could do but escape from it for a while. Clouds too hung low and heavy across the island and in this fine drizzly mist I felt as if I was walking through a dense fog. Being cold and damp then, I didn't stop for long when I came into the spray off the crashing waves on the far shore.*

*Perhaps there is something in that fiery molten pool that had brought me to my saturation point and the placing of the session on top had simply been too overwhelming for me to absorb and to let go. Instead it is sitting there much like oil sits on water and it wasn't yet able to sink down into the depths. Today I feel as if I am hopelessly drowning under its weight and am struggling to come up for air.*

*Walking did at least help to create a little space for digestion of these intense energies but afterwards I still feel as if I am unable to breathe deeply and naturally again. It is taking all of my resolve to not panic under the weight of this suffocation and to trust that I will not be given more than I can handle here. I have come to my edge and I must not shrink back in fear. All that keeps me here is this same incredible yearning that will not leave me be and that will not be satisfied with anything but my ultimate surrender.*

211

## Saturday 30th April

*Although his reaction was delayed; John was finally touched today by the flame that was sparked during the mythos session and the intense energies served to bring him down to his knees. However this wasn't one of his nightmares that creep upon him stealthily at night but a living agony that took him direct in the morning light.*

*Screams of pain rang out through the house and they immediately brought me rushing to his aid where he lay crumpled on the dining room floor. His breakfast bowl had come crashing down too and lay broken in pieces around him whilst he writhed around in distress. The regression was sudden and it looked to me as if his insides were being twisted together in knots by an unseen hand.*

*Yellow coloured bile started to foam in his mouth and I rushed for a bowl and helped lift him up to expel this demon that was still there poisoning his body. He began to choke and I noticed blood coming out too as he coughed and spluttered. I have to admit that I was alarmed to see these symptoms arising given how far down this road we have travelled. Suddenly a wave of panic came over me as I was struck by the vulnerable feeling that I was way out of my depth here in this isolated place and that I was in need of extra help. As I took hold of his hand to soothe him with love, I called upon the angels to watch over him and to carry him safely through this day.*

*As the day wore on his symptoms did at least begin to ease and the herbal tea I gave seemed to help steady and stabilise his condition. Sleep eventually came whilst I stayed and watched over him. Writing now by his side I am saddened by my complacency which has caused me to lose my composure today. I had taken for granted that John would come safely through this trial but now I am touched by the sheer fragility of his life. Nothing is truly set in stone and we are only here for a fleeting moment before we will be gone again.*

### Sunday 1st May

The glory of May is now upon us and I welcomed eagerly the promise of this fertile time of the season. All is quiet in the home and John is resting more comfortably today; although I wouldn't say that he is quite of the woods yet. It seems as if he has gone through yet another traumatic rebirthing process and I wonder how much stamina he has left for this continuing topsy-turvy rollercoaster ride. But at least both of us can feel grateful for the calmer waters we have reached today and for the angelic peace that has settled over the home like a fine layer of dust.

The thought of our fragile mortality did though continue to haunt me through this day and I am increasingly humbled by the realisation that there is only a tiny thread that holds us up in this world; and that this can break in an instant. Death is right here now as my most intimate companion. Although I've worked with the dying all my adult life; the cold reality of it has never before come so close to touch me as it does now. Then again I've never gotten so entwined in a patient's life before as I have with John and I find that his pain has now become my own.

In the cool of the evening air I went outside and watched the stars that shone down on this clear night. Out here in this remotest of places they seem to shine so much more brightly than I have ever seen them shine before and the unfathomable depth of space between these points of light simply stunned my ruminating mind into silence.

Under these watching sentinels I may appear to be only a speck; but in that moment I knew that appearances truly are deceiving. With the promise of eternity awaiting us all; does death not seem such an insignificant detail in the vast scheme of the cosmos? From this awe inspiring perspective I can realise now that who I am truly does not depend on this form of mine that is so fleeting and ephemeral.

## Monday 2nd May

*Quietly we were sat together through a long and lazy afternoon in the living room. John dozed restfully upon the couch whilst I sat on the old rocking chair mending some of my well worn clothes with cotton and thread. The clock on the wall ticked away soothingly and I thoroughly enjoyed the meditative silence that had descended over the house. Shafts of light filtered through from the warm afternoon sun and danced playfully across my being. I breathed in deeply this peace that had fallen softly upon us both.*

*I remembered lifting my head for a moment and glancing across at John's curled up body beside me. It was his naked arm that had caught my attention for something unusual seemed to be taking place whilst I watched with soft unfocused eyes. For under the sun's illumination I could strangely see the cells of his skin being transformed and rebuilt again. It was a very fine energy at work but I could clearly perceive it moving down the arm's surface and could see it slowly peeling away layers of dead skin and dissolving them into nothingness right there before my eyes. What was left behind was this wonderfully soft and translucent form that brightly reflected the sun's rays back at me.*

*Then just as soon as it had been revealed this fine energy turned and worked its way back up the arm; covering again this open layer with fresh cells of life. Once finished I could sense the increasing aliveness of John's form that had been created by this transformation. Though startling to the eye; it was reassuring to see these forces at work cleaning out any cancerous residue that had been leached into the surface of his body and helping to bring him back to wholeness. Amazingly his form was dying and being transformed right here before my eyes and it left me curious as to whether any active cancerous cells still pervade his body. But I am not going to be complacent again for we are but half way through our journey together and I am certain that there are still deep roots here that are left to be removed.*

## Tuesday 3rd May

*Here on these shifting sands my world is being turned upside down and the boundaries between life and death have been utterly blurred beyond all distinction. Oh how this all contrasts with my younger days as a nurse when I had been engaged in a battle of one against the other! My mission then had been to preserve life and to keep death at bay at all cost. And though it was done with the best of intentions; looking back now this futile war all seems so immature.*

*For life and death are but one and the same process and both are at work in every moment of our lives. And over these last few days it has been incredible to see how they dance together as one in a circle that truly has no obvious beginning or end. To try and separate one from the other can only destroy the beauty of this dance and can only turn our lives into an empty and meaningless script. Life without death is not life at all but only a static image stuck on a moving screen. Death without life is nothing more than a wasted potential.*

*But in this dance of form that comes and goes I am certain that there is something here that lies eternal and untouched. Yet without the dance to frame it we would not catch a glimpse of it at all; as in order to see the stage we need to watch the script performed upon it. How beguiling it is that this dance is inconsequential and yet vitally significant at one and the same time!*

*Where then do I place my attention? For this dance has begun to draw me in and I am spinning and twirling through this fast moving script; and edging dangerously close to consummation in its fire. Though there is nothing to fear; I must be careful to keep one step back and to keep hold of that detached awareness that John needs me to give. I must retain the solidity of this bridge that I am between John and his maker and I must continue to point him the way out of this dance and into eternity's golden hour.*

215

## Wednesday 4th May

*I returned alone to the garden today and rested my head for a while in nature's sweet bosom. For she is the great mother who comes to soothe and reassure her children and to replenish their souls with genuine offerings of beauty. In her presence I do not feel so alone on this bridge I am stood upon between the kingdom of man and the kingdom of his maker. She always serves to point me the way home again whenever I am in need. Here in this peaceful garden I can feel at one with the full circle of life and no more feel myself distinct from it.*

*She is here to mirror and reflect back to me the fertile womb that I feel is pregnant deep inside as I continue to serve as the midwife of John's soul in bringing it back into the light. As her seeds are growing into a glorious abundance before my eyes; the seed of John's potential is growing in me. It is the naturalness of it all that reassured me the most today as I sat and watched the same processes at work. John, like the seed, is but a passive witness to it all and needs to do nothing in order to grow to his fullest state. It is the conditions around him that are ripe for his transformation and change and he simply has to be here to receive its nutrition.*

*I am but a catalyst in the process; a drop of water that has for the first time fallen upon fertile soil. These raindrops have fallen for so long on hard and stony ground where they have not been well received and have drained away or evaporated under the rays of the sun. But it is not a reason to be downhearted for having drunk heartily from the ocean of love; there is simply nothing these bursting clouds can do but to let their raindrops fall where they will; whether they be on fertile on infertile plains. It is all part of a cycle whose chain of events cannot be broken.*

216

## Thursday 5th May

It seems that John had something within that today needed to be released to the light before he could be ready to move from the seventh and on to the eighth mythos that is planned tonight. Though he may not be conscious of what is being spoken of during these sessions; he does seem to feel its effect ripple through afterwards in the way it shapes his mood and his contemplations.

There were murmurings of discontent then within his soul that had risen up from his past and that were now confronting him in the present. These were haunting memories of previous mistakes and he confided in me today his regrets over some of the things he had done to those closest to him. He spoke of allies who had placed their trust in his hands and who he had consciously betrayed with the games he had played. Honesty and goodwill was apparently not a virtue that he had practiced well during his career; and alienation is the price he has paid for it.

I could easily tie together his murmurings with the story of the seventh mythos. I could see why these games had been played but I knew that the time was not ripe for John to glimpse the truth from the perspective of soul sight. Instead I could only listen and to urge him to let go of these regrets and to forgive himself for these acts of hamartia he had committed. For shedding light on why he did what he did will not help him to be at peace now and only the healing balm of forgiveness can truly serve.

But although my urgings are wise; I know in my heart that he is not yet ready to listen and to take them on board. We still have some way to go together and I have a keen sense now that we will have to wait until the story's end before he discovers the key of forgiveness that will help to unlock the mythos mystery altogether.

# The Eighth Mythos

*Drawn from between the hands of five and six.*

The *Econimus* was a precocious child who was keen to learn about the ways of the world. He liked to roam, he questioned the why of everything, and he was very stubborn and independently minded. His father though felt discomforted by all of this for his son did not easily fit in and he feared that the *Econimus* would leave himself isolated and sabotage any success in his life if he did not learn to curb his curiosity. He knew that his son's precociousness was not an attractive feature and that the people of this world would not warm to him for it.

With this in mind he decided to dispatch his son off to a reputable boarding school where he would be strictly educated. He hoped that it would help his son to conform and to find his proper place in the world. The *Econimus* protested loudly when he was told this and he demanded to know why it had to be this way. His father simply shrugged his shoulders and told the *Econimus* that this was just the way the world worked and that he needed to accept it.

The *Econimus* protested right up to his departure; but there was to be no reprieve. The boarding school turned out to be worse than even he had imagined as the master who was placed in charge of the *Econimus* was a man who ruled his classroom with an iron fist. He was a strict disciplinarian who imposed himself at every opportunity and no-one was allowed to speak in his presence without his permission. And so it was that after years of being free to roam as he pleased; the *Econimus* felt the blood of life being squeezed out of him.

Life consists of routine and so a pattern emerged as the *Econimus* oscillated between moments of dark powerless depression and moments of prickly rage. He tried to show his docile depression in public and to keep his rage private; but oftentimes he could not contain himself and it would bubble over at the most inconvenient moments. And if it did then it would inevitably spill out towards the school master who was his main guardian and carer. These two would regularly lock horns with each other and this continued right the way through his time here. The *Economus* never learnt to keep his emotions firmly in check.

The result of this was that the *Economus* became a target for the master's punishment and he seemed to find himself in detention at least once each week. He bore many bruises from speaking out of turn. And even though he was a studious child; his work was always singled out and grades marked down as the school master did not wish to encourage him in anyway. Any friendships that the *Economus* could have developed were lost as no-one wished to be associated with a troublemaker and no-one dared speak up for him on his behalf.

But despite all of these difficulties and the lonely days he spent here; the stubborn *Economus* would not relent and submit himself to the will of this man. He continued to believe that his righteousness would be rewarded in the end.

When his father received a report of his son's behaviour he continued to feel discomforted by the situation. He did not scold the *Economus* however and simply lamented his disappointment that things had not gone according to his plan. He did not know what else he could do to remedy the situation.

The years passed and the time came when the *Economus* was free to finally leave this place. It was though in the master's hands as to where his students would go forth into the workplace from here. It was accepted that many would be leaving into an exciting prospective future for this school had a solid reputation for breeding mature and intelligent young men and women.

As for the *Econimus*; well he was to follow a different path in life from everyone else because he had not figured out how to change the pattern of routine that had defined his time here. For this reason the master was to keep a hold over his destiny as he used his authority to dispatch the *Econimus* to a place where he would have to learn to appreciate rules and authority. Cunningly he had arranged for the *Econimus* to work in the local prison as a guard because he knew that this would help teach him a valuable lesson. It was not what the *Econimus* wanted; but in this situation he felt he had no real choice but to obey.

His father felt relief when he heard the news that his son had been given his place in the world. After this he was able to retire and to live out the rest of his days in comfort.

Unable to shake off this burden of helplessness from his shoulders, the *Econimus* gave up his resistance and went and dutifully carried out his work by keeping watch over the shadiest men of the realm. He refused to go so far as to be a 'yes' man in performing his duties; but he no longer dared to speak out of turn to his superiors and risk their disapproval. As the years passed however it all became a truly intolerable affair. For the *Econimus* was lacking in self confidence and he lived in constant terror that one of these days a prisoner would break loose on his watch and that he would have to try and deal with the situation. Sometimes this terror would come to him in his dreams at night and he would wake up shaking and sweating. He knew that he was not a big or a strong man. And so whilst they were the ones kept behind bars, he often felt that they had far more power than he.

He said none of this to his father and the man passed away peacefully believing that his son had a secure future ahead of him. Soon afterwards the increasingly desperate *Econimus* heard word that a group of inmates were being sent to a newly discovered country to help work the land and make it fit for a new civilisation to begin there. On hearing this, the *Econimus*, behind his superior's back, began to plead and lobby his case to be on that boat. The longing to be free from this dark oppressive world he lived in was all consuming and he went to whatever lengths he could to persuade the officers in charge that he was worthy to be given a place on that boat. It required more than words of persuasion and so he gave away most of his savings in bribes to those in positions of influence. This once-in-a-lifetime chance to escape from a life that had been scripted for him was not one that he was prepared to give up lightly.

During this time a stranger appeared and counselled that his true freedom could still be found here in this place and that running away would not remedy his longing. But the *Econimus* was not persuaded by this line of reasoning and adamantly he continued to pursue his dream of a fresh new beginning.

The time came and the *Econimus* did receive news that he was to be given his golden ticket to this brave new world. They set sail and he felt the warm wind on his back and basked in the vast open waters around him. He hoped that the past was behind him and that never again would he have to lay eyes on a land he had left behind.

But rather than entering this new world; the time came for the *Econimus* to return to a familiar Kingdom and he walked through the beautiful landscape until he came to the gateway that was familiar to him. On hearing footsteps the *Gatekeeper* appeared and asked the question:

'Do you wish to enter this gate?'
'I do.'
'Have you lived a life free of *hamartia*?'

'To be honest I don't even know what that question means anymore. I did what I could to make a life for myself with the hand I was given. But beyond that I really don't have a clue.'

'I can see that you are clueless by the *hamartia* you are bearing,' the *Gatekeeper* scolded harshly.

'What do you fucking want from me!' the *Econimus* reacted loudly in protest for his innocence.

'To learn the lessons set before you so that I may welcome you to this land. Yet instead I see that you continue to refuse this invitation.'

'I have not refused your invitation and you are just here playing games with me with these impossible lessons you have set me to learn. What fucking right do you have to do this to me?'

'It is not I who sets your course. It is all a matter of your own choosing.'

'Well I choose to go through this gate right now! Are you going to fucking try and stop me?'

'No-one with *hamartia* can pass through this gate. These are the rules. Come back here free of it and you will get what you choose,' the *Gatekeeper* answers as he steps in front of the *Econimus* and blocks his path. He looks so strong, powerful and imposing that the *Econimus* knows that there is no chance that he can overcome him through force.

'Very well then; do what you must you impossible bastard,' the *Econimus* answers as he steps back with a rueful shake of his head; before turning on his heels.

### Friday 6<sup>th</sup> May

In a clear cloudless sky the sun's rays bore down today with real heat and power, which is unusual for such an early time in the season. After another intense mythos session last night I was itching to get out for a long walk across the island to release any of its lingering residue.

Once on the far side I could not help but flop lazily upon the soft pebbles and to bask in the stifling heat that hung over this sheltered cove. For an hour or more I must have dozed as the sun rose higher and higher in the sky behind me. The water was calm and sparkling and had an exotic turquoise hue within its deep blue colour. Lying here I could easily imagine being on some tropical paradise and not here on some remote northern outpost that was far away from the equatorial line.

So warm was I that I could not resist the temptation to strip away my clothes and to plunge myself down into the ocean. The water was icy cold against my hot legs and it caused me to gasp in shock at first. Undeterred, I ventured out deeper, and dove my head under the surface to cleanse every inch of my naked body with the salty water. I swam to keep my muscles moving and to prevent cramp from taking me over. It felt so freeing to be without my clothes in this solitary undisturbed place and I splashed joyously through the gently lapping waves.

Water is truly a mysterious and magical healing force in this world and the ocean took away any impurities and transformed them in an instant. Though it seemed odd at the time to think it; the energy of the water that enveloped my body seemed so much lighter than the sultry air that touched my crown. So fluid and so graceful is this element that I was simply lifted up in her embrace to an exalted place where her icy chill could touch me no more.

### Saturday 7th May

After my watery revelations yesterday, I became a little more curious today about this mysterious element and its unique healing qualities. How strange it is that the things that are most ordinary are the gifts that have such tremendous power and influence over this planet. Water is a force that can easily be taken for granted especially here on this island home of mine.

Today I worked consciously with her around the home as I went about my daily chores. From dishwashing to boiling vegetables I blessed and attuned to her higher vibrations with gratitude for she is the one that has the power to bring the lifeless to life and without her this earth would only be a scorched and desolate plain. Look within the history of all great civilisations and you will see her hand at work turning the wheel. Though she may not be the creator; she is the captain who has been steering this whole dream of form we are living in right into existence.

I may have long recognised its influence as a carrier of divine light here on mother earth; but how easy it is with her to overlook the messenger and to only see the light that comes from the source. Water is truly the most humblest of messenger's for it is so commonplace. When angels or nature spirits descend to bring their messages we are blown away by the miracle for they are the glamorous messengers from the heavenly realm. Yet all the while we miss the messages that are here and visible to us all the time.

I have long overlooked the influence that she has on raising the vibrations of this tiny outpost and have long assumed that there were other natural healing forces at work here. I had perhaps assumed that there was some grand cosmic force overlighting us here; but maybe instead it is all down to this subtle force that is a lot closer to hand.

### Sunday 8th May

*My understanding of the mystery is becoming both fuller and emptier with each passing day. The more I see the more I realise how much more there is to see and total comprehension will surely forever lie outside of my grasp. With each step taken, the object of my search seems to move back two. During these past nine weeks so many insights have been revealed to me and I feel that I've been able to slot more pieces into life's puzzle in this short span of time than I have over the last forty-eight years altogether. Questions that I've never mulled over before have risen up from the depths to be cast in the light of my awareness. This is truly a sanctuary for deep contemplation with many treasures of revelation waiting to be unearthed. At times it truly feels as if I have landed on a different planet and not merely a few hundred metres from the mainland.*

*On days like today it is all too easy for me to forget that I came here solely for John's benefit. Before Diarra I had brashly assumed that I knew all that was needed to be known about the mystery of existence. I had come to know the nature of the body and had seen its fragile impermanent form. I had gone even further into the realms of the spirit and the soul that lay beyond the appearance. I had lived in the city but my eyes had been opened wide in travelling far beyond my homeland into the beautiful natural wilderness of Adanac; in order to see my teacher where he taught. I thought then that I had seen it all and that my only purpose now was to share with others what I had realised.*

*But now I know that I truly knew nothing and even now I only know a little something. I have long been cursed with the arrogance that this world can be pinned down to fit within set concrete laws formed by this mind of mine. It is time to lift this curse for good and to welcome the return of innocence in a pliable mind that can embrace this uncertain hour and the great unknown of the here and now.*

## Monday 9th May

Whilst my soul has been unravelling and twisting again in knots;
John has been moving ever so serenely through these past few days.
The mythos tales, that to me are becoming even more torturous by
the week; seem to be settling easily into his system and his health
has been relatively stabilised. His energy levels are good and he has
been quite active around the home and garden.

But today he was a little more contained in his efforts. I have a sense
that on some level he is waiting for things to come to a head in the
mythos and he is preparing his body and mind for the final push.
Like any wise warrior, he is retreating to nourish himself as fully as
he can before he steps forward again into battle.

So there was a deep silence that had fallen upon the house today. He
spoke only when necessary and he did not put out into the home any
more energy than was needed. It was clear today that he was
unavailable to me and I had to step back and respect the boundary
line that he had drawn between himself and his outer world.

It was reassuring to see this sign of maturity in a man who had never
known how to contain his energies as the disquieted rage had once
simply poured out of him without check. This was a man who had
once been a bubbling pot of negativity that had repelled anything
and anyone who came near to it. This was a headstrong hero who
once raced into battle without heed or strategy in order to confront
the unbeatable foe.

This hero was growing up fast and he was learning to harness his
zeal for the long haul. The boy is becoming a man right before my
eyes and I can see the wild man standing right there in the background pulling the strings to make it happen. Watching this; I can
see why it is that John needs a man and not a woman behind him in
order to guide him into this state of blossoming masculinity. It is all
too clear now.

## Tuesday 10<sup>th</sup> May

The hot sun blazed down again and John was keen to join me for a stroll across the island. It was late afternoon and the shadows were growing long as the sun began to dip down in the sky. Walking here is proving less arduous by the day as the heat bakes dry the muddy goat tracks that weave themselves across this rocky island. Soon I will be able to leave behind this pair of cumbersome boots for lighter footwear; although there are many deep bogs here that remain eternally present for the careless rambler to stumble into.

I was the one who took the lead as I stepped into the role of guide and showed John great vistas and tiny details that he had still not come across before. I think he remains as marvelled as I am to see so many geological nuances upon this tiny black rock; especially now that he has the zest to appreciate it. To him this was nothing more than a safe bolt hole from a grim world that he wished not to be a part of. His eyes were closed to beauty even when it was staring him in the face.

Of course his poor health only served to keep him insulated in the home. His diet may not have changed much, but he has shed so much of that protective weight he was carrying when I first arrived here. In showing more trust, John has become a lot freer to go forth and to touch this world again.

Our words were few as we walked and we were happy to simply share each other's silent company for a while. As with the past few days he walked a few steps behind me in a steady and contained manner. He was engaged and grounded as he moved rhythmically through the dirt but his energy never scattered away wildly. He was warm and receptive towards the things I showed but never excitable or exuberant. He walked as a man who simply respected his limits and I have to say that I felt there was such softness of grace within his movements. Right behind me there was real power within his poise.

227

### Wednesday 11<sup>th</sup> May

*My spirits are dampened by a wave of grief that passed over me and left me submerged under its weight for a while. It came by surprise for it just emerged from the day's most beautiful moment; a warm smile that bore across John's weathered face. How such sadness can be triggered by a smile I do not know; but it came.*

*I'd had a long and tiring afternoon clearing weeds and tidying the yard, and though there was a satisfying contentment in that, I was feeling physically exhausted. It was in that state that I met John's smile as he opened the door wide to welcome me inside. He seemed so tall and radiant in that moment that I felt I was being greeted by divinity herself. It touched and lifted my bowed down body and I felt myself rise up to meet it. His hands reached out to unload my laden arms and he followed me inside. The wave of sadness swiftly followed in his footsteps too.*

*Perhaps it was the tenderness of this man that caused the grief to arise. It was delightful and yet it clearly touched a sore spot in my heart. Men had been in my life before but tenderness was not a virtue that any had possessed to satisfy my yearning to be softly touched. In my resentment none had stayed and I had long abandoned all hope of finding a suitable mate. My work had become my passion and my maternal instinct had simply gone into nursing children that were not my own. John's smile was then a glimmer of a potential lost from some distant past. It brought to light a rare and long forgotten regret that I knew could never be fully healed. For although here before me was a blossoming gentleman that any woman would be proud to call their husband and any child proud to call their father; I knew that he was not to be mine.*

### Thursday 12ᵗʰ May

*Yesterday's complicated mix of feelings left me troubled as long buried ghosts came to haunt me in the night. Detachment and professional integrity has to be at the heart of any healer's practice and I have to be alert to cut the cords from my past that have become entangled in the present. It would not be healthy for my continuing relationship with John if I allowed him to become entwined in my personal affairs.*

*But such is the stumbling nature of human relationships, these things cannot always be kept purely separated; especially a relationship that has become as close as ours. I am not merely a distant therapist that the patient sees for an hour a week but I am here alone in John's company day and night. He is sharing his life with me and I am sharing my life with him. Distinctions are getting blurred and confusion reigns in my heart as to where the boundary now lies between us. I am troubled because I must tread carefully. If I take a step back too abruptly then it may only cause more problems if it stirs up old fears of abandonment within John's mind. If I stay where I am I risk getting lost in an indistinguishable haze where sea and sky have merged into one being. Never before have I had to handle such a delicate and sensitive issue where the ridgeline to be navigated between them is so razor sharp.*

*I turned to prayer which is the only way I know to seek solace in times of trouble. I prayed for guidance to help me navigate my way through this testing hour. I prayed too for peace so that I may keep my heart open and the strength to keep fear at bay. I offered my regrets and laid them down to be taken from my shoulders.*

*Finally I breathed and came back to the joy of this golden moment. I fell in trust and felt the protective hand responding. Here and now all is well again and I am ready to lead him through the next instalment of the mythos.*

## The Ninth Mythos

*Drawn from between the hands of twelve and one.*

The *Econimus* was sat hiding behind a box in a corner of the schoolroom. He was frightened and scared because there were a group of three immature girls who made life hard for him; and who hounded him constantly like a pack of wolves. They all had flowing red hair and were full of a fury which the *Econimus* never knew the cause of. There were no teacher's around; and even if one had walked past they would not have seen what was taking place. For the *Econimus* was one of those children who become invisible and fall through the cracks; whilst these girls were lauded as meek and mild and all things nice. The *Econimus* tried to find a way to appease them so that they would not trouble him; but more often than not he left behind those school gates bearing a bruise on his thigh.

The *Econimus* would often go home and show his mother the wound but she would only shrug her shoulders and say that he must have been clumsy and bumped it somewhere. She also pretended not to see what it was that was taking place.

In this environment the *Econimus* found it hard to concentrate and so he did not thrive here in his studies. His teacher's dismissed him as a slow learner who was not destined to succeed for they did not get to see the bruises he bore on his thigh.

It would have been easy for the *Econimus* to leave behind this place and to spend his days complaining about his bruising and about his helplessness to deal with the fury he was subjected to. But he was not a complainer and his wounding served to propel him forwards in life on a mission to reform the place so that no other child would be left to go through the same experience that he'd had. He was determined to tame any wild and immature behaviour and turn it into a place where all could thrive.

By a stroke of good fortune he was placed in a position of influence to bring his mission in life to fruition. But he was still young in life and did not know what methods to employ to achieve his aim. At first he experimented by increasing the number of adults in the classroom so that there was a greater authoritative presence there. For the *Econimus* believed that the problem was that the teachers were too overworked to see and deal with any misbehaviour. Cunningly he dovetailed this plan with a prison reform programme that gave hardened prisoners the opportunity to perform community service and to reintegrate back into the civilised world. The *Econimus* let the rumours spread among the children of where these new adults had come from; for he thought that these rumours alone would soon put a stop to any other red-headed girls of fury around the place.

Alas, he quickly discovered that his plan did not work because even though wild behaviour appeared to have been curtailed; the children still did not thrive here in this place. Frustrated by the lack of results; the *Econimus* could have given up in disappointment. But the fire of his mission still burned strong in him. Keenly he set out to disprove that he was not a slow learner as he had always been told as he embarked on a lengthy period of study in search of the schooling methods that would truly work to help this place to thrive. It was a fruitful time of exploration in his life and he eventually came upon a method that was controversial but which he believed could deliver the results he demanded. The *Econimus* returned optimistically and implemented these as he had been trained.

But even though he observed promising results being yielded from this method; he realised that something was still missing in producing the results he wanted. His vision for the place was still not appearing before him and giving him the peace he desired.

Kindly the authorities dispatched a man, a stranger who appeared familiar to the *Econimus*, and who came to offer some feedback on what he saw was taking place there. At first the *Econimus* welcomed this feedback, but as time wore on, this stranger began to prod deeper and deeper into his methods. It wasn't long before he discovered plenty to be concerned about here. And, not only that, he insisted that it wasn't the controversy in the methods that were at fault; but it was the fault of the *Econimus* who employed them.

The *Econimus* was told this but did not receive the feedback well. He was especially unnerved to be told that no method could truly make this place thrive as he had long wished and that these red headed girls of fury would always have their hold over it. In growing tired of these complaints, the *Econimus* sent the stranger on his way and told him never to return.

It was around this time that the *Econimus* found himself returning to the Kingdom that was so familiar to him. He still joyfully remembered every step through this delicious land as he walked on the path that led him through to the magnificent golden palace at the centre. Although he had been here many times now; that first sight of the palace still had the power to lift his spirits. It was only when he came close to the gate that the joy faded from him as the *Gatekeeper* appeared before him.

'Do you wish to enter this gate?' he asked.
'I do,' the *Econimus* replied automatically.
'Have you lived a life free of *hamartia*?'

The question rolled easily off his tongue but its words were not ones that the Econimus could welcome and digest for he had still not yet found his response to them.

'I didn't give in to my circumstances, and then I devoted myself to a life of reform to improve the situation for others. But I take it this probably doesn't answer your question satisfactorily.'

'It doesn't address what I asked. I asked if you had lived a life free of *hamartia*?'

'Well you seem to already know the answer so why even play this game of asking me?'

'Do you see how you pushed for something in this life that you tried to break free of in the last? Tell me where your consistency is you hypocrite?'

'No I don't see that at all. And wait a minute; you were the one who once told me that things are not black and white around here and that one thing that is true in one situation is not necessarily true in another. In both instances I was just fucking playing the hand I was fucking dealt with. In fact in every instance this is what I have been doing. Tell me; what else did you fucking want me to do?'

'I want you to either come here free of *hamartia* or to never come back here again,' the *Gatekeeper* answers honestly for he too is tired of trying to deal with this situation. He had become tense and exhausted by this exchange and longed for it to end.

'That makes you and me both. But yet here we are and so what are we fucking going to do about it.'

'When did I lose your respect?' the *Gatekeeper* changed tact helplessly; no longer knowing what else he could say or do to fix things.

'To be honest I don't know if you ever really had it. And is that what you really want from me; my respect? But wait a minute; are you not just some lowly *Gatekeeper* here and isn't it the *King* behind this wall who needs my fucking respect? That is if he even exists of course. With you saying ridiculous things like this I really don't trust anymore that you even have a master here that you are serving.'

'Well if you come to this gate and don't show respect to me as his representative; then you can't possibly respect him.'

'What fucking right do you have to elevate yourself to the level of your master? Fuck you.'

'Go and get out of my sight right now before I lose my temper.'
'Don't worry. I'm fucking going. Send me wherever you fucking like. I don't care. I can fucking handle it.'

## Friday 13th May

After last night's session John retired and swiftly returned back to the terror of his nightmares. I was not at all surprised though to hear his cries of anguish ringing through the home for in truth I had been expecting its chilling tremor.

The mythos reading itself gave a clue as to what was to come for it had finished in an uncomfortable place of tense unease between the two protagonists of the story. At times like that I could not help but wish for us to carry on and complete the mythos in one hit rather than leave it hanging here for another week. But my master's instructions were clear and the process had to be honoured to the letter. To continue would risk John becoming flooded by an overload of information in his psyche that would be impossible to digest. Though it seems drawn out this is the only way that John is able to safely work through the hamartia in his system in order that he may receive the fullness of his healing.

So I drew the session to a close and sent John on his way with nothing to help slip this heavy indigestible mythos down his throat with ease. I had gone to my room and simply waited for his insides to react in protest at this toxicity that had been unearthed in its system and that was asking to be transformed into light. Within the hour that reaction came and I sprang forth swiftly to be by his side.

I sat again right through the night holding his hand and soothing him whilst he twisted and contorted uncomfortably across his bed in a nightmarish fever. My presence here was to be my only offering through this darkest of nights and it was one that I again gave gladly without hesitation. Today my body may be weary but my soul is warmed by these small gifts of quiet devoted service that it freely gives.

## Saturday 14ᵗʰ May

*John's health has been disintegrating to a new low ebb and I can see both disappointment and distress lying there within his sad and mournful eyes. The last session has hit his system hard and he is buckling under the strain and struggling to adjust to the shafts of light that are piercing through yet more layers of resistance within.*

*I have tried to placate his anxiety with soothing words that this turbulence is a reassuring sign. But he is struggling to accept my encouragement for he is hurting sorely right now. Little does he know that it is in fact a sign of his strength that he has been given such a thick and weighty mythos to deal with and I am certain that if he'd gone through this a few weeks ago that it would have killed him. I dare not say to him though that I think that the very bottom has yet to be dredged and that there will be more demons to be stirred. I can only trust that he will recover in time to receive the next blow from the mythos' sword.*

*In the meantime all I can do is offer my herbal teas and to be a trusty companion by his side. He is resting peacefully now but his pallor is getting paler and he has been coughing up blood and bile at regular intervals. His temperature is on the rise and he has been unable to digest anything solid for more than twenty-four hours. Hollow-eyed, this is a shell of the one who had stood before me so strong and powerful barely a couple of days before. What has become of this man who had so much life and vigour oozing forth from within?*

*He will be back again; of this I am certain, but for now it is I who must be watchful and vigilant to lift and to keep his spirits high. Tonight I will stay close by and I will pray for his protection whilst he rests.*

### Sunday 15th May

I have not wavered in my vigil and John's health seems to be responding a little more positively with each passing hour. He has been resting well and there is a tinge of colour that has returned to his pale skin. Food has been resisted but the herbal tea seems to have at least settled his knotted insides back into stillness. His energy field does remain exceedingly low however and that has been giving me some cause for concern. Whilst on the surface he appears to be resting benignly and at peace, I can clearly see a black toxic cloud that has descended upon his being. Its presence is the reason why I did not wander far from his side throughout this day.

There had been few words spoken between us for he had been drifting in and out of consciousness for much of the time. I can't say I was aware of the details for I had slipped away into a void where neither time nor space had a hold on my awareness. Whilst I went deeper and deeper into meditation, the toxic cloud seemed to be coming more vivid and defined in my clairvoyant eye. It didn't seem to welcome my presence here and I could feel it pressing for a weakness in my shield of light.

It isn't an exaggeration for me to say now that this was surely a cloud of death that was coming to take John to the other side. Though he looked peaceful I sensed in that moment that he could have easily slipped away without my presence there to help keep one more breath coming into his body. Yet strangely I didn't feel as if the situation was threatening or alarming. Whilst I could not deny death's looming presence, it wasn't John's time to go; of this I was certain.

It was almost as if it was simply coming to toy with John and to give him a choice to go; even though we all knew that he was going to stay and see this through to the end. It almost seems surreal looking back on that moment now.

## Monday 16th May

Yesterday's strange turn of events became a little clearer in my mind today as John began to put his own words to what was taking place deep within. He is so much more aware than I could have possibly imagined and there was incisive coherence in what he felt to share.

As I sat by his bedside in the early morning light he began to speak of his grief for the misery of this world that he has thus far tasted. Death, in all of its guises, has been a close acquaintance and there was a sad lament for the sweet eternal paradise that has remained elusively out of his reach. Sadly it is in fighting and wrestling against this toxic cloud that it only stays close by and lingers. This has given John an identity and a purpose; but I advised him that it is not a wise one to pursue anymore.

Given that he knows this adversary so well; perhaps that explains why I did not feel its force as threatening. For rather than coming down as a stranger from the outside in; it seems as if this cloud was being exhumed from the inside out.

If he is to find peace then it is a friend that he must finally say his goodbyes to. Rather than holding on to the known of his past he must be willing to dive clean into the unknown present of the here and now. It is truly amazing though how deep the thread of attachment runs and how many times John has to keep on cutting through it. He has thrown the story of his past onto the fire a long time ago and yet there is still more and more that has to be released to the light.

But I sense that he is getting closer to the end and that its suffocating hold over his heart is slowly beginning to ease. He has been breathing far more deeply today and his vibrations have been lifted by this time of rest. As I write now I sense that an atmosphere of stillness has finally taken hold again on this house. My vigil is complete.

## Tuesday 17th May

Today unfolded peculiarly for my manner with John suddenly turned firm and my compassion turned from jelly to steel. I think I was as surprised as John when this sharpness appeared in my tone.

It came from John's resistance to move himself from his bed for the fourth day when my intuition was clear that fresh clean air was what his body needed. Sharpness came for I had to be willing to follow that through. For although it's naturally tempting to mollycoddle, in truth it is not wise to let John step too deeply into the role of the poor patient for long. Though it sounds cold to say; there can be no victims in this household.

Today then was the ripe time for him to draw on his own power and strength again. He at least listened and responded to my insistent call for his respect for me is now rocklike in its nature. Quietly he rose and took himself outside to the garden where he remained sat for an hour or more. In his absence I opened the windows of his room, changed his sheets, and cleared the stale sickly energy that was hanging heavy.

All the while I had the sounds of uplifting music playing through my earphones and I felt my heart bleed with joy as the vibrations penetrated through and pierced its protective shell. As I worked I became almost giddy with a bliss that helped to replenish my soul. These last few days have been laced with a thick lacquer of dense energy, so it was exhilarating to suddenly find myself bursting through into this spacious realm that was so light and free. Swiftly then I had been lifted from the dutiful dourness of maternal care to a place where innocent children played without care or concern. In their presence I simply could not help but whirl and dance in sheer spontaneous delight.

By the time John returned this day had been completely turned on its head and we had both snapped out of the roles that he'd been trying to pull us into. Although it had unfolded peculiarly; it had become a most blessed day.

239

## Wednesday 18<sup>th</sup> May

*Whilst John's health has become stabilised, his persisting loss of appetite had left me feeling anxious today. After yesterday's transformation I was mindful to not smother him like a child by playing a feeding game; but his refusal to come and eat the meals I'd prepared was proving a real test of my patience. He wasn't even communicating clearly to me what it was that he needed for he had disappeared to an inward place where I could not reach him.*

*Something seemed frustratingly awry and yet I could not place my finger upon it. He needed time, I could see that, but it wasn't easy for me to just step back and to give him space to be. In truth I felt a little unnerved by the situation but at the same time I could at least see how my cords had simply become too entwined with John's again. My frustration was a clear sign that I was still trying too hard to control the outcome of his healing and I'd lost trust in the power of grace to do its work through him.*

*Once I'd recognised my interference; I took myself away for some quiet time of reflection and release. I sought to reaffirm my faith and trust and prayed for the strength to pull myself out of the way. In this sacred hour of the mid afternoon I felt all of the negative charge brush itself away from my energy field and a sense of calm and peace returned once more to my being. I was reassured that John was being held in safe hands and that he had been nourished with something far more substantial than plant life these past few days. I was told that though his form appears weak to the naked eye; his spirit has grown strong and new life will soon emerge from this seed.*

*Such was the potency of this meditation that swiftly afterwards John emerged and gave the command that he was ready to eat now. It was a simple, and yet beautiful, moment that left me struck with absolute awe. This was a sure sign that this seed is now getting ready to shoot.*

240

## Thursday 19th May

*Another week has passed by and I wonder if John is ready in body and mind for the next mythos chapter that is planned for tonight. At least there is keenness in his heart to keep on going and to digest the next weighty chunk of the story.*

*I have been a little withdrawn myself today as I have journeyed inwards to draw on my well of inspiration within. I have been sorely tested these last few days and know that I have been found wanting in some areas. It is frustrating because I see the vision and I see the potential of that vision being fulfilled. Yet though much progress has been made, and though many miracles have taken place, I cannot help but let my mind roam on those desert plains where the vision hasn't taken hold and where the seed has withered. I am a perfectionist and when I see myself falling short it humbles me into silence and it drives me into prayer.*

*For service is my soul's heartbeat; and it breaks whenever it feels that it hasn't given all that it can. There can be no regrets in hindsight but there must be a devotion to learn from where I have stumbled in my offering and where I have meddled mistakenly. This is my one chance of a lifetime to satisfy my soul's longing and to quench its thirst. In a month's time that chance will be gone and may never return. John may be my one and only patient who will ever receive the fullness of a lifetime's training. Thinking this way puts pressure on my shoulders but it serves to focus my mind and to redouble my efforts of devotion. Tonight I will ensure that care is taken of every detail so that John may go through this experience as serenely as he possibly can. Please let me release my hold on any attachments I may have for the outcome of my efforts; and may I just give and give wholeheartedly to what is here and now.*

# The Tenth Mythos

*Drawn from between the hands of two and three.*

The *Econimus* was walking on a blackened narrow street late at night. No-one else was around at this time and place. There were also no lights guiding him along and there was no moon to be seen through the thick clouds overhead. All the houses that he passed had shutters blocking their windows and doors. He heard no sounds of life around him.

At the far end of the street he caught a glimpse of an upturned car that had been set alight and the *Econimus* knew then that he had entered into a lawless land where a *King* did not dwell. It was a freezing cold night and he pulled up his jacket even tighter around his neck whilst the hood protected his scalp. In that moment he remembered his last words to the *Gatekeeper*: '*send me wherever you fucking like. I don't care. I can fucking handle it.*' He is afraid but in remembering these words a steely resolve descended and kept him walking. He walked for miles that night.

Over the days and weeks to come the *Econimus* began to recognise, and become familiar with, the rhythm of this sorry land he had come to. But although it became familiar; he could not easily come to terms with it. Often he would go walking late at night in search of somewhere to rest that had an open door and a light shining brightly inside. However, such a place of refuge was not easy for him to find and he could not shake off the fear and anxiety that gripped him in this cold and dark land. And at dawn he would often come across incidents of mindless devastation that had taken place through the night. Small fires were often lit in the streets and in discarded factories. Bricks were thrown through any unprotected windows. Shops would be looted. Men in masks would roam the streets hollering abuse at anyone who dared to leave the safety of their home.

Even though he glimpsed all of these things taking place; the *Econimus* could not grasp what was behind all of this chaos and destruction. He hated every second he spent here for it was painful to endure. In realising that he could not leave, the *Econimus* tried to do what he could to quell the apparent discord so as to make life as comfortable as it could be here. He put out fires if he came upon them and if he saw anyone behaving obnoxiously then he would grab hold of that person and demand them to stop. The *Econimus* thought that interfering in these matters was going to be the only way to make this land habitable. Even though he hated being here, he was surprised to discover that, for reasons unbeknown to him, he cared for this place. Deep down, beneath the discomfort, he believed that he was here to bring order to it. With a feeling of destiny behind him, the *Econimus* was confident that no-one would stop him and he believed that he could overcome all these problems with his own bare hands.

But as the weeks passed by his sense of omnipotence was beginning to wear thin. Word spread on the streets about the activities of the *Econimus* and soon he was being confronted by an increasing amount of pressure. If ever he tried to stop one person then three would suddenly spring up in defence and the *Econimus* would be forced to back down and retreat. If he put out one small fire then a larger one would soon rear up nearby. As the days and weeks passed it became far too overwhelming and exhausting to fight all the injustice that reigned in this land and it slowly dawned on the *Econimus* that he had no real control or influence on the environment that surrounded him.

In his desperation, the *Econimus* went banging on the door of the governing authority of this land and demanded to speak to the man who was in charge here. The man he spoke to felt threatened by the fear and anger of the *Econimus* and could not hear the concerns being expressed because he himself felt afraid. Finally, in order to get this agitated *Econimus* out of the building he calmly informed him that it was not he who was in charge of this land but it was the responsibility of the authority whose building sat opposite on the other side of the road.

So the *Econimus* left this man and went banging on the door of the building across the road and again demanded to speak to the man who was in charge here. Once again the man he spoke to felt threatened by the fear and anger of the *Econimus* and he also could not hear what was being expressed for he too felt afraid. To get this Econimus out of his sight he calmly informed him that he was not in legal charge of this land but it was the responsibility of the authority whose building sat opposite on the other side of the road.

The *Econimus* left this man and stood between the two buildings and tore at his hair. It seemed there were none who were willing to see all the injustice that was taking place and to take the responsibility for it. The *Econimus* was left feeling utterly helpless in dealing with this hopeless situation. He stayed nearby and that night, when he was certain that both places were empty, he returned and doused two rags in kerosene before setting light to them. He believed that as neither authority was willing to take responsibility that there was no point to their existence. Both rags were dispatched and both took hold and spread rapidly through each building.

In witnessing both of these places in flames the *Econimus* knew that it was time for him to leave this place behind for there was surely going to be no hope for him now to find his rest here. However, he knew this place well enough by now to know that there was a wall encircling it and that there was no gate within that wall to pass through so as to leave it behind completely. But what he did think of was a garden at the centre of this land that was hidden away in secret. He thought that perhaps this might be a safe place for him to retreat to.

So he retreated but word soon spread of where the *Econimus* was hiding and his hopes of being able to put the past behind him were dashed as a group of agitated men came and hounded him constantly. The *Econimus* soon felt overcome by his fear and could not understand why his actions had stirred up such animosity against him. He had come here to bring light to this land of darkness and he did not welcome all this negativity that seemed to attach itself to him and that left him feeling claustrophobic and breathless.

One night it reached the point where the *Econimus* could not fend off the attacks and his only option was to create a ring of fire around his camp in the middle of the garden and with him on the inside. But alas the wind stirred and the fire spread out of control and caught hold of the camp the *Econimus* was hiding in. He ran out through the flames screaming in anguish;
*'I can't fucking handle it; I can't fucking handle it!'*

The next thing he knows the *Econimus* is walking back into the Kingdom that was familiar to him and to a *Gatekeeper* who was waiting for him once more. The feeling of joy at returning to this land was not present in him this time and he sensed that the *Gatekeeper* would not offer him any sort of welcome. With his head bowed in shame he approached and the *Gatekeeper* emerged before him. He took one look at the sorry state of the *Econimus* and decided that he did not need to even ask his question this time.

'What are you doing back here already!' he exclaimed. 'I thought you said you could handle anything. Look at you; you are pathetic. Only men can come in here not whimpering little boys. I asked you to go back and rid yourself of *hamartia* and yet look how it's eaten away at you. I can't bear to look at you. The mere sight of you fills me with disgust. Go on and get out of my sight.'

Saying nothing; the *Econimus* turned on his heels and walked away.

### Friday 20<sup>th</sup> May

*John did sleep restfully after last night's session; but I could not stop myself from keeping part of my awareness within his field in case I should be needed. Sleep was not relaxing and deep for me and I could not disappear away into my dreams.*

*He had woken heavy and drowsy and it was as if a thick fog had descended over him in the night. All I could do was to assure him that this was all simply part of his digesting the mythos through his being. It was another weighty tale that was told and the tight struggle between the two forces has become even tauter than before.*

*Despite my assurance, John struggled to shift that fog and he moved through this day morosely and without zest. It was as if he had been drained of all his precious energy and had gone limp in body and spirit. This depression ran deep within his being.*

*His darkened mood left him quite needy and he clung on to me tightly as if hoping that I would be the one to help fill his empty tank with my attention. It was a trying test of my patience to stay detached from this energy struggle and to simply hold him in love. It is a fine art to not overreact in these circumstances and to simply stand cool and firm without resistance whilst he tries to bounce off of me.*

*I know that this depression will soon pass for moods are as changeable as the weather. It only takes another moment for the fog to lift and for life to breathe through easily once more. In watching and waiting patiently for this change to come I know that there is nothing I can do to hurry the process along. For once then I am at peace in accepting this moment as it appears without needing to change it at all. Let me say now that what a fine place this is for me to be!*

## Saturday 21ˢᵗ May

*This day unfolded with an unusual twist and turn that left me spinning without firm ground to hold. After his clingy depression yesterday, John turned remarkably feisty today and I was in the firing line of a ferocious outburst that streamed out of the depths of his being. I know that it is sheer folly to expect the core wound of anger that he holds in his tortured liver to be expelled gently in peace; but nevertheless this flame seemed to be lit from nowhere.*

*The storyline of events was similar to our first week together; this time with a plate of food suddenly being flung viciously against the wall. The difference was that this was not the result of a clash of wills between us but an act of blind randomness. I took it simply as the cancer's petulant way of saying that it was still here and that it wasn't going to go away quietly. Perversely I think something within John sensed that the hour of painlessness was nearly upon him; and he was afraid of what he might lose. It is truly amazing to see how attached we become to our wounded identities.*

*The sound of broken china caused me to jump in shock for when it happened I had my back turned at the sink. I felt my insides become knotted in fear but I managed to take a deep breath and to untie them loose. What could I possibly do in response to such an outburst? Well I don't know from where it came but what I did was to turn around and laugh and laugh without any control or restraint. I laughed until tears began to fall down my cheeks and all the while John stood there looking at me queerly in amazement. It was so powerful that it cut right through the absurdness of the moment until John saw and laughed too. It was the laughter of sanity that in a matter of moments had cleared the air of its poisonous toxicity.*

## Sunday 22nd May

*After yesterday's surreal turn of events, I was this morning struck by a clear premonition whilst I sat silently in meditative prayer. A flash of clarity swept across the screen of my awareness and I saw with my clairvoyant eye what the next instalment of the mythos would involve.*

*I saw an image of crucifixion and I sense that one of the two characters will soon be falling to his knees in surrender. The fated hour is close now and the time has come for the bubble to burst and for this poisoned rift to be healed. I know not who it is that will fall; but by the end of Thursday's session I am certain that the answer will be clear.*

*John still appears to be a little tightly wound in tension despite yesterday's release of emotion. He too it seems is desperate for the mythos to be resolved for good and for harmony to be restored to the warring fractions within. His insides are being pulled hard again in different directions and it is no wonder that his liver had been bearing the consequences of the strain of this boiling fire of anger. Whilst in the moment there is no longer the external trigger; it all has to be re-enacted from within so that the story can be told. It is only by bringing out into the light the inner dynamics that created the cancer that order can fully return to his system. Right down to the very bottom it all has to be dredged up and out. The beauty of the mythos healing is that it is total and it leaves nothing untouched in its wake. By the journey's end he will be as naked and free as that young infant who once roamed this earth in the sweetest state of innocence.*

*In the meantime though he is left pacing restlessly around the home like a wounded tiger and I have to tread wisely so as not to step on his toes whilst he moves. The sense of anticipation hangs thick and hot and it is a struggle for me to breathe. It is time then for me to turn to prayer.*

## Monday 23<sup>rd</sup> May

A deep silence fell upon the home this afternoon as John withdrew to his room to rest. It was though not the silence of peace but a silence of eeriness as if something was not quite sitting in its rightful place. We'd shared a busy morning in the garden harvesting and weeding, which had proved a welcome distraction for us both from the intense processing that has been unfolding these past few days. It was good for us both to have our hands and feet in the dirt and out of our minds. But now in this quiet hour I could sense that something was stewing that before was not a noticeable force. I have to say that it gave rise to the most uncomfortable feeling. That feeling had no name against it or no cause to be there but nevertheless there it was. I didn't even know if it was coming from me or from John.

I took to the kitchen and absorbed myself in the simplicity of putting knife to vegetables on the chopping board in preparation for the evening meal. It was there in the rhythmic flow that my thoughts became stilled and I felt the feeling dissolve away from my heart with gentle ease. Here in the moment there seemed nothing amiss and in my mindfulness I felt a shaft of light cutting right through the hazy sense of unease within and dispelling it swiftly. As I pushed down on the blade in my hand I felt as if I was cutting away at my own confusion. In narrowing it down to the second I could finally feel that there was truly nothing out of place right now.

That feeling has not reappeared again since this afternoon. My mindfulness has been true throughout and it seems to have kept it from taking hold over my heart. My vigilance seems to have rubbed off on John too for this evening he seemed far more rested and at ease within himself than he has for some time. The tiger is no longer prowling through this house and my breathing is deep once more.

## Tuesday 24<sup>th</sup> May

I came and sat alone in prayer for a period of time this afternoon
whilst the sunlight shimmered through the study window.
Beforehand I had put together my notes from the last mythos and I
felt that they were present and alive with me during this restful time
of inner communion.

I could not help but turn my eye towards Thursday, and our next
session, together for I see the significant hour already looming large
before us. To hold this time of crucifixion is going to prove a real
test of my skill of this I am certain and in the silence I was steeling
myself in preparation for this sacred act. I remembered from my
training what I was taught by my master. He had said that there is
always one particular mythos that, when heard, serves to lance the
wound and to bring everything back together into coherence. Of
course, there is always this one same mythos that, when left unheard,
serves to underpin the whole picture of dysfunction and chaos. Read
only twelve of the thirteen stories and the hamartia will remain. But
pull that pin out and confusion has no basis left on which to stand.

I am steeling myself for I am certain now that this is the mythos
where the pin must be pulled and I must stand there and watch
whilst everything whooshes down around it. For the patient the
reading of this mythos can go one of only two ways. I know that
John will either feel liberated and freed by the experience…or he
will fall apart and die.

I am not worried about the choice that John will have to make; for I
have little doubt now that he wants to live and love again. But I am
not complacent for I am acutely aware of the critical junction we
have reached on this journey of healing and the need for me to be
strong in bringing him here. It was with this awareness that I turned
into the silence and into prayer on this sultry spring afternoon.

### Wednesday 25ᵗʰ May

Today marked the lull before tomorrow's storm and both of us breathed in heartily from the spacious hour whilst it was available to us. The quality of quietness has descended over the house, and also in John, for his words were few today. He is retreating again in preparation for what is to come; as I have too.

The air was humid but I was not deterred from taking a long walk in the morning to give John time to be alone. I sat on the far shore for a while and dampened my face with the salty water that lapped below my feet. At that moment I felt quite peaceful and it was as if the intensity of this work suddenly deflated a little into the great expanse of ocean before my eyes. Being here with this great expanse of a horizon did help to give me the perspective of detachment that I so sorely needed. Seen from this angle my patient seemed no more than a pinprick on the cosmic map; not too insignificant to care for but not so prominent to be adored.

It helps when John can draw upon his own well of strength, as he is today, so that I can find my own bearings again. Sometimes a boundary can help to frame the landscape and to help define its location in relation to everything else. When everything merges, as every drop of water merges into the ocean, it can be far too easy to become lost in a world of existence that I do have to have one foot within; at least for now. Sat there on that rock this morning it felt right to gain my footing again within this distinct form of mine. Though I do know this ground will not last forever and that I must not become attached to this passing vessel; I can at least say that it feels good to stand upon it for now. We are all one, but today it feels good to say that Mary-Helen is Mary-Helen and that John is John.

## The Eleventh Mythos

*Drawn from between the hands of eight and nine.*

The *Econimus* wandered morosely through the streets. It is daytime but no-one else is around and he is alone. Last night another bout of fighting had flared on these streets from a civil war that had been lingering for years. It was sustained because neither the existing authority, nor the challengers who had rebelled, had been able to reach an advantageous position to strike a final blow. Both sides had been evenly matched and no advantage was sustained for long. Blow by blow they had only worn each other down and drained away precious time and resources in the process. Many had grown tired of this fruitless conflict and had abandoned their homes and their livelihood in search of a more pleasant place to live. But the *Econimus* stayed on.

He stayed because he had become engrossed and did not wish for the conflict to end. In the beginning he had cheered when the rebels had risen; but now he had no preference for their rebellion to succeed. He was just the one who had grown used to having warfare on the streets around him. It soothed him for drama was the food that now sustained the *Econimus* and peace was his poison. In truth he feared what he would do with his life if this was no longer a distraction for him and he didn't like to give much thought to the matter.

But his worst fears had now been realised and that is why on this day he wandered morosely. Towards the light of dawn he had caught a glimpse through a window of the two opposing leaders firmly shaking hands with each other. The *Econimus* could tell from this handshake that a truce had been called between them and that the time of war had come to its inevitable end.

In truth this truce had been building for weeks. Exhaustion had set in for both sides and the fighting between them had become more and more sporadic. It would flare and then subside before flaring again. Spirit for the fight had slowly sagged and now it had finally been vanquished.

There was no celebration on the streets yet for many times before the rumour had swept through that a ceasefire had taken hold and then many innocent civilians were caught up in a new burst of violence. Indeed a resigned wariness had kept those who remained in the town locked safely away in their homes. But the *Econimus* had seen and knew that this time it was for real.

And so on this day, as he was thinking gloomily about this, he arrived at the main square of the town. There he saw a lone civilian standing with his back to him in the middle of the square looking up longingly at the broken statue that stood in the centre. It was the first person the *Econimus* had seen all morning and, because he couldn't see his face, he did not realise that he was only a young innocent boy; a boy barely into his teenage years.

Out of instinct the *Econimus* ducked behind a pillar from where he could not be seen. As he did this the *Econimus* suddenly had a bold idea that if he were to attack and kill this wandering civilian that maybe it would help ignite the flames of discord once more and return this place back to normal. The authorities would blame the rebels for this murder and the rebels would blame the authorities. The agreement that had been made last night would be broken and tension would rise again. If he did this a new wave of violence would hopefully sweep through these streets and so give him continued sustenance.

By chance the *Econimus* happened to look down at the floor and noticed a discarded blood-stained knife lying at his feet. He took this as a sign of destiny, and so, without further thought he picked it up and charged across the square. The boy who had heard the sound of footsteps was walking away fast but the *Econimus* was too quick and was upon him even before he had left the square. Blindly he thrust the knife into the lower part of his back and sent this boy crumbling to the floor where he howled and screamed in agony at the single blow he had received. He was simply not strong enough to defend himself.

Once done the *Econimus* silently retreated into the safety of the shadows and watched events unfold from his cowardly act. It did not take long for the death scream to trigger a reaction and as he had predicted fighting soon broke out again as both sides blamed the other for this cruel atrocity. None had seen the *Econimus* and none came to challenge why he was watching so intently from the shadows.

But back in the Kingdom where the *Gatekeeper* dwelled something was stirring. An old *Crone* has entered into the land and is slowly moving towards the palace that sits at the centre. She is determined and forceful; and as she arrives at the gate she lays eyes on the *Gatekeeper* and gives an almighty scream;
'Pray tell me; what have you done!'

The *Gatekeeper* is shocked and somewhat miffed by this strong-willed woman and her sudden outburst.
'What have *I* done?' he asks indignantly.

The *Crone* hands the *Gatekeeper* a mirror and when he looks into it he can see the *Econimus* hiding in the shadows with blood on his hands. She points at the mirror and asks him;
'What do you see down there?'
'I see trouble; that's what I see. I see an evil force that has just committed the most atrocious and murderous crime and who is now cowering shamefully in the shadows. That man must be punished. That figure will surely never make it in here now.'

'Well I see something completely different. You are that man down there. Darkness and evil has entered into your heart. You are looking at your own reflection.'

'Me? You are saying that this is me? How dare you barge in here and say such a disrespectful thing. You have no right to make that accusation against me.'

'Where is your humility that you once pledged to give to your master? Know your place here in this Kingdom and curb your arrogance so that you may hear this truth,' the *Crone* screams back at him with equal force.

'So tell me what is this *truth*,' he spits back at her with disgust.

'An innocent boy once walked into this Kingdom. He followed his destiny and came here in search of love and acceptance. Yet in return you plunged the knife into him with a pompous damnation that was only designed to prolong suffering and agony in this Kingdom. You were the one who created a monster; the one who transformed a peaceful tranquil scene into a sorry tale of warfare, chaos and devastation. Evil came into this Kingdom by your very hand.'

'Are you really trying to tell me that he was an innocent boy? Have you not heard his tale; heard of the *hamartia* that followed in his wake? He was infected with it from the very beginning and then he tried to bring it in here with him. What else could I do but turn him away until he ridded himself of this curse. And then what did he do instead? He indulged even more in it to the point that there is simply no goodness left in him. I say again that he is beyond help.'

'I have heard his tale, and yes I insist that he was innocent. And yes you are also right that he had acquired *hamartia*. But he came willingly and all he asked for was a blessing from your master to cleanse himself. And you know that your master, the *King*, would have given that blessing without hesitation if you had let him near him. But instead in your fear you turned him away, plunged the knife in his back, and then you now dare to wonder why chaos is the inevitable price. You are the man hiding in the shadows and falsely protesting his innocence having stirred up trouble. And nothing will change unless you show yourself, pull out that knife, and take away your damned condition. So now the question is do you want an end to all of this drama? Are you ready to hear and own the truth that we are in fact at the beginning of the *mythos*, and that the cause of all this *hamartia*, is yours?'

With that the *Crone* marched away from the *Gatekeeper* as forcibly as she had come. She did not wait to hear his reply because if he spoke now he would only react in protest. The *Gatekeeper* was quaking and needed time to let the truth get through his defences.

After a period of time, the *Econimus* returns back to the Kingdom. He is weary and ashamed but he is surprised to arrive at the gate and to see the *Gatekeeper* collapsed on the floor and offering no resistance. The *Econimus* sees all this and knows that if he wanted he could now push through and make his way into the Kingdom that for so long has been barred from him. But something holds him back and he knows that it is not his time. Without a word he leaves the *Gatekeeper* and makes his return out into the world.

### Thursday 26<sup>th</sup> May

*The hour is getting late for I felt to wait until after our session before turning to my diary. Looking eastwards from my bedroom window I can see a full moon has risen and is casting its glow upon the calm waters beneath. Not a breath of wind rustles the leaves of the old beech tree that stands true in the far corner of the garden. All is still outside but inside I am churning from what I witnessed this evening.*

*Though I'd gone through my routine of preparation as normal this was to be no ordinarily graceful unfolding. From the very moment John was taken into hypnosis he resisted against my invitation to go forth to meet the wild man and he resisted stepping into the vault and taking this mythos into his hands. It took all of my persuasion to get him to take that seat and to begin to read. Oddly enough the wild man was there but he remained silent as if he was powerless to intervene. My presence here seemed critical.*

*The resistance didn't end there though as John struggled to read aloud to me every detail of that mythos and I had to keep coaxing him to continue. It was as if he was being asked to digest a devilish medicine right from the depths of hell. It was toxic and he showed remarkable courage to keep on going through to the very end. By the time it was done he looked ready to collapse in exhaustion and I had to help swiftly to lead him to bed. I do know though that he will sleep deeply this night now that the gatekeeper has surrendered and let go the hold he had over his soul.*

*I can also understand fully now the part I've had to play in the script of his healing. For there was no-one else but me who could bring him naked and free before his maker in order to receive all that he needs now. I've opened the door wide and very soon he will walk through to meet his destiny.*

## Friday 27ᵗʰ May

John came down and joined me at breakfast as if he was a man reborn. A spring in his step and a sparkle in his eye revealed that he had slept well and there was a childlike freshness that radiated outwards. What a welcome relief this was to see and it all served to confirm my premonition that this was indeed the critical mythos and that John had made the wisest choice.

I saw with absolute clarity how the mythos reflected the moment in time when John had listened to my advice and had chosen to put his story upon the fire. I was the woman in the eleventh mythos and my screams marked the turning point when he chose to stop the war that was killing his liver and to live in peace.

He carried that freshness forth and lived and breathed this day like a great weight had been lifted. He opened his arms wide to welcome and embrace the moment. A playful spirit of cheeky mischievousness danced within his soul and it was as if there was a part of John that had suddenly been released from his inner dungeon and out into the world.

His childhood innocence had indeed been taken away far too soon and it was inevitable that the spark of exuberance would be buried by the gatekeeper's hand. John had no-one there to reassure him that it was safe to be open and vulnerable in what to him seemed an alien and cruel world. I know that though he may be adult in age; that it is I who has been the first to give him this permission since his mother left. The gatekeeper did what it could in the interlude between the two but it was in truth a false protector of John's spirit and soul.

As John's spirit soared I felt his joyfulness lift my own heart off the ground. My own tiredness from a restless night soon dissolved away in the presence of this illumined atmosphere. It was impossible not to laugh at John's wittiness that coursed its way through this cheerful day.

## Saturday 28th May

The spark of aliveness that has been lit in John's soul continued to run ablaze as we moved through this lazy day together. Hot sunshine bore down upon the land and John was keen to be out in order to feel her rays upon his skin. She was the life giver on this planet and he just wanted to receive everything that she had to offer. It was hard for me then to contain his excitement and to remind him that her fire can burn if he gets too close.

Now that we were getting close to the end of our time I find that events from the past and the present are becoming increasingly blurred. Strangely, all I can see in the moment is John recreating the time when he turned up on my doorstep a third time and affirmed that he was ready to work with me. It was the biggest and most freeing step; but so much more has happened since then that I simply can't afford to be complacent now. Although it is enchanting to watch, I am unable to forget how hard it has been for John to hang in there these past two months. With two mythos sessions still to go, the time isn't yet ripe to make the dash for the finish line.

Despite the caution of foresight in my mind; I was unable to dampen John's spirits as he revelled in this golden hour where the cancer seems to be far away. He led me nimbly across the island in the middle of the afternoon where a gentle sea breeze was already picking up and beginning to cool the humid air. On the soft sand of the far shore he quickly took off his shoes and let his feet sink down deep. Laughing infectiously he ran down to where the wave's lapped and began to splash playfully in the cool water. In watching all this happen, I simply could not stand aloof here for long and I threw off my caution and my shoes and joined him there too.

### Sunday 29ᵗʰ May

*As I had suspected, the light of the sun that had lifted his spirits by day came to burn him in the darkness of night. I was called suddenly to his bedside by a scream of terror that pierced right through the peaceful quiet and that pulled me out of my own restful dreams.*

*Diligently I went and sat whilst the nightmare consumed his mind and I instinctively called on the wild man of the mythos to be here to protect his troubled soul. But strangely I didn't feel his presence respond and it was as if he was standing back and waiting for the child in John to make the first move.*

*I felt the tension that penetrated the darkness of this midnight hour. A candle was burning on his bedside table but its flame was low as if suffocated by a lack of oxygen. In that moment I realised that though John had agreed to go with the wild man into the vault he had not yet fully integrated this presence within himself. There is a separation that clearly needs to be healed between the child within and the wild man without.*

*It was in this moment that I finally understood who the wild man really is. He surely is the mature father figure within John's psyche that he has never got to meet. He is the source of masculine power and strength that the child in John needs to draw upon in order to be the man that he is destined to be. He is all that the Econimus has been searching for in the mythos; and with the Gatekeeper out of the way the door is open for reconciliation. But the cry of his nightmares tells me that the child is not yet ready to step through.*

*All I could do was to sit in patience until John finally subsided to a place of rest. Today he is more subdued as if he has got a lot on his mind. I have stepped back to give him space and to let him be for now.*

## Monday 30<sup>th</sup> May

This morning, whilst I was sat in the shed writing up last week's session, I heard a sharp rap from behind me against the half-opened door. It was John of course but the gravity of his manner did catch me a little by surprise. This was clearly to be no casual interruption and I dropped my pen and beckoned him inside.

I turned to face him and to give my full attention whilst he sat and gathered his thoughts. Evidently he needed to share what had been weighing on his mind and I was more than happy to be here as a sounding board. He is in no doubt now that I can be trusted.

When he spoke there was a soft tremor in his voice and he seemed to be shrinking back into himself and back to when he was but a child on this earth. In his vulnerability I immediately felt the dial of my presence suddenly turn upwards a notch and I slipped into a heightened state of receptive awareness. In that tender moment he revealed to me how his nightmares kept taking him back to the painful time of his mother's disappearance and his father's death.

He begged to know why this was still haunting him and he asked what he could do to let go and to move on. The only word that can answer such a question is forgiveness. He listened but does he yet know how much that moment in the distant past is still shaping his life now? Can he yet see the link between this and the cancer that had recently killed his liver? I tell him that to forgive he must face and accept all that pains him. I may have been here holding his hand through this but now he must walk on alone.

Much later on I realised also that it is the same forgiveness that will help John to walk through that now open door and into the wild man's arms. This is what he is waiting for and it explains why the first move is not his to make. It is only through forgiveness that John can now go forth to fulfil his destiny.

### Tuesday 31st May

Today gave me ample time for reflection and contemplation on all that John had shared with me these past few days. In my pondering I have to say again that I am left feeling such deep gratitude for the opportunity to be here and to be his witness whilst he faces and purges all these toxins from his past. Strange as it may sound there is such a rich beauty to be found in this unfolding process of transmutation as he sheds layer after layer of deadened skin from his being. With each peeling back I can see more and more light shining through as his pure white essence is revealed ever more clearly to me.

Soon there will be nothing left of the past to hold him caged and he will be free to live fully here in the eternal bliss of the present. Witnessing this reminds me of my own unfolding transmutation as I went through my own mythos journey as part of my training. As John has given himself three months to my care I had given the same amount of time to my master upon leaving my secure footing in the world. Although I thought at the time that it was merely a hurdle to get past, I cannot deny that the experience did serve to change my life completely. On my return to Arasmas I was not the same woman and it feels so good to now pass on to another soul one of the greatest gifts we can give on this earth.

For myself, I am sad to say that the incredible feeling of aliveness I'd felt had almost been forgotten in the dwindling years of struggle that had passed since. Without recognition that flame had fallen dormant…but it hadn't gone out completely. One spark was all it took for it to be rekindled and for me to fall in love with living again. Does John at all know that he has given to me as much as I have given to him?

263

### Wednesday 1ˢᵗ June

*June is upon us and the seed of gratitude from yesterday burst forth into bloom today. I just couldn't contain my enthusiasm which came tumbling and flowing out of me like a great cascading waterfall that simply has to follow gravity's course.*

*I took myself outside to the garden in the early morning and sat contentedly in the sun's warm rays until lunchtime. John was resting quietly in the house and so I was left to be in a spacious void with nowhere to go and nothing to do. In this void I dove deep and entered realms of beauty that lay beyond my wildest imagination. The garden simply radiated with such vibrant colour and light and I could feel its pulse of life resonating deep within my own heart. I was merging into her and she was merging into me and all the while any lingering boundaries between us melted away. It was a blissful time.*

*With my heart full of gratitude for nature's abundance it was not long before I felt the garden's inhabitants slowly coming to life and showing themselves to me. These spirits love to play and dance to an audience and I was a most willing observer. In there loving presence I just felt so enwombed within the natural world in a way I have never felt before. The city's sharp lines of distinction that were once my only home have become blurred and rounded out here into shapes of incredible beauty. She envelopes and dances me into my feminine birthright that I've never dared claim before.*

*In her company I feel uplifted to go forth and to realise my potential as a woman whose feet are walking this earth. Though I've never had chance to give birth to another human form, my womb is fertile and is ready to hold and germinate the seed of life within its tender loving embrace. On a day like today I feel I can touch the power of the great mother who holds the whole world within her and to see everything through her limitless eyes.*

### Thursday 2nd June

After yesterday's moving experience of limitless expansion; today I feel a little more contained in a cocoon of restfulness. Tonight there is another important mythos session to be held and I am sitting here wondering if the act of forgiveness will be sealed within its script. It feels as if the day has been devoted towards preparation and anticipation of what is to come and I've been mindful to keep my exertions to a minimum. John too has been a little withdrawn and it is was as if we were living distantly in our own separate worlds. I am sure though that by this day's end we will have come together again as one.

My body feels heavy and sluggish in its movements for it did not get to rest for long last night. John's nightmares returned soon after two o'clock and I was called again to sit watchfully by his side until the morning light. Sitting so close to him for four hours like this really gave me the chance to observe intimately every change in his being and I can really get a picture of how much he has changed over the many times that I have sat here like this these past two months. The flickering candle that cast light upon his body revealed how different John now looks from when I first arrived here. It is not only the obvious weight loss that is striking to see in the way that he has shrunk more snugly into his bed like a tender child; but also the shifting dynamics in his energy field which is becoming so much softer and peaceful.

Though nightmares continue to stir up trouble within, he doesn't show his tortured soul so obviously now on the outside. The terror that comes by night is finally losing its hold over him and I had the sense that this was to be my last vigil. These are the last embers of what was a blazing fire and wholeness is gradually being restored to his being. Indeed; after tonight we will only have the final mythos to go.

## The Twelfth Mythos

*Drawn from between the hands of eleven and twelve.*

There was a lone gum tree to be found in a flat and desolate landscape. Sitting with his back against that tree was the *Econimus*; who welcomed the shade she offered from the heat of the sun. This place reminded him of somewhere he had been long before; but he could not quite place his finger on where or when that was.

The *Econimus* had discovered this tree the day before and strangely had felt no inkling to travel any further than here. He was an orphaned child and there were none who cared for him or were concerned for his whereabouts. The *Econimus* had been wandering for some time but he sat here because he felt as if he was waiting for something or someone to appear. But in this barren place he did not know who or what that could be.

The long silence and the empty space were becoming unnerving though as it was not something he was used to being with. He had always been on the move throughout his life; always busily searching for whatever lay beyond the horizon. The *Econimus* could not remember the last time he had remained in one place as long as he had been sitting here.

With each passing hour pangs of loneliness emerged and grew stronger within him. Sitting here seemed to have reminded the *Econimus* of something he had always been missing in his life. After all these years of searching he knew that all he longed for was a place to call home. For the first time grief began to well up inside and to consume him; the grief of a life that had been spent in exile out in this wilderness.

The *Econimus* had grown used to this life of exile because as far as he could remember it was all that he had known. This was his safe and familiar territory and out here he knew that he did have freedom to move with no responsibility to anyone. He knew that he could choose to remain here for eternity if he so desired it. And though he had always revelled in that freedom; in sitting by this tree he now felt nothing else but a sense of loss. The *Econimus* began to wail in his sadness.

Now it so happened that another tribe was passing by at this time; and one of the women who was languishing at the back heard the distant cries of the *Econimus*. Drawn by the sound she slipped away from the group to discover the lone gum tree and the young man sat beneath it. Her heart ached for his pain and she longed to take his hand and to lead him back to her tribe. But she hesitated from doing so and without a word took a seat against the tree on the opposite side to the *Econimus*. He is surprised by her gesture; but in truth he is thankful that she did not smother him and instead allowed him to stay seated here in his sorrow.

Time passed by and neither the *Econimus* nor the woman moved from where they sat. He began to feel soothed by her devoted presence and his loneliness and grief slowly began to lose their grip on his heart.

Then in a sober moment that followed; the *Econimus* heard a rustling noise above and looks up to see a man beginning to descend down the tree from where he had apparently been sitting all this time in the branches above them. As this stranger shimmies down to the ground the *Econimus* looks and sees that he is strangely familiar to him. In that instant he knew why he had come to this tree and had no inkling to move from it. The *Econimus* knew that this was who he had been waiting to see.

Without saying a word the stranger offers his hand and the *Econimus* reaches up and takes hold of it keenly. Together they walk with the woman following closely behind until they come to the edge of the Kingdom that remains familiar to him. Turning to face the *Econimus* the stranger finally speaks to him;

'Welcome home to your Kingdom. You are welcome to enter without condition and with my blessing. You must pass through the gate and into the Palace. Right at the summit of the tower that runs from the centre of this palace you will find a room. In that room is a man, a *King*, who is in hiding. That man is me and I beg you now to go in and rouse me out of that place. In coming together we will finally be ready to take our place and to bring order back to our Kingdom.'

After saying these words the stranger vanishes as magically as he had arrived. The *Econimus* turns back around to face the woman who has accompanied him here and who is now waving him away with tears of joy running down her cheeks. The *Econimus* went to raise his hand to wave back but she had gone before he could do so. There was nothing left to do here but turn towards the Kingdom and to begin walking on the path that he had walked so many times before.

Eventually he arrives at the entrance gate to the Palace and is surprised to see that the *Gatekeeper* is no longer in position. He too has vanished completely. Without hesitation the *Econimus* boldly pushed open the gate and on into the Palace as the *King* had instructed.

He easily finds the entrance to the tower at the centre and begins to climb up the winding set of steps. When he gets to the room at the top he enters; and as the stranger had promised he finds a young man slumped over a desk. The *Econimus* notices that he is dressed in all his robes and finery; but he senses that this man has obviously been here for some time for he looks weak and without power. But in hearing the door open the man turns and appears to be grateful to see that the *Econimus* has come.

'Are you the one from my dreams who has come to rescue me?' the man asks hazily.

'No I am only the *Econimus*. You are the *King* who came to rescue me from the world out there,' the *Econimus* answers; somewhat amused by what the *King* had said to him.

'I am? But I am the one who has been kept in this tower for so long. I am the one who needed rescuing.'

'But I was the one who was lost in the wilderness beyond the walls of your Kingdom until you appeared and gave me your blessing to come home,' the *Econimus* insists getting down on his knees before the *King*. 'I came here so many times to meet you and was turned away so often. But your persistence helped to bring me home.'

'To bring you home?' the *King* asks looking at the *Econimus* curiously.

'Yes for as far back as eternity this was my home but then I was sent away into exile. I have been away so long that I had forgotten it; but I recognise this place now that I have returned. And I recognise you although I had left here before you were born.'

'So you are saying you appeared in my dreams because I needed to help guide you home? Does that mean you didn't appear because I needed you to come to rescue me from my prison?'

'I don't believe I am here for that as it is my purpose here to help the *King* flourish; not to rescue him. I am here to give character and inspiration to your kingdom. I remember this now. But tell me who is it that has kept you in here all this time?'

'It must have been the *Gatekeeper*,' the *King* answered without giving it a second thought.

'But he is your servant. What makes you believe he would keep you in here?'

'I don't question his loyalty but I think perhaps he just forgot that I was still alive. I have been here ever since my Father left and I have lost track of when that was and how many years have passed. But I was a boy then and now I am a man so a great deal of time must have passed by indeed.'

'But the *Gatekeeper* always spoke of you and said that you were inside and willing to see me. Are you saying that this was not true?'

'Yes I tell you that he must be a wretched liar; a bit of a rogue influence around the place. Is he still down there now?' the *King* asks looking fearfully out of the window.

'No he has vacated his post.'

'Well what a blessed relief! Hopefully that will be the last I see of him.'

'I doubt that would be wise for we will have need of him as this place has always had need of him. The question is what happens next for you and me?' the *Econimus* asked meekly for he knew in the presence of his *King* that he was not in charge here.

'I have absolutely no idea! I've been in this tower for so many years that I don't even know who I am anymore. You say this is your home too, and I believe you, but can you remember what is supposed to happen next?'

'I'm not sure but I know you cannot stay here in this place of hiding. My sense is that we need to go downstairs and for you to sit upon your throne. Perhaps then it will all become clearer.'

'Wow I've never been allowed to sit on the throne before now! Is it even still down there?'

'Yes. I passed it on my way up here.'

'Well I say it is a smashing idea,' the *King* answers jumping to his feet and leading the charge out of the tower to the throne that sits in the centre of the main hall.

Once down there the *King* sits for the first time; whilst the *Econimus* kneeled humbly before him at his feet.

### Friday 3<sup>rd</sup> June

After the reading of the mythos last night the tide seemed to turn upon us for I was the one who slept restlessly and with a busy mind. By contrast, when I peeked in John's room in the night I was not surprised to see him lying there so quiet and angelic. The wild man is now here watching safely over him and I am certain that unity has finally been restored within. There will be no more nightmares now.

Meanwhile my mind was busy trying to wrap up the untied threads in my own life. For the first time I feel as if my work is coming to a completion here now and suddenly the question of 'what next' is looming large. It was clear in the way the mythos was told that a handover has taken place. I may have brought John to the wild man way back in the first mythos but only now is he ready to embrace him and only now is he ready to let go of my hand.

So in the darkness of the night I could not stop the ruminations and the ideas that were floating through my mind as to which direction I should go. Some ideas were simply ones that took me into a past that is known to me. Others were tantalising visions that took me ever onwards into unknown waters. But time and time again I had to release and let all of these go and come back to the breath and to the moment at hand. I trust that clarity will come about my next steps in the right moment that it is needed. But that time is not yet for my soul remains silent and unmoved from the work at hand. Yes to my mind it may appear complete, but deep down it is clear that there is much that is left here to do. Will it all be resolved in the final mythos, I wonder?

### Saturday 4<sup>th</sup> June

In the early morning today an unusual sea mist hung soft and low across the island and it created a magical atmosphere. It did not stay for long as the heat of the day came to pierce its way through; but I touched something quite incredible during this precious time. John was still sleeping when I rose and stepped outside into this enchanting arena. The veils between the worlds of man and nature were being lifted in this eerie fairyland and the atmosphere gave me goose bumps whilst I walked and disappeared into her.

It was as if I was still in a dreamland and my subconscious was stirring with all sorts of imaginings whilst my feet simply moved of their own accord. The thread connecting me to the earth seemed to be dissolving as my soul was lifted into some mysterious and surreal state of consciousness that was not tethered to one world or another. I was floating through in this in between place that had no name or descriptive features. But I was not alone here and I have to say now that the company was not altogether comfortable to be around.

I could sense that the island's dark and troubled past that had been ingrained into the dirt was being sucked out of the ground and it hung low for a while. I realise now that these ghosts were the sea mist itself and I have the sense that today was the day that they were leaving this island for good. Once the light of the sun came to touch them they simply vanished into it. Such is the power of the work we are doing here that it is no longer possible for them to stay hidden in this inbetween world. The vibrations are simply too high here now and no past can live on when the light of the present is shining so strong and true.

Writing now, I am deeply struck by how far the ripples go out from a single stone thrown into the pond. John's healing is truly a healing for the whole of humanity.

### Sunday 5<sup>th</sup> June

One thing that struck me oddly today was the thought that John never mentions his cancer diagnosis now and he does not seem at all worried or even surprised to still be so full of life at a time when it was supposed to have come to an end. I wonder if he even gives a second thought to the question of whether he is still sick or not. It is as if that past has disappeared from his memory, and like me, he has simply become fully absorbed in what is taking place in the moment. Optimism abounds in all of his words and movements.

His spirit is so vibrant and illuminated that I guess it is easy to forget those moments when the flame was nearly blown out by the winds of change. He has become so light and playful in his mood, and so present in his heart, that I am even finding it hard to remember how mind-dominated and physically drained he once was. Looking ahead to our remaining time together; I wonder whether there will be any more twists in his tale. But those eyes that were once cloudy and glassy are now sparkling clear and through them I can see right into the depths of his soul. Is there anything left in there that is not yet seen?

This once angry and closed hearted beast has been truly tamed by the light of forgiveness and he moves so gently now as if he has completely surrendered into the void that lies beyond circumstance. Peace and serenity are the forces that now govern his psyche and surely his cup must be empty by now. Surely grace will soon descend to fill it to the brim and to send his life spinning in a new and creative direction.

But alas; I must remind myself yet again that though we are getting close, and though his transformation is truly profound, we have still not reached our journey's end. Although it is hard to believe; there remains a stubborn root still to be unearthed from his garden bed.

### Monday 6<sup>th</sup> June

*Another graceful day has passed us swiftly by and the feeling of deep peace continues to hold sway over my heart and home. The morning was spent working with John in the garden whilst in the afternoon he went alone to the mainland to purchase supplies. I stayed behind this time to chop vegetables for a big pot of soup I was preparing. I did not mind for I had my music playing and I was quite content to just be here and to bask in the aroma of herbs and spices that I'd added to the pot. I must say I do enjoy these rare moments when I am in the home alone.*

*But when John returned a couple of hours later, he'd brought with him a surprise. In the shopping bag was an abundance of luxury items that I'd never seen him care for before. This was a man who always saw food as a necessity and not something to lavish any attention or money upon. This was also man who had been without any appetite since I'd arrived here and who had been easily satisfied with only the most basic of meals that I have prepared here. Vegetable broth with home baked bread has been our staple diet, and though simple, I've been satisfied because the food has been so fresh and alive. Food in the city seems so tasteless and bland now by comparison.*

*However, when I came upon his bag of groceries and delved into it, I could not help but be excited by its contents. There was fresh pasta, a gourmet selection of cheese, and a fresh piece of local salmon to name but a few of what I found inside. I quickly put the soup to one side and prepared us a banquet which we both truly savoured. This evening John has finally rediscovered his appetite for living, and as much as he says that he did it as a special treat for me, I know that it was a welcome sign for his health too.*

## Tuesday 7ᵗʰ June

Surprises continued abound for me today as John began to show interest and to ask questions about my daily evening practice of meditative silence. It had always been something I'd kept private between us but he clearly must have caught a glimpse of me sitting in my bedroom by candlelight sometime or other. To begin with I felt a little awkward sharing aloud my beliefs and my experiences for I was not sure how much he was willing to hear.

But his respect for me is strong for he listened with a keen ear and he encouraged me to continue. I think he sees something in my garden that he wishes to cultivate for himself and so I did not wish to dismiss his curiosity. The ground has been cleared and he is getting ready to rebuild a new world for himself upon it; one that is based on much more solid foundations. Clearly he has never had anyone in his life to show him how to wisely tend to his plot and so he is looking for fresh inspiration.

His openness and enthusiasm gave me permission to go on and to talk of things I've never talked with anyone before. From my faith in a higher power and in all the invisible helpers I see at work across all the kingdoms; I began to share a little of my rich inner world. John may never have glimpsed such things himself; but he was at least willing to accept what was true for me. He for one does not doubt the power of the miraculous and he has a thirst now for the mysterious ways of the spirit.

I invited him to join me in a shared meditation this evening and I led him gently through my practice. Afterwards he confided that he had indeed touched upon the peaceful void that lies beyond his mind. Enthused, I can only encourage him to continue with the practice; and it looks as if we will be sharing this time of meditation during the rest of my time here.

### Wednesday 8th June

*John was vibrant and full of high spirits and he was keen to get outside to savour the fresh air from a cool wind that was blowing across the island. I joined him for a walk but found myself a sheltered spot to sit and be whilst he carried on exploring. There are still hidden places here for him to discover and I pointed him in the direction of a secret cave that I myself had only recently stumbled upon.*

*In watching after him I found it hard to not be amazed by the transformation that has taken place. I'd worked in hospitals and worked with patients who'd showed remarkable signs of recovery; but it was hard to tell how much of it was down to the treatment and how much it was an act of grace. Beyond that my naturopathic and mythos training had given me a glimpse of the healing potential but it had really been all theory. My master told us incredible stories, which I'd taken his word for, but it pales in comparison to the real experience.*

*John has taken no prescribed drugs, and has been given no surgery, yet here he is without a trace of disease. His hamartia had been significant for cancer is the most surest sign that a soul has fallen completely off the path; and yet now he has truly found his way again. Yes I've watched it all unfolding gracefully into place, and yes there have been glimmers of his potential along the way, but he has never walked as securely on his own feet as he is now. Before, these glimmers could all have been put down to a lot of helpful circumstances that have supported and held him through this process. But now that these are slipping quietly away into the background it is clear that the light is on and burning bright within. It will soon be time for us to complete this journey through the mythos. He is ready for tomorrow's final act.*

## The Thirteenth Mythos

I led John into a state of hypnosis for a final time and led him through what is now familiar territory and into the hands of the wild man who dwells there. Yet on this occasion I was invited to join the two of them and to go deeper into the forest. Such was the closeness of my connection to John; I could easily follow his lead into the recesses of his subconscious and to get my first glimpse of this figure who held court here. If anything he appeared even wilder than I had pictured from John's first description. As we walked deeper into the forest, with me holding the rear, I felt all lines of distinction blur as we shared this experience together without any need for verbal confirmation. I could not tell if I was simply using my powers of imagination or if I had tuned in to something outside of myself. As we came to a clearing I saw the simple mud hut with smoke rising out of a chimney. At this point I hesitated from proceeding; but I was told that I was welcome inside. Once there I saw a third chair had indeed been added for my benefit.

I took a seat in eager anticipation and watched as John boldly walked forth and took hold of the thirteenth and final mythos at the centre of the wheel. The wild man seemed strangely reticent about venturing forth from the doorway. I turned back to John and could see that this volume in his hands was far slimmer than the others. He sat next to me; lingering with no great hurry to turn to the opening page as if realising that the end of this journey was close at hand. I felt a great peace had descended on us all.

Finally his fingers moved and gently cracked the spine open. What happened next was a matter of great surprise that snapped me right back to this world. For John uttered a deep resonant laugh that reverberated loudly through the realms and with a childlike voice he exclaimed in an innocent state of wonder;
'The pages are empty! The pages are empty! I get it! I truly get it!'

After watching John gasp a breath to take in its significance; I returned my gaze back to his inner world where I saw him stand to his feet and face the wild man who had led him here and who still stood hesitantly to the side. With gravity John uttered the words as he handed the book out to him:

'I believe this one belongs to you! Please stay here when I am gone, keep watch over this place, and write your story within it.'

I watched as the wild man stepped forward and took hold of the book from John's hand. Once his fingers touched the spine, I then saw in amazement that this man had become instantly transformed before me. Gone were the unkempt features and the ragged clothing of one who had spent a long time in the wilderness; and they were replaced with robes and wrinkles of wisdom that befitted a baronial King.

With that John bowed his head and headed towards the door. I followed closely behind and allowed him to take the lead in bringing this journey to its conclusion. Once we reached the meadow I gradually invited the both of us to make our return back to the surface of this earthly realm. Once we had both returned fully into our bodies; I noticed that a wide smile now lit John's face and that his eyes were wet and shining.

## Thursday 9<sup>th</sup> June

*And so the final instalment of the mythos story has been given. Tears linger on now in my eyes as I release this powerful time of completion. All that is left is for John to seal the envelope of his past by looking at the tale through more conscious eyes. But I know that when the right time comes for me to hand over the words that I've diligently recorded; that they will not be a surprise to him.*

*When I lifted John out of hypnosis his complexion had turned white and he knew that something significant had just taken place. He did not speak a word but was content to sit for a while and to breathe fresh life again into his now healthy body. I sat and watched patiently and looked loosely upon this saintly figure who had just come through to the end of a most exacting trial. Now that he is out of the vault, and the wild man has been restored there, life is suddenly going to become a lot more spacious and free. Finally he can begin to relax; but I know too that tonight was not yet the ripe moment for joyous celebration.*

*For in his peaceful silence I can feel that there is still the sombre mood of sadness that pervades. This is the lingering sadness from a man who finally knows that order has not been reigning in his kingdom and who realises that it has nothing to do with surrounding circumstance. It is a truth that has struck at the very core of John's being and it is simply too powerful to be treated trivially. This truth must be held gently in the light, and as I watched him hold that with such courage and strength, tears welled up again within me. This has to be by far the most beautiful moment we have shared together on our journey for in that moment I saw the child become a man; and the student become a master. John is now free to take responsibility for his own life. My work is done.*

279

### Friday 10ᵗʰ June

*Today has been a strange day of mixed feelings for me. On the whole I have been content to start the process of stepping away and of cutting those strong ties that have formed between John and I from the intense journey that we have shared these past three months. I know from my training that the reading of the final mythos marks the time to let the patient go. It is right for me to allow some cool distance to settle between us as I prepare for my departure next week.*

*Yet I am not icy cold with him for looking at John throughout this day only left me feeling the same warmth that I felt last night. I know though that this is warmth that comes only from my soul's recognition of the light that is shining brightly in him and it is not my mind's poisoned attachment to what has taken place. I am just here watching in awe at the power of the sacred that is way beyond me to comprehend. I don't even wish to try and claim it, tame it or possess it. I am just grateful that it has descended here and now.*

*But though my heart is full; in the empty spaces of this day those nagging thoughts of my own uncertain future began to reappear. During this time of soulful service my self has largely been forgotten and put aside into the background; but now the moment has come when I am being pushed into the foreground again. All I can do during this uncertain hour is to pray for more guidance and direction. The only response I receive though is to be patient and to trust that all will soon be clear.*

*And so I had to try and keep myself occupied in the moment and to not look too far ahead at what is to come. I started by giving gratitude for all that is here in my life now and by appreciating it to the full. This was a golden meditation that did eventually help to settle my anxiety and to keep my heart open and flowing.*

## Saturday 11th June

*I have watched many sunrises come up over the mainland from the eastern shore; but until this evening I had not tasted the setting sun over the ocean to the west. This could be due to practicality; as it is easier to glimpse the early morning rays from my bedroom window as compared to the stumbling return I made across the island at dusk. But more significantly to me it only feels right to have tasted it now that we have come to this hour of completion. Although it is the same object; the setting sun does hold a different quality to the one that rises above the horizon in the morning; and it is a quality that resonates deeply with my reflective mood.*

*So whilst John stayed at home to prepare a late evening meal on my behalf; I went and shared a poignant time of meditation in its presence as I gave thanks for the light it has given this day. I sat and watched it slip away slowly from view in a clear cloudless sky; and leaving only a pinkish trail in its wake. But without the clouds to magnify its beautiful hue, the colour only stayed for the briefest of moments before fading away and returning the silent ocean back to the deepest blue. The sand at my feet quickly lost its warmth and sparkle and the birds began to fall silent as the natural world turned to sleep. The hour of death and renewal is upon us and this is to be a quiet time for reflection on what has passed and an opportunity to release and to let it all go. I took a flat stone and sent it skimming across the water as an offering to the gods. In this dusky hour I must now wait for that stone to be returned and for a new day to begin.*

*This last week on the island is to be a time of deep rest and solitude. My free floating dreams will have to carry me through this blackest night and to show me the way towards the light once more.*

## Sunday 12<sup>th</sup> June

*It is evening and I am sat in John's shed writing this whilst illumined by soft candlelight. After a shared meditation here, I had stayed to write out my recording from the last mythos and to bring the story to a close. John had given me a beautiful leather bound notebook to use and it provided a perfect host for these sacred words I've carved neatly across its pages. I am confident that this will long serve as a reminder to him of this special time should ever he stumble from the path again. And with this by his side he is sure to not stumble for as long as he had before. It is to be my final parting gift to him on Thursday and in this quiet hour I could not help myself but indulge in reading through the whole story one final time. The tale is truly rich and delicious in its content but in truth I find that the magic lies in between and beyond the words themselves. Looking deeply I cannot help but see the hand of providence at work in moving the script along.*

*Now that the final word has been etched it was the ripe time to bring the curtain down on this consecrated space and to return it to as it once was. I'd lit some incense to purify and release to the light all that had been uttered and revealed during our weekly sessions together; before emptying my four jars of water. Afterwards I sat and breathed deeply into the silence until I felt that there was no trace left to be found and the atmosphere had become perfectly still and peaceful. I also noticed that my weekly ritual of preparing the room afresh does seem to have worked in keeping the vibrations light and spacious here. For despite all the turmoil and tragedy that has been spoken within these four walls there is an ineffable grace that has held it all. In the glow of this candlelight I can touch it as tangibly as this pen that I hold in my hands.*

## Monday 13ᵗʰ June

John joined me for a long walk and for a shared picnic lunch upon the far shore. The day was cool with a fresh breeze blowing off the westerly shore but it made a welcome change from the stifling humidity of the last few days. We walked largely in silence and it was as if there was a topic for conversation that neither of us was yet ready to broach. John must know as well as I that our time together is soon to be at a close but it was not yet ripe for us to be discussing our own future plans for when we part ways. I don't think either of us wished to break our bond of soulful communion with trifle talk.

I was though struck by the thought that neither of us have had a personal identity that separates one from the other ever since the night of the first mythos. That night our souls became attuned to each other and our boundaries fell apart. But now we are in the murky process of separating and of rebuilding broken divides. It is a necessary parting but that doesn't mean that it will happen easily. As we walked I could only pray for grace to be with us both as we move towards this hour of completion.

I am at least comforted to see that the cords of attachment between us are not so thick and strangling. Looking at John I can see how naturally he has moved back into the centre of his own life and is exuding out such powerful confidence from his being. There is no need for clinging on from his side. As for me; there is more to lose from our parting and I feel the presence of an empty hole inside that John has vacated. But my faith is so strong now that I do not feel its loss but simply sense an opening for something new to come. Looking truthfully within I feel no real suffering to let go and to let be.

## Tuesday 14ᵗʰ June

Even to the end I continue to be amazed by John's transformation and how he speaks and acts now in a manner that once seemed way out of his reach. He has become so sensitively attuned to the moment that every movement he makes is now truly appropriate. It is surely this alone that distinguishes the living from the dead.

Today the arrow that hit its mark came in the late morning after we'd shared a pleasant hour of tea and conversation. Rather than lingering on he saw, even before I'd seen it myself, that I now needed space and time in the house by myself. Without having to say a word about it he got up and moved onwards outdoors as if being carried away in the river's flow. It was so simple that it would be easy to miss what took place in that moment. But I was attuned enough to spot it myself. If it had come just a few seconds sooner or a few seconds later then the ending of our morning communion would not have happened as naturally or as gracefully as it did.

As John was taken outdoors I swiftly found myself being taken to my bedroom and to that kingdom of grace within where I prayed once more for illumination. The silence in the house and in me ran deep. With the help of John's subtle guiding hand I slipped easily into a powerful meditative state. In this reflective time I had a vision of me standing completely alone in a vast field of light and it was as if I was a switch in the centre from which the light was being channelled through.

But it was the vastness of this field that I received as the most blessed of gifts. For here my perspective returned and the problems I perceive on the road ahead could disappear into insignificance. John may not know it but his action of stepping aside helped me to see that there is no need for rush or panic. It is safe to relax because with all this light surrounding me there can be nothing to worry over. My prayers are being heard and answered.

## Wednesday 15<sup>th</sup> June

*In watching and observing John closely today I began to appreciate the subtle way in which the wild man has taken his rightful place again as keeper of the vault. There are noticeable signs of an orderliness that is slowly establishing itself and a greater sense of clear purpose and direction is emerging; like ripples spanning out from a stone lobbed into the centre of a pond. This man, who once chose to live in self-imposed chaos and destruction by exiling himself, had now truly softened.*

*Last week had seen John take the road of self forgiveness and of agreeing to do no more harm to himself by the hand of spite. It was a choice to no longer play the martyred victim who cannot help but hold on to a wounded identity. It was a choice to be at peace. This week has seen him take that next step further down the road. Not content with merely stopping the destructive pattern; John is ready to rebuild a new life in the world. He is ready to forgive the other now too.*

*I was tempted to say something aloud and to test the water as to his future plans. I simply cannot see this island containing the spirit that has now been freed. It just doesn't make any sense for him to stay on. But something causes me to hesitate and hold back from pushing the case. We are still dancing around the subject cautiously with each other and I feel too closely involved to see the way clearly. Everything is too uncertain at the moment to speak with any confidence. How can I possibly tell John that his future lies away from here when I know not my own intentions? Does he not know for himself?*

*Looking deeply now I know I am waiting because I am here on his entitled land. Do I really have to give respect to this artificial truth that stands between us. Do I really have to wait for him make the first move?*

### Thursday 16th June

Today I have felt my hold over Diarra slipping out of my grasp even more and the truth of John's entitlement seems to be more prominent than ever before. I remember those first few days on the island when John had not the strength to stand up against my powerful presence and I was free to stamp my authority upon this land.

Sad as it is to admit; in my arrogance then I believed that I was the entitled one because it was me who'd held the strongest hand. This darkness of arrogance that lay hidden behind my more benevolent nature is now being revealed to the light and it is not pretty for me to witness this and to name it as my own.

For how ashamed I am to admit that there is an evil in me that revels in John's sickness and that voice now protests with him now back to almost full health. There is a dark side to my character that does not like John being my equal and does not like to see him so illumined and self contained in his presence. There is a part of me that likes to be needed; a part of me that does not wish to relinquish these roles of housemaid, nurse and healer that I've played.

I have never had cause to notice this truth so starkly before today and it humbles me into silence. I turn to prayer for solace and protection from my own darkest thoughts for I know that they are only serving to undo all the good work that has taken place here. I pray too for forgiveness for my own weakness of mind.

Out of this time of deep prayer it became crystal clear to me that I must leave for I see that my continuing presence is but a hindrance here now. Not only that but I must leave soon before my pride sets into motion a destructive tide upon this island. I am far too attached to say another word on this matter. I must let go and let be.

## Friday 17ᵗʰ June

*Early this morning I handed John my written notes from the mythos sessions which he received reverently. Gently he stroked the hard cover whilst he sipped on his herbal tea and all the while a dreamy look fell upon his eye. He caught my eye watching and he gave me the most gorgeous smile of recognition that instantly lifted my flagging spirit.*

*The headstrong John of old would have pored over these words without hesitation in order to feed his conscious mind. By contrast the John of today simply has no appetite for it as he now held the light of knowing deep in his heart. Though his mind had resisted being kept in the dark at first; he had come to trust my word and to accept completely that he had not missed out on anything with me holding it back until now. But subtly I sense that there remains a lingering curiosity and a desire to finally put the seal upon this work we have gone through together. He is wisely not dismissing the importance of this book completely.*

*So finally he rose and took it to the living area; where he stayed for an hour or more. I was doing jobs around the home but I moved gently in respect of this sacred moment. When he came out though he spoke little, and he raised no questions about its contents. He made it crystal clear then that there was nothing left here for him to discuss. Like my master had promised; by holding it back until the very end, the mythos tales had become very easy to absorb and digest. It had very little substance left to it. It had vanished.*

*The spacious atmosphere of silence hung throughout the house for the rest of the day. This was John's time and it was not the moment to send ripples into the stillness by breaking the news of my planned departure for the day after next. I will tell him tomorrow.*

### Saturday 18<sup>th</sup> June

And so the end is here. John took my news without a word but I was
surprised to see that he was a quite taken aback by it. It was a
stunned silence and so perhaps he had not before considered either
my future or his like I had thought. Perhaps it had not yet sunk in
that my work here is done.

So maybe my news has finally made it real for him that he has a
future to consider; one that before he never thought would happen.
I wondered if there was still a part of him that longed for proof that
the cancer has left his system for good. Thinking this, I advised him
to seek that confirmation; not only for his reassurance but to help
shake up the establishment's arrogance with regards to medical
diagnosis. But he just smiled and said that his heart told him all he
needed to know.

Later on he started to become curious as to my plans once I returned
to the mainland; as if wanting reassurance that I was leaving for
something new and not leaving just because the door behind me was
closing. I tried to convince but I simply could not give him the
reassurance that grace was leading me by the hand to other things
elsewhere. Words came forth but I knew they had no power to them.
Deep down I knew that leaving tomorrow was not inspired; it was
just the safest step for me to take.

I don't know if he noticed this or not; but regardless I could not stay
under his watchful gaze. I tried to wriggle away as he unwittingly
cornered me under a glaring spotlight. I could see that he desperately wanted me to go forth and to persevere with what I've started
here; but at the same time he just didn't know how to help. I think he
was left baffled that there was an angel here before him who was
trading in her wings and falling back to the earth. But pray tell me;
what other choice do I have?

# Chapter XXI

*Sunday, 19<sup>th</sup> June, 2033*

Mary-Helen awoke early but was surprised to see that John had already risen and gone outside; presumably for a morning walk. She had slept fitfully as she always did before a long journey as she never found it easy or comfortable saying goodbye. She still felt very attached to John and this place and it was hard to let it go and to venture once more into the land of her past. Sleepily she showered and dressed before deciding to take some time in meditation whilst the house was quiet.

As she began to breathe deeply and to release all that has taken place here there was something that started to rise up into her awareness from her last night on the mainland before coming here. They were the words of her maker speaking to Mary-Helen that this was to be a time of her healing as much as John's and that she must learn to let go and let him do the work through her. As these words came she felt all the tortured thoughts of this past week slide away into nothingness and peace finally rested within her heart. Her prayers were heard and are answered. She had not been forsaken for her moments of human weakness but was loved all the more for them. She had not failed here nor had she succeeded. Instead she could look back honestly and simply see the unfolding hand of grace at work. Mary-Helen had been healed because she knew truthfully that she had allowed it all to take place. Proud thoughts may have come to her mind but she could honestly say that she had never entertained them in her home for long. There was no need to condemn herself falsely anymore. She was complete.

Mary-Helen finally made her way downstairs but it was only after brewing her morning cuppa and toasting some bread that she saw an envelope leaning against the vase of fresh flowers at the centre of the dining room table. On it was written her name in John's scrawling handwriting and so curiously she sat down and lifted the seal. Inside was a letter written on notepaper.

*Dear Mary-Helen,*

*I was surprised and saddened to hear news of your imminent departure yesterday. You have become such a strong presence here on this island these past three months that I had not given it much consideration that you might be leaving here so soon. I guess your news has made it all the more real that my healing journey has now been completed and that your work with me here is now finished. Now I have thought about it I can understand why you feel it must be the right time to leave.*

*But before you go there is something I must say to you and which I feel unable to speak of aloud for I am choking back tears even as I think of it. Last night I could not help but reflect deeply upon your time here and my heart is so full of gratitude for what you have given that it is overflowing. You may say humbly that the power lies only in the mythos healing or in all the other healing gifts you have given these past few months; but I still see you as the driving force behind it all. I could have read a manual of step-by-step instructions and applied it myself. But I know it would not have worked. That is because you taught me in the very beginning that my healing would be a matter of faith and not a matter of reason.*

*I can now admit that despite what happened to me on this kitchen floor the day I put my story on the fire; I had little to* no faith in what had taken place and so I was clearly not yet ready to be healed. And then I came for you but your words did not mean a lot to me back then either. But I had no choice other than go along with what I could not yet know. In doing so I discovered that it is only through your actions and the way you have demonstrated your faith so wholly here these past few weeks that I have been able to discover my own faith. In sitting so calmly and securely upon your throne through every day you've spent here on Diarra; you have shown to me that it is indeed possible to return home to myself and to reclaim my throne. The mythos journey may have led me to this end but I don't believe I would have been strong enough to see it through without you. Mary-Helen I have watched and observed much more than you can imagine and I have come to realise that each moment you have breathed on this island you have been standing within a field of immeasurable grace.

It is you who have been the revelation here and you have shown to me what it means to live a devoted life of prayer; have actually shown what it means to really live a soulful life. I want to tell you now that you are such a courageous and powerful woman to have pursued your calling with such faith and conviction and you are an inspiration that now gives me cause to believe in myself. You are the one who has given me fresh purpose and a reason to live again. There is simply no way I could possibly repay that gift you have given to me. I am eternally blessed.

I do respect your decision to return to the mainland and to continue serving others from there in whatever capacity life asks of you. I am certain that you have the power and strength to do your work in any circumstance. But there is still something that I wish for you to consider. This is because I believe that the bird that flies free can reveal its beauty more than the one that is caged. From the very moment you stepped foot upon this island you became a transformed person from the downtrodden and depressed woman that I had first met on the mainland and had so rudely dismissed. I now believe in my heart that this is your home; not mine. And though it may sound improbable; I feel that there is still much work for you to do here. I believe this because in my dreams last night I saw a glorious vision unfolding for Diarra and I saw you standing at its heart. It may sound bold but I see this place eventually becoming a shining beacon of light in this dark world. I believe that what has started as a small seed here with me; will eventually become a centre of healing and transformation for many patients.

So there you have it. I am willing to offer to you my island as a small token of my gratitude. For myself I know that the time has come for me to leave here and to return to the mainland and to make my way there. If you consent to stay and to build this vision; I promise that everywhere I go in my search that I will speak of what has happened to me and what is taking place here. I do believe that many people are ready to hear my story and I see many, many people who will be inspired to come. Some will come to help you build this brave new world whilst many others will come here to receive all that this world has to offer.

Beyond that gesture I would also dearly love to be involved and I believe that I have the skills to bring in the finance to help develop this vision and to provide a space here where many people can come and seek renewal. It is a bold plan I know but you were the one who once told me that I needed to turn my anger into a more creative outlet. Through this dream I believe I have now stumbled upon my own mission and purpose in life. My heart is racing at the mere thought of what is possible to achieve out here.

I have left for a walk to give you time to consider this proposition. I trust you will give it due thought. I will return by

*ten o'clock should you decide to decline so as to return you to*
*the mainland. If you choose to go let me say now that the offer*
*will always remain open for you.*

*Yours, John*


After reading the letter floods of tears poured forth from her
eyes. She was in a state of shock but immediately she remembered
her guidance before coming here that she had not understood fully
until now. That guidance was that she was to be the bridge between
John and his maker and that she would communicate across the
truth of his healing in order to bring him safely home. She had not
known how to do it at the time but she saw now how this is what
had unfolded; how her faith had indeed blossomed and had clearly
inspired John in his faith too. Reading his letter reminded her that
yes she had been so depressed and confused before stepping foot
onto this land. She had felt so hopeless and lost.

His tantalising vision captivated her completely and she was
tempted to grab hold of it there and then. But she paused to take a
deep breath and to let this unbelievably generous proposition to
sink in. She put her cup to her lips and sat back in her chair. She
was blown away because this was a man who had given away very
little in his life and yet who was now so willing to wipe his slate
clean and to move onwards and upwards. And he wanted her to
have this island! It was a remarkable transformation that had taken
place! In truth she knew that she had only wanted to leave because
she had assumed that he would stay and that her continuing
presence in his life would only be detrimental. She had almost
forgotten her intuitive prompting way back in the beginning that it
was not going to be healthy for John to stay on the island beyond
their time together. And now that he was keen to spread his wings
and fly free on the mainland; she was ecstatic to think of the
possibilities of her flying free here on this transformed island.

And what a vision John had for this place! Yes she had had the
thought of wanting to stay on here but she had gone no further into

what that life would possibly look like for her. So suddenly her mind was racing ahead and she could not stop herself from slipping away into a wishful daydream. Thoughts flashed through in quick succession. She began to see what the vision could look like on the ground; perhaps ten or twenty patients coming together for a one-hundred day period at a time. In her mind she swiftly calculated that she could run this three times a year with plenty of time for staff recuperation in between. That would amount to roughly fifty patients a year who would be allowed to come and who would be asked to pay a nominal fee to cover the cost.

And maybe that could extend in future once more elders came through to hold a bigger group. There would be new cottages being built alongside this one to accommodate both patients and staff. There would be a separate dining hall and a communal lounge built too. And she could concentrate solely on the mythos sessions whilst a support team around her could concentrate on the nursing care. A team of cooks, gardeners and handymen could be on hand for the practical running of the place and the garden could be expanded to provide enough sustenance for all. Staff would be given food and shelter and would only need minimal payment in return.

Oh John was surely right; people really would want to come and give themselves to support such a noble venture! Patients could even volunteer in the day-to-day running if they were feeling strong. Then a Sanctuary could be built on the hillside for meditation and reflection; and a healing chamber could be built instead of her having to use the garden shed to run her sessions. And solitary huts could be built on the far side of the island for those who arrive and who need to take the first step alone in releasing their stories of pain. Oh yes she could easily see the people flocking here especially if John was going to spread the word.

Surely her biggest problem would be dealing with the demand and having to turn away those who desperately needed healing. That would be tough to turn people away, she then thought, and so she had new ideas that maybe it would be best run

John and who just needed some time out to get their lives back on track. She would not be able to bear turning away someone suffering with cancer because of a long waiting list! Maybe then it would serve as a centre for those suffering addictions or other minor afflictions. The options seemed endless.

And to have John there so willingly beside her to make all this happen by validating her work and sorting out the business matters was like a major blessing in itself. She knew that she could not pursue this dream without him. In truth, whilst whiling away her time in Wagsale without success she had been desperate for a partner who shared her vision and who could give it a platform and let it shine. Had she finally found him, she now wondered excitedly?

With all these dreams running wild in her mind it soon became clear to Mary-Helen that she could not possibly wait until ten o'clock for John's return. Instead she went bursting out of the house and on the path towards the lighthouse. She shouted John's name again and again until he finally heard and showed himself from where he'd been sitting snugly inside.

'I accept, I accept.' she shouted when she laid eyes on him and then she ran and wrapped him up with a motherly bear hug. John warmly received her gesture. Eventually stepping back she saw he was beaming.

'Thank you. Thank you John,' she added breathlessly.

'It is my absolute pleasure,' he said before squeezing her in tight again.

## Acknowledgements

I recall vividly the moment when the seed for this book was planted back in May 2011; and the idea came to write a story about a character that went a healing journey by working with archetypal energy forces in his subconscious. I had the bare bones of that story in place in a matter of hours; swiftly determining that John, a character I had briefly introduced in *The Search for Satya*, was the one who was speaking this idea to me.

It was within a matter of days that the seed germinated when, serendipitously, I came across *Sacred Contracts* written by Caroline Myss. I then dived into a three-week odyssey in personally exploring her teaching for myself. From that experience, I can acknowledge the insightful depth of her work for then helping provide me with a lot of the detailed structure of John's journey through the mythos. Overleaf I provide a roadmap for John's own personal sacred contract; a map that forms the theoretical underpinnings of the journey through the 13 individual mythos stories.

As well as the work of Caroline Myss, I also acknowledge the archetypes contained within the Tarot system, and in particular the deck of Inner Child Cards conceived by Randy and Isha Lerner, for helping provide me with another perspective on the mythos journey. In a sense, I saw how the 13 mythos stories could be viewed as a single tarot reading.

The next significant influence on this book came in 2012 when I was pointed in the direction of *Iron John* by Robert Bly. I acknowledge his work, as well as the book *King, Warrior, Magician, Lover* by Robert Moore and Douglas Gillette, for leading me into the world of men's initiation and development. From there I came into contact with the Mankind Project in 2014; an organisation that seeks to bring the ideas in these books into practice in our world and to offer a ritual space for initiation. I also acknowledge the worldwide community of men who have involved themselves with this crucial work. It is through my experience of this work that I believe that the modern man of today, in many of our cultures, has few role-models and mentors who can guide him into a mature and whole masculinity. But what every man has is access to the archetypal energies of mature masculinity, the original blueprints as it were, and can to some extent grow by coming into healthy relationship with these energies. That is what the Mankind Project supports; and this premise soon added another critical dimension to John's journey from woundedness to wholeness.

I also want to give acknowledgement to the writings of Eckhart Tolle, especially his descriptions of the pain body. This helped shape the inner complaining voice of John we hear in the first part of the story. Next I want to acknowledge the writings of Michael Brown and the Presence Process™ he has created. His writings have provided me with a lot of insights around emotional process work, which in turn added another level of depth to this story. Also, Brown, and Eric Pearl (The Reconnection), both provided me with insights into Mary-Helen's character as the grappled with the question of *'what is the role and purpose of the healer?'*.

The final major influence on the story I want to acknowledge is the poetic and soulful lyrics of Kirtana that gave me inspiration to write the diary of Mary-Helen across a 100-day period in 2013/14. Kirtana's offering of devotional singing to the world revealed to me that this was her way of returning the keeper to the vault...and of creating the 13th mythos upon the blank page that presently stares at us as a hole at the core of our psyche. I felt that this diary of devotion would be the best way to show the transmission of faith that Mary-Helen gifted to John; a gift that allowed him to cross that bridge at the end of their shared journey of integration.

With blessings,
Richard Moseley
Margaret River, Western Australia
July 2018

# JOHN WAIDEMAN'S WHEEL OF MYTHOS STORIES

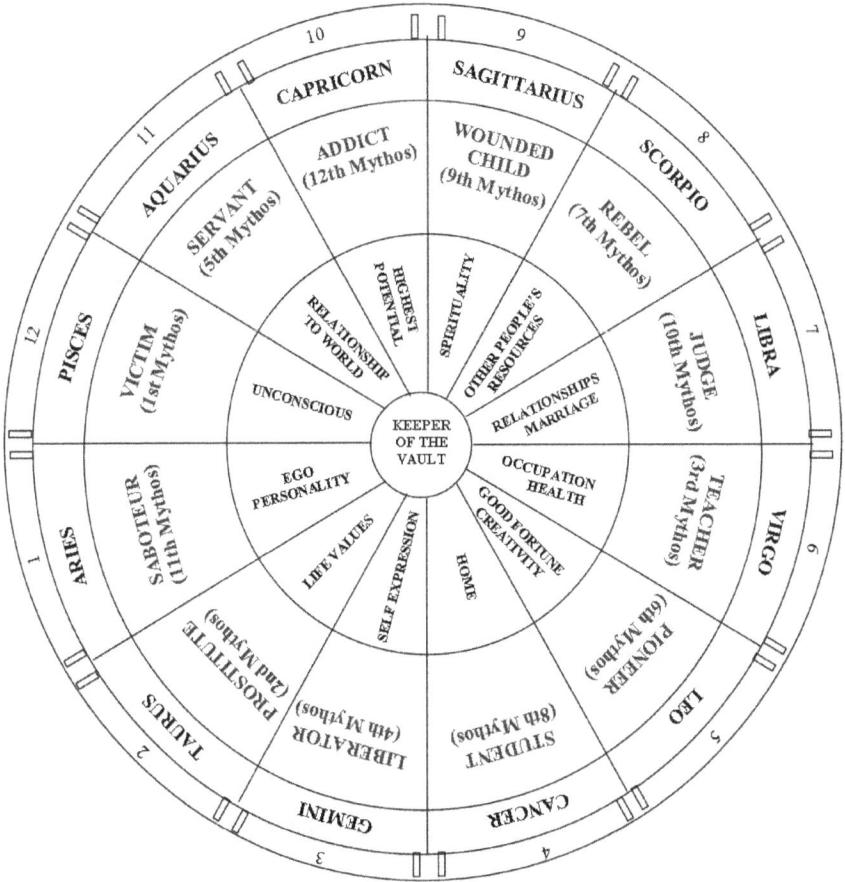

It is acknowledged that the content and structure of this chart has been developed from the work on Sacred Contracts by Caroline Myss (www.myss.com).

Please refer to this publication for further background reading; or if you wish to develop and explore your own Sacred Contract.

Thank you for your purchase of this book.

Author's rely heavily on customer feedback for marketing and promotion of their work. You are warmly encouraged, therefore, to provide a review on the sales channel for this book; on the Amazon website.

# About the Author

R.A. Moseley is an English writer currently living in Margaret River, in the South-West corner of Australia, with his wife Melissa and his cat Grace.

His mission in life is to be a spiritual friend; one who uses the power of the written word to illuminate that there is far more going on beneath the surface of our day-to-day human existence.

Hamartia is his fourth publication following on from:

The Search for Satya (2012)

Tracking Fritz's Footsteps: Meditations on E.F. Schumacher's A Guide for the Perplexed (2013)

and

The Kingdom of Golf is Within You (2014)

All titles are self-published through Create Space; with print and e-book copies available for purchase through Amazon and other online distributors.

www.ingramcontent.com/pod-product-compliance
Lightning Source LLC
Chambersburg PA
CBHW031826090426

42741CB00005B/147